Benedict Allen read Environmental Sciences at the University of East Anglia and in the year of his graduation joined expeditions to Costa Rica, Brunei and Iceland. In 1983, aged twenty-three, he crossed north-east Amazonia – a journey on foot and by dugout canoe through some 600 miles of virgin forest. It is the subject of his first book, *Mad White Giant: A Journey to the Heart of the Amazon Jungle*.

By the same author

Mad White Giant
Hunting the Gugu

BENEDICT ALLEN

Into the Crocodile Nest

A Journey Inside New Guinea

PALADIN
GRAFTON BOOKS
A Division of the Collins Publishing Group

LONDON GLASGOW
TORONTO SYDNEY AUCKLAND

Paladin
Grafton Books
A Division of the Collins Publishing Group
8 Grafton Street, London W1X 3LA

Published in Paladin Books 1989

First published in Great Britain by
Macmillan London Ltd 1987

A CIP catalogue record for this book is available
from the British Library

ISBN 0-586-08761-3

Printed and bound in Great Britain by
Collins, Glasgow

Set in Times

To the memory of Laura Brightman,
a friend of much the same spirit

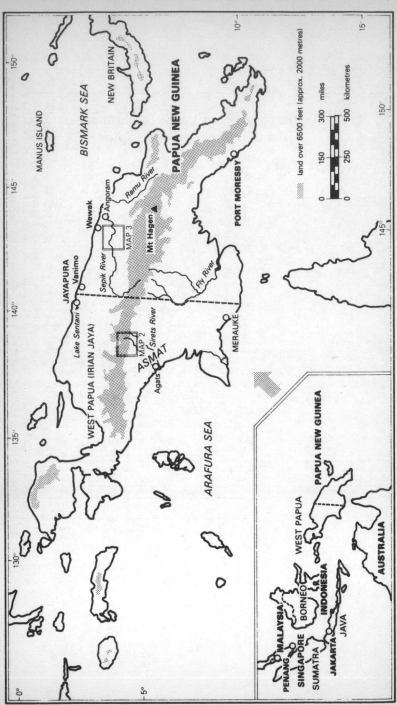

The island of New Guinea, composed of West Papua (Irian Jaya) and mainland Papua New Guinea

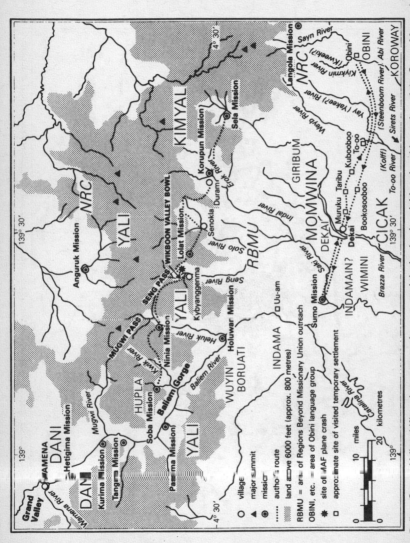

The Baliem Gorge, Yali and Kimyal country to the east, and the lowlands neighbouring this portion of the Snow Mountains

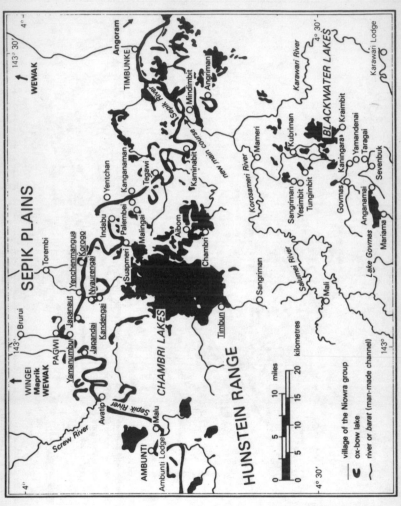

The Sepik River in the region of Chambri Lakes

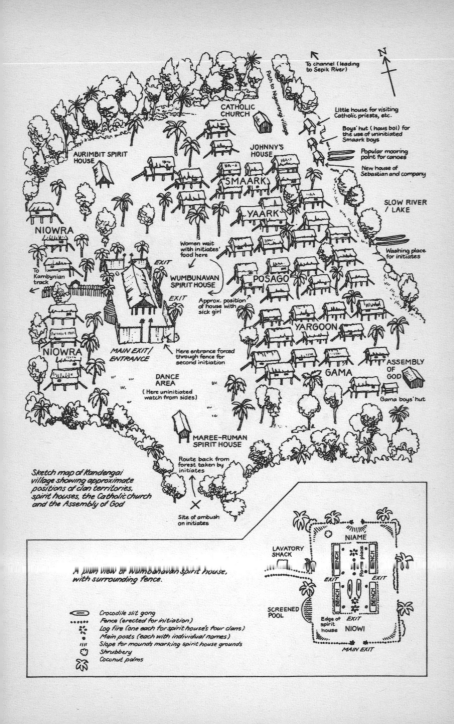

To channel (leading
to Sepik River)

N

CATHOLIC
CHURCH

Little house for visiting
Catholic priests, etc.

Boys' hut (haus boi) for
the use of uninitiated
Smaark boys

JOHNNY'S
HOUSE

Popular mooring
point for canoes

AURIMBIT SPIRIT
HOUSE

SMAARK

New house of
Sebastian and company

YAARK

SLOW RIVER
/ LAKE

NIOWRA

Women wait
with initiates'
food here

Washing place
for initiates

To
Kambynian
track

EXIT

WUMBUNAVAN
SPIRIT HOUSE

POSAGO

EXIT

Approx. position
of house with
sick girl

YARGOON

NIOWRA

MAIN EXIT/
ENTRANCE

Here entrance forced
through fence for
second initiation

GAMA

ASSEMBLY
OF
GOD

DANCE
AREA

(Here uninitiated
watch from sides)

Gama boys' hut

MAREE-RUMAN
SPIRIT HOUSE

Sketch map of Kandengai
village showing approximate
positions of clan territories,
spirit houses, the Catholic church
and the Assembly of God

Route back from
forest taken by
initiates

X

Site of ambush
on initiates

NIAME

LAVATORY
SHACK

BENCH

Fire place

EXIT

EXIT

A plan view of Wumbunavan spirit house,
with surrounding fence.

BENCH

BENCH

SCREENED
POOL

Edge of
spirit
house

EXIT

NIOWI

MAIN EXIT

Crocodile slit gong
Fence (erected for initiation)
Log fire (one each for spirit house's four clans)
Main posts (each with individual names)
Slope for mounds marking spirit house grounds
Shrubbery
Coconut palms

Preface

In Papua New Guinea I was privileged to be made welcome by a Sepik tribe and to be allowed to take part in the initiation ceremony by which their boys traditionally enter manhood. The description of what it was like to undergo that ceremony forms a major part of this book. By its very nature, however, much of such a ceremony is secret – even from the women and the uninitiated of the tribe. In describing the rituals I have therefore sought to respect that secrecy and have unveiled only those details which have already been guessed by other tribal members and which the elders have given me permission to reveal.

In general I have not thought it necessary to alter names, dates and other particulars; exceptions are one Indonesian official and 'Cursacaik', whose names have been changed, and the Missionary Kid called 'Carol', whose real name I unfortunately could not remember. This is a personal account of my experiences, based on my diaries, correspondence and photographs, and to prevent distortion of my own impressions I avoided reading anthropological literature on the Sepik until after the text was written. However, I am grateful to Dr Allen Abramson of the Department of Anthropology at University College London, who kindly read and commented on a draft of the manuscript.

My very sincere thanks to Tan Yoke Sim for her support in Singapore, to the quite indomitable Sjovald Cunyngham-Brown, who, with 'Tekha' and Anna, gave crucial assistance while I was visa-hunting. I hope the RBMU missionaries, who were equally generous and hospitable not only those mentioned in the text but also Mike and Carol Meeuwse at Wamena, and Martha Reimer of SIL at Sumo (whom I had no room to mention, but who appeared unexpectedly before I left) – will understand my quest and where it led me. Their sincerity and dedication impressed me deeply. I hope all these people, the 'Sepiks', and in particular the very tolerant and kind Jeff Liversidge, will forgive my inclusion of some personal details. I am indebted to all those of the government's Migration and Citizenship division at Waigani, Port Moresby, for my extended visa, and to Andrew Strathern, Director of the Institute of Papua New Guinea Studies, for his friendly co-operation.

I would also like to thank Michael Alcock for his encouragement over the initial draft, and I am especially grateful to my stoic and ever-dedicated sister Kate Allen, to my exceedingly patient editor Brenda Stephenson and to Peter James for his intelligent copy-editing.

Since my return to England the missionary post at Sumo has been re-occupied by Les Henson and his family, and the regular RBMU publication *Horizons* has mentioned that the Obini people have been contacted by that organisation. Life has returned to normal at Kandengai village, and I have sent off presents of boxing gloves, wristwatches, books and football gear as requested – and as a token of my profound gratitude to the whole community. As I write, Augusta has left the village to commence a typing course.

The island of New Guinea was originally settled by successive waves of peoples – principally those related to the present-day aborigines of Australia; Negritos; 'true Papuans' and Melanesians – when, as a legacy of the Ice Age, lower sea-levels considerably aided navigation. Today the island's population can be divided into two main linguistic groups: the highland Papuans and the coastal Melanesians. The label 'Melanesian' is also an overall one attached to the peoples of the archipelago that begins in the west with New Guinea and extends eastwards to New Caledonia and Fiji.

New Guinea's awkward topography – the coastal mangrove swamps, the thick freshwater nipa and sago palm forests, and the central mountain ranges peaking at 16,000 feet – inhibited communication between peoples, frustrating mutual cultural stimulus through trade and preventing the establishment of unified political systems. Isolation bred suspicion between communities, which became culturally introspective and defensive; no change from stone-age technology came about.

Early in the sixteenth century a Portuguese explorer, Jorge de Meneses, became the first European to set foot on New Guinea. He called it the *Ilhas dos Papuas* because of its 'fuzzy-haired' people. In the 1540s the Spaniard Yaigo Ortiz de Retez named the island after the Guinea coast of Africa. During the next three centuries New Guinea's terrain discouraged exploitation of the island by European traders and governments. The Dutch, however, wishing to reinforce the eastern flank of their lucrative East Indies trading empire (today's Indonesia), recognised the unlikely claim to New Guinea of their vassal the Sultan of Tidore and so in the early nineteenth century themselves became rulers by proxy. Britain acknowledged the Dutch claim west of the 141°

meridian but in 1884 took the southerly portion of eastern New Guinea to provide Australia with a buffer against other European powers. Within days the Germans named the remainder, along with the Bismarck Archipelago, theirs. In 1906 British New Guinea was renamed 'Papua' and control was transferred to the new Commonwealth Government of Australia, which also seized the weak German colony during the First World War.

After the Second World War the Dutch were ousted from the East Indies by the pre-war independence leader Sukarno, who won sovereignty for an Indonesian Republic in 1949. Before long his Java-based government required a national cause to boost its wilting popularity and clamoured that western New Guinea, or 'West Irian' as they called it, was also theirs. After some unsuccessful military agitation, Sukarno began leaning towards Moscow and the US hastily piled pressure on The Netherlands to relinquish their part of the island. The resulting New York Agreement was ratified by the United Nations in 1962. The Indonesians took full control on 1 May 1963, having agreed to allow the Papuans a referendum on their future. In 1969, with General Suharto now in office, 'West Irian' became 'Irian Jaya', the twenty-sixth Indonesian province. In 1975 Australia launched their island half to independence as Papua New Guinea, with a democratic parliamentary government and an economy based on Australian fiscal support, copper mining and plantation crops, notably coffee. When I visited both sides of the island ten years later, the independence movement was growing, erratically, within the mainly non-Muslim province of Irian Jaya, and those who believed in its right to self-determination called it West Papua.

Chapter One

The sound which signals my return is enough to send shivers of apprehension through the village. We press our dripping paddles to the grey wood of the dugout to listen. From where we are across the water, we watch as even the oldest women are drawn from the dark of the huts. They merge with the agitated figures rushing to wait for us on the river bank. Sprinting behind are half-naked children with hands up to their faces and maybe tears in their eyes — it is impossible to tell from so far away. We lift our paddles again and the gap between us and them continues to shrink.

Concentrating hard, I can picture which slit gong in particular the village elders are beating, the carved head of which crocodile it bears. The roar we hear comes as if from that crocodile's soul, reverberating from deep inside the central spirit house, rattling between the village huts, through the hot chatter of women lining the river margin, and shimmering to us across the water. It will travel beyond this canoe, beyond the channel we have just paddled. Depending on the breeze, it could even travel some miles along the silty waters of the large river, the crocodile telling everyone who cares to listen that I'm back.

Time drags, and I watch the twisting and untwisting of the man's spine as he stands working the long, male's paddle, just in front of me. From an otherwise black skin the sweat glistens in countless raised dashes of silver up and down his back where his initiation markings catch the intense light. Just now it is easy to dwell on the pain he endured earning these ancient patterns — carved into his skin in emulation of the crocodile, of course.

I feel a touch of remorse — or is it guilt? Some women must have been hoping I would break my word, not return. Others, the older, the acquiescent, that I would keep it, make this simple act of homage to their culture, if that is what it is. Well, now they know for sure, I *have* returned, and so preparations *will* begin.

As for me, I cannot help but think back to the man whose idea — or fault — it was. My slowness in comprehending the intricacies of his art as a witchdoctor — there was fact to be filtered from superstition and trickery – and *his* in divulging those darker rituals he normally keeps close to his chest, meant sluggish progress. That was predictable. His suggestion which came in the end, quite out of the blue, was not. He simply said I should go through the ceremony. It would be the crowning of his (in my opinion not very informative) lessons. I scoffed at the idea. You have to take Cursacaik with a pinch of salt – his dead-pan face and empty stare. Even so the seed of the idea he had planted remained fertile and, soon after, germinated.

It does not bother me that Cursacaik has not been through the initiation himself. It has been outlawed in his village and anyway he has enough on his plate with other activities. Most of these account for his criminal record, which, he is the first to admit, is extensive: twenty-one times behind bars. But after that last really heavy sentence, which was imposed for a particularly colourful crime, he decided on a clean start. Once released he sought out a distinguished old witchdoctor whose reputation is said to be great in spiritual circles even now, long after his unfortunate death. The ancient witchdoctor lived a hermit's life in the jungle some miles along the untrustworthy track from Timbunke towards Wewak, the track that locals say was partly built by one white man, a zealous overseas volunteer, with the help of a wheelbarrow. In the bush, among seasonal mosquitoes, sharp grasses and ant mounds lying around like heaps of abandoned cement, the old man from time to time took on young aspiring witchdoctors as apprentices. Cursacaik in turn learned many rites, then went back home to Mindimbit, downriver from here. He has been helping his neighbourhood understand the vagaries of the spirit world ever since.

Usually he is healing the sick by advising them to confess what they might have done wrong to upset the spirits, such as sleeping with another man's wives. It is easy to be flippant about all this, but not necessarily wise. The other day he saved a child. The hospital had given her up – it was one of those mysterious jungle lurgies. What is more, it seems as though Cursacaik's prestige is increasing by the year. Even the Seventh Day Adventists, with their strong grip there at Mindimbit, tolerate his activities now. Best of luck to him, I say.

Silence interrupts my thoughts. The rumbling of the slit gong has ceased. There are the last hollow echoes from the hut walls. We should have reached the crowded river bank by now but across the sepia water there is wind, the one they call the *bara*, I think, and islands of weed spin into our way, slowing the nodding progress of our canoe's crocodile-headed prow. Beyond its cowrie-shell eyes and the snout, we can now see the details of the villagers – even their feet dancing through the grasses, and who is making the most noise.

And yes, there *are* tears in the eyes of the crowd. No one seems to be bothering to show any restraint.

The other canoes have been taken by the women for fishing, so there is plenty of room in which to tie up. We stab our paddles into the knotted bank roots, and chuck the mooring line to the only older boy here. He pats my back as I step ashore. Although most women are murmuring, softly as if in sleep, that they have missed me, I suspect that their crying is born of relief – the waiting is over.

But *my* waiting, is that also over with? Am I on the verge of finding whatever it is that has drawn me halfway round the world to this backwater? My excitement at the thought – that this could be the end of my journey – is dampened by a new and quite unexpected feeling, that of uncertainty: I am suddenly aware of how very far I am from home.

'You really won't forget to water the cacti, will you? About once a month should do the trick. Remember they don't like being prodded. And the ugly hairy one that looks dead, isn't. And if you could remember to return the library books ... Thanks. I've left your Christmas presents in the sitting room by the telly. They're rather on the cheap side, I'm afraid.'

'You've got everything? Passport? Tickets? The jungle boots? Auntie Joan's and Uncle Geoffrey's apple and tomato chutney?'

My father drove me to Heathrow in the Renault, leaving my sister on the doorstep to comfort my mother. It was my last view of them as we swept down the hill, out of the downland Hampshire village, a gusty November wind playing with leaves around their feet. They turned abruptly, shutting the door behind, and alone on the step were left six empty milk bottles.

Why leave that scattering of flint cottages, the sandstone war memorial, the village pond with its inbred carp, St Mary's Church with the avenue of yews and company of leaning gravestones? And why go to *that* place, of all distant places, and to a region of West Papua which the more perceptive ruling officials thought was roamed by subversives, and the less perceptive thought stalked by ever insatiable cannibals?

This was the western half of the second-largest island on the globe. The other, eastern portion of New Guinea was newly independent, trying to stand on its own feet, having been launched off by Australia ten years before,[1] when the inhabitants of that 'land of a thousand tribes' had to an extent learned to communicate with each other in Pidgin English. Another tourist brochure cliché ran that Papua New Guinea was a 'last unknown', which it was not particularly.

For my purposes that contact with my culture mattered, so I decided to head next door, to West Papua, the Indonesian-controlled, less frequented portion of the island. It made sense to go to 'jungle', if only because I had already learned how to survive in it, and to *this* jungle in particular because its people were, by and large, the least familiar with our world, the remotest from it. Refugees from this island half trickled and often gushed across the frontier with colourful stories. And they were not all that came over. A corpse, someone said, had been reported floating its way downriver, patterned with bullet holes, and once it was the sound of mortar fire from what, according to the map, should have been a palm-hut village.[2] The Indonesian presence in West Papua was reinforced by multinational petroleum and mineral companies, and by one superpower in particular, which shared the Indonesian fear of communism.

Of protest from the West Papuans the world knew little. At least some of those who had raised the Papuan flag had been tried, and armed resistance to the Indonesian Republic by the West Papuans, usually in the form of arrows, was often returned in the form of automatic gunfire. This helped explain why the Indonesians were coy about the remote interior, and why obtaining permission to wander there was not necessarily going to be straightforward. The London Consulate had already turned down my application for an extendable visitor's visa – and that without even bothering to look up at me through the security glass. I flew from Heathrow around the world, heading towards New Guinea but stopping off at Singapore, where I unsuccessfully tried four more visa queues at the Indonesian Consulate. In the longest queue were a couple of Norwegians who were hoping that the *Indonesia Handbook* was banned in Indonesia for its stance on drugs and sex: once there, they might be able to sell it at a neat profit on the black market.

Time to try elsewhere, I thought, and boarded the night train, a red diesel, bound north towards Penang, Malaysia. My contact in Penang was Sjovald Cunyngham-Brown, a man of Shetland-Scottish descent and a veteran of South-east Asia who, though in his eighties, each dawn swam twenty lengths of his club's pool before a substantial breakfast. He had been taken prisoner of war by the Japanese and the ship carrying him had been sunk by an Allied torpedo. He spent the war in and out of death cells; once his camp was liberated, he borrowed a full colonel's uniform and, coming across a Japanese regiment, accepted their surrender. After the war he was appointed Consul-General in Penang for France and by now had been awarded a Légion d'honneur (he also had an OBE).[3] On my arrival he took me for a coffee with the Indonesian Consul, who, flustered by the unannounced arrival of the legendary figure limping in with his stick, put a big stamp across my passport.

While drinking a third congratulatory gin and tonic at Penang Swimming Club, we chanced on a young British expatriate with a bright white Moss Bros. shirt. He wanted to see my visa. 'I like to pride myself I'm something of a specialist on Indonesian bureaucracy.' He took my passport. 'Hey, this is good. Where did you get it?' He looked at the document in the light. 'Of course to get into West Papua officially you'll also need a *surat jalan* pass from Central Immigration, Jakarta. But you'll be unlucky if they check. Though coming from Papua New Guinea, and leaving that way . . . I don't know. Then you'll need a *surat jalan* for the interior – you'll have to play that one off the cuff on arrival. The police wages are calculated on the assumption they'll be topped up with a certain large percentage of bribery,' he hinted darkly.

The man was reading my passport, flicking through the pages. 'Mmm. And when are you leaving?'

I said I would spend three months in PNG toughening up then fly over the border to the provincial capital, Jayapura.

'Trouble is,' he said, sucking a finger-tip like a pencil, '*Berlaku hanya apabila mendarat di Indonesia dalam waktu tiga bulan terhitung tanggal pemberlan.*'

'Sorry, didn't quite catch that.'

'Your Indonesian can't be up to much.'

'It isn't yet. It will be when I get there.'

'Well, you'd better pull your finger out. This is only valid for a one-month stay, or three in total if you get it extended when the month has elapsed. That month is starting from today.'

It wasn't actually, but he said so, Cunyngham-Brown mulled it over and thought so, and I was unsure. It looked as if I would have to get myself smartly to Indonesian West Papua, skipping all jungle preparations in PNG. Was that really wise?

The young man said, 'You'd better move your behind.'

I did. I packed my holdall that day and boarded the murderous night coach, with its headlights flickering from a very loose connection, for a roller-coaster ride down the peninsula to Singapore – a ride which I want never to repeat. In the departure lounge at Singapore airport I sat apart from the other passengers, who were mainly urban Papuan New Guineans excited to be homeward bound. I was uninterested. Ahead lay the prospect of flying straight across PNG, then over the border to West Papua, getting through the local Immigration without a *surat jalan* for the province, then facing the police for travel permits, first in Jayapura, then in the interior – all this with only a few dozen phrases of Indonesian. And that was not to mention having skipped my jungle training.

I pulled out my pocket *Say It In Indonesian*, and began thumbing through its 'over 2100 up-to-date practical entries'. '*Mobil saya terperosok di lumpur*,' I mouthed. 'My car is stuck in the mud.' On my right shoulder leaned an intoxicated Australian with a loud shirt and louder voice, and over the left mewed a Papuan baby with a quiff of liquorice-brown hair.

5

From PNG's capital, Port Moresby, my apple and tomato chutney destroyed by health officials, I flew to Wewak on the northern coast, from Wewak directly west to Vanimo, then, arching out to sea, skirting the refugee-strewn border, descended after a few minutes to West Papua and Sentani airport, near Jayapura. The pages of my phrasebook were already wearing thin between restless damp fingers. I wasn't ready for this.

I crossed the stickily hot tarmac towards Immigration, accompanied by a herd of radiantly clean North American children: dresses for girls, jackets and corduroy or brushed cotton trousers for boys. Their leader was a man with a wide and white smile, who shared his attention between two women, either of whom could have been his wife. 'Come on, you guys, keep together will you?' cried the women alternately. I said they were a well-behaved bunch.

'Well,' one of the women said, 'they're not all bad. Not for MKs.'

'MKs?' I mused to myself whether M.K. was the founder father of a local borstal.

'Oh sorry, that means missionary kids. They go to be educated in PNG, and now they're back in Indonesia vacationing with their parents. Say, you got all your documents?'

'No.'

'You'd better stick close to us.'

'Thanks, I will. Can I carry a suitcase for you?'

'Yes, that would be much appreciated.'

'Uuump!' I said, lifting a case up. 'What's in here – a stack of Bibles or something?'

'Yes, that's right.'

The little white immigration cards were handed out with great deliberation by a sympathetic Indonesian with dry lips and passive, Chinese, opium-den eyes. In the office three officials had their legs up, a smoke haze all around them. I was inserted halfway into the queue by the missionary. As I moved into position I trod on a thick-legged girl's white Kickers. 'Oops, sorry.'

'Mind your big, fat feet, will you?'

'Carol, please.'

'Sorry, Mom.'

The Indonesians seemed to look upon this weekly flight from across the border as a penance. They were dragged from Jayapura, which was miles away, to handle the incoming and outgoing missionaries; their only hope of 'extra income' lay in the occasional oddball – such as myself. The officials spotted miles away that I was not an MK, though I was just as well scrubbed as they were, my hair was respectfully short, and my blue jacket was obviously unsuitable for a backpacker. I was waved to stand aside while all the others were processed. The two women said not to worry, they would wait a second to see if I got through all right.

I was summoned to the desk, during the missionaries' passage through the next stage in the vetting, the luggage search, but the MKs created such a din when their Christmas presents were unwrapped for inspection that my interview never really got off the ground. Never to know what a catch they had missed, the Indonesians backed into their smoky office after a quick rummage through my rucksack. 'It's your lucky day,' the missionary said. I had got over the second political hurdle. The third, tomorrow, would be harder.

At Moresby airport, the Papuans had been everywhere – sleeping, staring, sewing, chatting; here in West Papua the only indigenous people were those sculptured in murals. Chunky male warriors were depicted going about their daily lives, gathering jungle produce with spears from among the crocodiles.

'So, you've made it here. Now what?' the missionary said.

I told him I was going to Jayapura – tomorrow I would see the police for a permit to the interior. I asked why the Indonesians in Jakarta, who were mainly Moslems after all, allowed Christian missionaries to work out here.

'You could say we've got a sort of understanding going. We both believe there's one God.'

Along the road towards Jayapura the only signs of the indigenous lake people of Sentani were their huts, raised along the shoreline on stilts. This stretch of lowland bordering the sea was now also inhabited by immigrants. They came from overpopulated Java, starting afresh, encouraged here one way or other by the government. No Papuan 'fuzzy hairs', no skins as dark as burned sugar, these people are light-boned, with smooth, black hair, Mongoloid eyes, and teeth large for the jaw; their skin is the colour of fallen bamboo leaves; typically they have longish, clean fingernails.

My minibus taxi took to a road flanked on the right by lakes and on the left by hills covered with brown grasses, scrub and tacky houses. The boy conductor pestered anyone who passed within earshot, calling my first destination, Abepura: 'Abé! Abé!' We stopped repeatedly to pick up passengers; these were invariably women, dressed in batik or some brilliant cloth brought along from their homelands and bearing food on yokes. Some roadside dwellings were bordered by beaten-out metal petrol drums, red with dust and rust. Tethered goats skipped over dry ditches filled with plastic wrappers. Cock-hens rutted in the dust, others were fluffed up in cool dirt nests. On one corner the buckled remains of a car were mounted on concrete blocks as a warning to drivers; on another stood a memorial statue of a helicopter crew. Looking right, there was a leafless coppice which had drowned in water; elsewhere the roadside was just grit and powder, tramped by lines of children carrying empty buckets to nearby brooks.

There were shacks and more shacks, a haze of road dust, and motorbikes overtaking us on blind bends – men with sunglasses and glossy black jackets, girls riding sidesaddle behind, their cotton dresses peeled away and flapping. Jayapura itself nestled in a coastal bay of white sand and turquoise water. Shrubs and frail huts were poised on hills around. A river which swilled past the onion dome of a mosque, then a stiff white church tower, was being filtered by children seeking what they could from the jetsam of crates, plastic basins, snagged fishing nets. Relics of iron installations left during the Second World War by the Allies under General MacArthur, from the time when the coast was his fighting headquarters, were still busily rusting away in the harbour waters. There were other relics, too, of huts abandoned by the original West Papuan inhabitants, many of whom had, with inducement, upped and left.

The taxi dropped me off in the square, and I sought out the cheapest hotel: there, two boys were stretched out asleep on the cool of the hall floor, all but naked under a sheet. They gave me a room with a padlock, loud with the noise of passing traffic. I lay on the bed under a fan and slept in its draught through the afternoon and through the night, until I was woken by the morning rush hour. I removed most of the dust from my suit, and put on a pair of white socks which I had been saving for this day, the day of my police interview. Although I still lacked the *surat jalan* pass for West Papua – and so was not entitled to be in the province at all – I was going to demand from the police a *surat jalan* to the highland town of Wamena, the next stage but one before I walked down into the forests.

The sun was barely up, not yet heavy, but I was sweating. At the government offices, rousing band music was being broadcast through loudspeakers on to the forecourts, where everyone was stretching, clapping, folding and unfolding not quite in time, getting the day under way. A bleak parade ground, alive with the clack of typewriters from the surrounding offices, lay before the police headquarters. From the sentry box came the scented mist of clove-perfumed cigarettes; on the wall outside were ten or so blue helmets like dozing tortoises. A uniformed boy leaned on a scrubbed wall, his eyes pursuing me as I made an initial inspection, walking by among the traffic. At a street stall I picked up a very old issue of *Newsweek*. A central article had been blackened out. Turning to the contents page, I saw it was an economic review of the Republic. A photograph of an Edwardian lady grandly riding her motor had also been partially inked out, but perhaps the censor had got bored.

I walked back to the police headquarters. The sentries, without getting up, nodded across the parade square to a squat office, from which tailed a queue of West Papuans – dozens of them. I stood in the obedient line for a while, before I was picked out and beckoned forward in the Indonesian manner, all fingers together and palm downwards. Uniformed men criss-crossed my path as I followed indoors. The office, lit by low-wattage bulbs, contained what looked like two classroom desks, around them shelves laden with dusty box files. A wooden bench was pointed out to me. I sat down. Overhead coughed the fan. Outside, policemen at morning parade were receiving orders.

'S'lamat pagi. Good morning,' I said.

'S'lamat pagi.'

A boy sat at one of the desks, stacks of folders on either side; he had no pips or stripes on his khaki drill and was fidgeting with a box of pins. We were alone in the room. It sounded as though the netting over a ventilator shaft was being sawed away by some sort of noisy forest wasps; and there was a smell in the room, besides cigarettes, which I guessed was boot polish. Though I was careful not to hurry the boy, it was hard not to. He was a slow thinker. Slowly he thought about the PNG exit stamp in my passport, and slowly he made movements that looked promising – no question of asking me for the extra entry papers from Central Immigration, Jakarta. He took up three surat jalan forms, interwove them with carbon paper and eased them into his typewriter. The forefinger of his right hand extended and hovered over the keys.

But the boy knew he had forgotten something. I clenched my fingers under the desk, while his brain clumsily attempted to grasp whatever it was. Finally he caught the answer – I saw his eyes light up, then his mouth forming words to the effect that I had come from PNG – where was my permit for entering this province? His browless eyes then said, 'This, mister, means deportation.' The forms in triplicate were removed from the typewriter, the carbon separated off, a draw unlocked, the papers inserted and the key turned. The carbon papers were piled on one side.

'Stay, mister.'

I stayed. The boy went. I began to grow hot, as if the fan had been switched off. An overweight man with a flat cap, plenty of glittering braid spreading like ivy from his shoulders, entered busily, the boy returning to watch. The newcomer removed his cap and merely inclined his head an inch to acknowledge me as I rose to extend my hand. Not to be put off I gave his in-tray my calling card, and sat down again. Black lenses joined by gold wire sat astride his nose, entirely obscuring his eyes. He stood by the desk.

'Inggeris?' I said that I was. 'You have not a permit please for Irian Jaya.'

'I was hoping it was not necessary.'

'No, it is a serious business. A *surat jalan* is very necessary.'

At what point might I dare offer to top up the policeman's wages? I wished I had had a chat with the missionaries about it.

'You are in a problem, Mr . . . er . . . Alin. How long is your length intended stay in Indonesia?'

'Three months.'

'But you present me no good documents. No good. Do you have many funds for your stay? Please let me see, please. Quick.'

I unzipped my money belt, stacking up my cash and sweat-soaked traveller's cheques on the desk. The boy said, 'Oh mister . . .', almost drooling, but his boss now looked as if he had been up all night.

'I think you will leave the country. You have not much money and not good documents.' Speaking behind his black lenses, and in the gloom of the office, ineptly painted green, I thought he could be seeing very little of my pleading eyes. 'I cannot see a way behind the problem. And there is no aeroplane until a week back to Papua New Guinea. I do not understand that you not come from Jakarta. I do not like this. Now I telephone to my authority and ask what is done with you.'

'Isn't there a special tax I can pay instead?' I said, suggestively, without actually winking.

At once J. K. Salkim – he wore a name-plate on his breast – took the boy's chair and slumped deep into its seat, his skin loosening as he relaxed. He thought about it. He thought about it very hard behind his dark glasses. I imagined his eyes working back and forward between the spread of creased rupiahs and my face. He came to a decision.

'I do not know about this tax. Maybe you have made a mistake. You will wait here.' He stuffed a fresh lot of forms, five sets of them, into the boy's hands. 'I now learn a little more about you.'

Salkim went to the black telephone in the corner, and stood dialling different numbers. The first was unobtainable, the second engaged. I looked at my watch and saw it was lunchtime. The boy handed me the five forms. 'Please.' His gaze followed my biro as it wrote out my life history. At the bottom of the form I was asked to provide five references, and I started off with David Marfleet, a missionary pilot I had talked to while he was on leave in England. By now David should be back in the interior of this province, near Wamena. His geographical knowledge, I had hoped, was going to be invaluable.

Meanwhile the policeman had got through to Jakarta via the operator.

He seemed to regard this success as a triumph. The boy at the desk fed all the carbon papers into his typewriter the wrong way round and I watched the backs of the five forms come up covered in type. Salkim looked into the receiver and dropped it down. He had been cut off. He chucked his watch an angry glance. Its case matched the gold of his sunshade frames. He put his elbow in the face of the boy as he tugged the sheets from the typewriter and fanned them out; the boy winced slightly as he received a sigh of dissatisfaction from his senior.

Quite suddenly, the top drawer was unlocked, the piece of paper labelled *Surat Keterangan Jalan* brought out. Salkim gave the boy's stool a kick, an indication that he wanted to get by. Wooden feet scraped on the floor and Salkim spun the papers down and was out of the office. I heard a motor start up outside and looked round in time to see him shooting over the parade ground on a white scooter to lunch – today, perhaps, *besengek daging sapi*, boiled beef in spicy sauce.

As I was leaving, slipping the pass into my wallet, the boy said, 'You take plenty photo at Wamena?'

'Yes, plenty.'

'Wamena got dirty men. No shirt, no pant. Like animal. You take photo. Many photo.'

In a back street, I had a rice dish with the hottest green chillies. It almost blew my head off. The water had ice cubes with specks of dirt caught in its twisted lines of bubbles. But nothing mattered: I was on my way.

In the afternoon, I went to the missionary office to check that David Marfleet, the pilot with geographical insights, had arrived safely. He hadn't. He was stuck back in England sweating in bed, 'the colour of Dijon mustard', stricken with malaria.

That night I sat in the hotel annotating the expedition provision list on my knee. *Bulk foods for forty-five man days. Trading items: salt, razor blades.* . . . A man was slashing the leaf sprays under the light outside my window. Slow, heavy strokes: swish, swish, swish. The fan drew in the sweet smell of bleeding foliage and it washed over me periodically as the fan turned left, right, left, right across the room, parting and reparting my hair. *Parang, matches – twenty boxes.* . . . A motorbike passed outside, its headlight streaking across the curtain. The grasscutter spat and stamped off into the distance. *Coffee, corned beef, sardines.* . . .

At the evening market I fingered sacks of beans, and pulled out kilo after kilo: groundnuts, rice, sugar . . . A boy ran behind catching all I threw to him. Even among the milling crowds I was easily noticed and children flocked around to watch. A girl with wandering eyes was serving at a chemist counter. She offered me an alarmingly intimate

11

smile – distinctly non-Islamic – but on noticing my attendant crowd slammed each item I pointed out on the glass counter with a hard crack: a box of safety pins, Band-Aids . . . While she was waiting for the next, she drummed her fingers on the till. Her fingernails were smoothed to an extravagant point, like fountain-pen nibs.

Outside in the dark all hell was let loose as rain came down. Street vendors rushed off into the night with their magazines, clothes or fruit. I left my boxes in the store until morning and took cover inside a food tent beside a hissing paraffin lamp. Women squatted with iceblocks between their knees, chipping off splinters with knives, as the tent flaps, though weighted with rocks on tangled strings, swung in the wind. Policemen strolled about on every street in casually polished black boots and tight khaki, black cords strung over one shoulder.

There were other Indonesians in uniforms, the state primary school children disappearing up the twisted unlit streets in impeccable maroon shorts or skirts and white sleeveless tops. Listening to their street chatter I found I could not decipher a word. It was no good, I would have to wait here in Jayapura a week at least to tune my ear in Indonesian. The hotel family patiently helped me work at the language, and the day before I left, the hotelier's overfond daughter, who smelt sweet but musty, carved 'BENIDIKT' drastically round and round the trunk of her father's prize tree, a traveller's palm.

From the lakes of Sentani one of the twice-daily flights was soon flying across level green canopies of leaves through which fragments of swamp water reflected back light. Occasionally, rivers could be seen looping through the wilderness. The pilots had done the route many times before and were reading newspapers, cigarettes hanging from their mouths, for a hundred miles until we reached the Snow Mountains in the central highlands, with their temperamental clouds and vicious summits.

'Well, we're almost here, everyone,' said a kindly, high-shouldered man to his wife and daughter, raising his video camera to film our approach into the mile-high valley. We had already introduced ourselves. They were the Bernheisels: Kathy and Art and their daughter Laura, an MK at the Regions Beyond Missionary Union (RBMU) hostel at Sentani. Art was newly in charge of the hostel, which looked after the children during term time, and he was now flying out to visit some missionaries.

'And what brings you here, Benedict?'

I told him how I was hoping to walk away from Wamena, south-east along the Baliem river from where it broke from the highlands and dropped 5000 feet to the jungle foothills thirty miles away. The river ran southward to the Arafura Sea, but I would walk east towards the border.

'If the local authorities give you permission.'

'Yes, if.'

'Do you mind me enquiring what you intend to do if you ever get to your forest?'

'That depends . . .'

'Oh?'

But I would not be drawn. Nonetheless, I wanted to let him know that my expedition was not lightly undertaken, so I told him, 'What I need to do first, anyway, is to reconnoitre along the Snow Mountains, overlooking the jungle.'

'Well, sad to say I can't advise you there. You're talking to the wrong person. We've never been in the interior before.'

'Have the pilots put away their newspapers yet, Art?' Kathy asked.

'Mom, they put them away hours ago. They know what they're doing, I keep telling you.'

Soon, as we were coming in to land at Wamena, there was a jolt as if the undercarriage had fallen off.

'It's okay. Everything's fine, Kathy. They were just raising the undercarriage.'

'Raising?' Laura said.

I said, 'My God!'

'Sorry, I meant lowering,' explained Art.

Beyond the rim, decked with clouds, rocks and crooked trees, which varied in height from 10,000 to 12,000 feet, nestled the Grand Valley of the Baliem river. It sprang from the mountain wall, wound through the plain for fifty miles, then plunged down a tight gorge. We were upon it quite suddenly. After the hostility of the mountains, all was peace: at the foot of the slopes, miles of neat vegetable plots, occasional pine-like casuarinas – shiny with dampness – open grasslands of gold and yellow and blue–greens, mottled by village compounds, each with half a dozen conical huts and rectangular sheds within the grass-thatched wooden palings. From these projected long-roofed pig stalls and pandanus and banana gardens. The brown, free-limbed figures of gleeful children were looking at our plane's belly and running behind as we touched down on the smooth black strip, long enough for the troop-laden Hercules transports.

I had read that this niche was discovered by the outside world only in 1938; it was inhabited by Dani-speaking peoples, 40,000 of them, who until then had tilled their sweet potatoes in 'garden' plots and fought peacefully for no one knew how long.[4] The men, scornful of attempts by outsiders to clothe them, were covered in pig grease to lessen the mountain chill. They wore gourds – *horims* – tubular extensions to the penis rising typically a foot up and out from the groin, held in place with a strand of twig fibre around the scrotum and lower waist. The girls had simple reed skirts called *yokols*; married women wore *yungols*, skirts of strands looping across the upper thighs. The first outsiders to settle had arrived in 1954; now a garrisoned town had grown up, attracting Indonesian traders who hated the chill but who could get a foothold in business out here. Each day power from the hydroelectric dam faded progressively with the daylight, as switches were flicked on. The missionary organisations used their own generators.

At daybreak the Danis wandered in from the hinterlands, wrapping their arms tightly up around their necks like scarves to fend off the cold, and goggled at the comings and goings; then they returned to their family compounds, *sili*, with a little cash earned from flogging firewood or from smiling (or glaring if required to portray 'a warrior') for tourists' cameras.

I trailed along to the airport building – an architect's impression of a *sili*? – hugging my supply boxes. Though I tagged behind the Bernheisels, who said they would introduce me to the Protestant missionary pilots, I was waylaid by the airport policeman, dressed in blue. He was rosewood-coloured, a Papuan, the first I had seen in authority this side of the border. I got out my *surat jalan*. He told me I would now report to the police station. I asked him when it closed.

'Twelve o'clock.'

What time was it now?

'Twelve o'clock.'

The Indonesian baggage loaders snorted loudly at the West Papuan's back. In the end I left him looking after my boxes while I went to the MAF (Mission Aviation Fellowship) hangar to find out what I could about the highlands. Outside it, light aircraft in red and white were buzzing about on the turf like hive sentry bees. Dozens of Dani children had their lips and round eyes tight to a metal window-grill at the hangar office. Seeing me, they shrank back, mouths open, or puckered as if for a kiss but actually in alarm. I pressed my own face up; at chest level the grill was hot and wet from Dani breath. Inside, a Cessna was having its engine stripped down and some North Americans were queuing to stand on weighing scales with their baggage; but there was no sign of the Bernheisels.

'That makes you fifty-six kilos. Or is that pounds? Bob, does this thing work in kilos or – oh, kilos – okay, good. That's three hundred and twenty so far. Now your turn honey. Just step on the scales there.'

'Excuse me,' I said, waving my hand through the window-grill.

'Sixty-seven. You've been eating too much candy. What are you going to weigh after Christmas?'

'Excuse me . . .'

'Oh, hiya! You need help?'

14

I said I had had a word with an English pilot of theirs in England. He had said he would proffer advice about walking in the Snow Mountains around Sela.

'Paul! There's a guy here says he's a friend of David Marfleet's. Can you come over a minute?' To me he said, 'Won't be a moment.' He turned to the woman. 'Can you get back on the scales, honey? We'll have to start over again.'

From the wooden office, a side door creaked open. The Danis took fright and scuttled away. The man who walked out had a firm parting through straightish, brown hair – now turning to grey – and two even creases dividing his forehead horizontally. When he saw me his tanned, strongly boned face shone affection; I might have been someone returning a long-lost pet spaniel. 'Well, hello! What can I do for you?'

Chapter Two

By a curious chance, Paul Kline was the RBMU man from Sela Valley, east across the cloud-forested ridges and crags of the Snow Mountains, through Yali territory and into Kimyal. The mountains' cold rivers flowed down into the jungle I was aiming for.

'Say, why don't you walk along to my house and join us there for Christmas? You should make it just in time.' Christmas was eleven days away. 'Half a dozen missionary stations lie between here and there. They'll be glad to put you up. I'll introduce you to Bundam Sole, my houseboy. He's walking back home to Sela. He can be a carrier.'

'Are you sure you want me for Christmas? I'm bound to be miserable with blisters.'

'No, no, don't you think that way. We'll be delighted to have you.'

'How many people have walked right through to Sela Valley from here? Westerners, I mean?'

'Through to Sela? A European travelling *singly*? Er ... Anyway, don't fear. There was a big earthquake in the Solo Valley in 1981 at my end of your route. That made the Yali people calm down a lot.'

'Calm down?'

'Yeah, now if there is fighting it's just inter-village.'

'That's something.'

'On the other hand, landslides have now took away the trails. From the air Solo looks a mess. I figure you are kind of strong but you better watch yourself. How fit are you?'

'Moderately. Trouble is I've come here rather suddenly, after weeks in towns chasing visas.'

'Well ...' He cupped his chin. 'Say, I take it you've done this sort of thing before?'

'Jungle mainly.'

'You possess good boots?'

'German paratroopers'.'

'There's a few Danis been shot on the first leg to Soba, this week. The exact number escapes me. You'd best skip that bit and take the plane direct to the Soba mission.'

I thought I would. 'When's the plane leaving?'

'Now let me see,' Paul Kline said, tapping his wrist watch. 'Five minutes?'

Five minutes! Five minutes in which to get a *surat jalan*, do a final check of all those stores, buy a few last-minute things . . . Paul Kline went over to speak with the pilot, who said it was okay, he had developed a 'gas leak' and would be another half an hour. But the cloud was coming in fast and they would not risk leaving it any later.

Bundam Sole was slightly built, in his mid-teens I thought. He wore shorts and a laddered shirt which hung limply as if bullying brothers had the habit of hauling him along by it. He had a friend from Korupun, the Kimyal valley before his own, called Diam – older, stockier, wearing the same limp clothes and a very large pair of gumboots. His eyes were bright, Bundam's were placid. Diam's thick skin looked dry and hard to the point of crustiness; Bundam's was still a boy's, elastic and unlined. They spoke very little Indonesian, but more than I did. I had to resort to speaking through Paul Kline, and no one was very impressed.

'I just haven't quite got my ear adjusted yet,' I said.

'Let's hope it's fully adjusted two days hence.'

Wages would be 1500 rupiahs a day; they could use money in the mission stores. Now to get the *surat jalan*. I headed back to the airport building and found the Papuan policeman leaning, half asleep, on my supply boxes, which were now badly crushed. He said we could try calling at the Captain's house. We deposited the boxes at the MAF hangar and ran; he did not enjoy the unseemly act of pursuing a foreigner through the clumps of onlooking fellow Papuans, but he lacked the will to take initiative. It was interesting that the Indonesians had chosen him for the post. We stopped, breathless, at a suburban detached house of craftily banged-together painted wood panels. I rapped at the door urgently. A baby started to bawl. Through the fly netting I could see a scrap of brown shadow rapidly buttoning up a white shirt. Still panting I strung a few Indonesian words together. 'Plane . . . missionary . . . leaving . . . five . . . minutes . . . Paul Kline . . . Soba please . . . very grateful.'

To me the Captain said in English, 'Come, please,' and I stepped inside. To the Papuan he said a dozen crisp words, which set him sprinting off – not dragging his feet now – in the direction of the Indonesian flag, red above pure white, beneath which were the police headquarters. The Captain offered me a plush cushion on the deep sofa.

'You speak good English,' I said, after five minutes of pleasantries.

'I see many foreigners. They like to look at the Irianese men.'

On a low coffee table I saw there were two *horims*, the gourds which the Danis grew and trained into an extended tube shape suitable for wearing. They were Cheddar yellow and clean, obviously tourist trophies. 'I am sending them home for a kid. They are cheap and light. Many of my men find presenting these an amusing thing to do.'

'Do the Danis often come to ask you to sort out their problems?'

'In practice, no. I do not know why. Perhaps they are still too Stone Age. They are free to come any time.' He paused. 'Of course, they are not permitted to come into the offices wearing one of these.' He laughed softly, amicably tapping a gourd with his fingernails, thereby unconsciously making the Dani man's sign for astonishment.

The policeman came back gasping for breath, as if just rescued from drowning. The form was signed. I surrendered my passport for the duration of my 'visit to Soba'. He had not asked if I planned to walk on anywhere more remote from there, so I did not trouble to tell him. But now I needed to make some more purchases.

The road to the market, of cobbles polished by highland feet, was laid with drainage trenches on either side containing black water which flickered with skating water creatures. Beyond these ditches were missionary houses with their gardens of springy turf, pea-gravel paths, nappies strung from washing-lines, water-storage tanks and netted doors with parrots on perches behind. Time was getting on. The blue mountains around the valley were becoming smothered by sinking cloud. Dodging uniformed Indonesians on motorbikes and in squads jogging with rifles, I came to a block of Indonesian stores, the ground strewn with plastic wrappings, here and there Danis selling firewood. Most of them had shining skin: it would be a stupid thing to wash in mountain water when it would only chill and remove the insulating pig grease, so they didn't.

The market square was boxed in by the shops, which were hung with spades, peanut butter (for the missionaries), salt (for the Danis, who previously obtained it by soaking banana palm pith in wells of natural brine), string, sweets and matches. The Indonesian traders had marked out a badminton court and some of them were knocking a shuttlecock back and forth, ignored by the Danis, who squatted in the way talking. I watched Danis hugging each other in greeting. They wore neck strings of cowries, or white cockatoo plumes trimmed like fern shoots as they arose from their tight mops of hair. One man had a *mikak* shell hanging from his neck like the bowl of a huge spoon, shiny leather thongs falling with it across the muscles of his chest; another man wore the iridescent plumage of an emerald bird of paradise which curled back over his head, his hair cascading down on all sides in twisted cords, heavy with fat. I saw parrot-feather crowns, tiaras of the brown and white banded feathers of hawks. Women sat with legs casually crossed under them, some bowed low under the weight of full string-net bags, which were

19

borne by every woman on the shoulders and neck supported by a forehead strap. I passed a female ghoulishly dry and white in mourning paint, which was beginning to come away in flecks, revealing a child's skin.

Those Danis not exchanging news gazed at the shop fronts or sat in the shaded alleyways while pigs scuffled here and there; women, occasionally with torn Western shirts, sat in the central covered market behind clutches of stubby cucumbers, sweet potatoes, tomatoes and groundnuts. I bought a cooking pot and four sacks to replace my boxes; then I glanced around, wondering if there was anything else I needed – I had been through my lists, but you never knew. I did not like being rushed like this. Next I was racing back to the airport.

The other passengers were the Bernheisels. Laura Bernheisel, standing on the weighing scales, said, 'You staying at the Webbs, then?'

'What are the Webbs?'

'They are the people at Soba. Soba is just their house and Sue Trenier's – she's a nurse – and wooden buildings like the church and school and nothing else. Apart from the village huts.'

'I suppose I'll be in one of the huts. The Webbs don't know I'm coming.'

'That'll be no problem. Mike Webb is an Englishman too. Expect he'll wanna find out just how your national coal strike is coming along.'

The little red Cessna trundled along the grass, crossed on to the mighty tarmac runway, and took us into the air. There were five of us: the pilot in a helmet,[5] Art Bernheisel beside him filming through the windscreen, Kathy, Laura and myself crammed between my copious boxes in the rear. We were out above the sweet-potato plots, the chocolate soil in deep beds, Dani compounds thatched with the same fawn grass as the pig fences. Further out, the Baliem river suddenly began to whiten and accelerate down a gorge. Round huts budded in clumps like mushrooms from the grassy, boulder-strewn slopes. We flew over the pale-green landing-strip and glaring metal roofs of a mission. Among the rocks cowered half-crippled oaks, pines and chestnuts, torn less by the weather than by the firewood plunderers of the recent years. We rose and rose, red moss forest rising with us up the mountain walls.

Kathy Bernheisel gripped her seat-strap grimly as we banked between sharp mountain ridges and flirtatious cloud. My boxes shifted, alternately crushing Laura and Kathy as we tilted this way and that. So loud was the engine, we knew the pilot was talking into his microphone only because we could see his lips moving. Art Bernheisel was getting very little footage; the cloudy air around us was a series of irritable flashes and the pilot was talking in haste to the Soba mission for advice. *Was the landing-strip clear or not?*

Light pierced through a chink in the clouds and lit a river gully into a silver cord. Somewhere down there was a nook at the side of the valley, and our airstrip, which was begun by the missionary Stan Dale just before he died from multiple arrow punctures on the trail I was about to walk. At a sharp angle we circled in search of the strip. Kathy looked repeatedly into Laura's face as we leaned and swung in blinding cloud. We straightened in our seats and the plane levelled into a final approach. When still nothing came into sight the pilot cancelled, and we flipped up and back towards Wamena.

I was put up for the night in the storeroom of the missionary guesthouse, and we tried Soba again the next morning, before the clouds joined and thickened. There was more to look at now, jagged strata beds and waterfalls pitching down shiny screes. Finally, we reeled left, north of the Baliem, flew up a side valley and dropped on to a strip of clean grass at its head. The approach was easy by MAF standards, but the pilot had to remember to accelerate rather than decelerate after touching down, because the airstrip ran up a severe uneven gradient. At the top of the landing-strip were two or three houses, which looked more like holiday homes than anything else, with cheerful flower beds around them. Smoke drifted from their chimney stacks. Behind was a hut built of boards – a church? – and scattered over the slopes were men with digging sticks, one or two with a stone adze.

The Webbs shook hands with the Bernheisels and the pilot. I hung back beside the plane. Virginia Webb had a Canadian accent, Mike had a beard – black rather than the red of Art Bernheisel's extravagant growth. Two girls in flowery white frocks – young Webbs presumably – chatted to Laura. While I fumbled with my boxes, little brown boys of the valley's Hupla population squealed and giggled at me with their hands in their mouths, most of them too young to wear gourds. Their parents were beginning to get back to work – the men using heavy poles to break up clods for new plots, the women gathering sweet potatoes into their net bags. The children's noise caught the attention of a sprightly woman with red curls. She said, 'I'm so sorry – I didn't see ya there.' She was Irish. 'Welcome to Soba. You're with the Bernheisels.'

'No, I'm just walking on through to Sela Valley.'

'Oh, I see, just walking to . . .' Her eyes looked to my cardboard boxes, whose bases were dissolving on the wet grass. 'Sela Valley? I hope your legs are strong.'

She took me over to the others. Mike Webb said it was good to see a fellow Brit. 'I get fed up to the back teeth with all these ex-colonials.'

'Careful, limey,' said his wife.

21

I explained again why I was there.

'Well, I hope you're fit.' I hoped everyone wasn't going to say that. 'You could grow a beard, like Art's.' Not quite like Art's, I thought, studying his splendidly rich, lichenous formation. Mike said I ought to because the Huplas, who spoke a dialect of Dani, respected men with beards. 'Well, bring your baggages along and come indoors.'

'I think I'd better work out some accommodation first.' I gestured loosely towards the sprinkling of huts on the incline above, their roofs steaming faintly through horizontal bars of morning sunlight.

'You'll have plenty of chance to live like that on your walk. Stay in our house, we don't often have visitors.'

The Webbs' house had a kitchen stove; huddled round it were half-clad and unclad boys being trained in domestic duties. Once the Bernheisels' suitcases were safely on their journey upstairs, we locked the door to keep out more Huplas, who had the habit of sneaking in, ostensibly to pass messages to the houseboys by the warm stove. The kitchen was homely: mugs on hooks, sugar jars, sets of saucepans and two animals.

'That's Nippy.' Nippy was a dog with the sort of coat a lion might have if it took a spin in a washing machine. He spent much of his day staring at the hutches by the porch. 'The rabbits are our meat.' There was also a fierce cat, Fluffy. We had tea by a fireplace of crazy paving. Sue Trenier brought some biscuits over.

'Cookies,' said Laura.

'Neat,' said Art.

The plate of biscuits was passed around as we sat in our creaky chairs. Above the fireplace I read the message:

CHRIST is the HEAD
of this house
THE UNSEEN GUEST
of every meal
THE SILENT LISTENER
to every conversation

But there was no conversation; not yet. On the wooden mantelpiece was a white rose in a brass vase with a sheen that reflected the two melting candles on either side.

'Well, this *is* a treat. We don't often get visitors.'

There was more shuffling silence. The two Webb girls said they would show Laura their rooms if she liked. Sue Trenier, Kathy and Vi Webb went to 'look at the kitchen facilities'. Art followed, 'I'll leave you two English people together. You must have lots to talk about.'

I had another biscuit. It crunched; the fire spat and crackled. On the bookshelf I spotted a slim volume, a handy guide to refuting the theory of evolution. Mike said, 'How's the miners' strike?' It emerged that his news was more up to date than mine; he could get the BBC World Service. He showed me my room instead. 'You are going to need every minute of rest you can get.'

After Mike and Art had fiddled with the generator, which was about to blow, Sue suggested we put on our wellies and go out to see the Huplas. I came in my paratrooper boots, which I was softening for the march, the Bernheisels in pumps, which were soon coming adrift in the greasy garden-plot soil. Sue gave us the rundown: sweet potatoes were the staple – there were goodness knows how many varieties. Pigs were generally kept for special occasions and there were greens, yams, this and that – and taro, of course. Fourteen hamlets made up the valley. The huts were not all in compounds in the Baliem fashion, but there were fences to keep pigs from plundering crops. The huts – only circular ones here – lacked chimneys, so the warmth escaped slowly through the thatch. 'Don't sleep in them if you can't take bug bites,' Sue said to me.

Inside the first hut was a boy playing a cane mouth harp. He froze as we stared through the three-foot-high doorway. 'Hiya,' said Laura.

An old man crawled outside to greet us; he looked confused when he saw her. He gave Art and myself a greeting, tickling our chins, 'Halabok.'

'That means, I value your excreta,' said Sue.

'And I value yours, I'm sure,' said Art.

'No, he's saying he's honoured to meet you. There are plenty of phrases like that here, though "Halabok" is borrowed from the Yalis, I guess.'

A man was constructing a rain cape, folding the pandanus palm leaves in the heat of the fire. It would last the wearer about one season, she said. The hut roofs of palm or grass lasted two, and the increased use of pandanus palm roofs perhaps reflected our nearness to Yali country, over to the east. Those giggling little girls were ten to twelve years old, their head bags stitched with a needle of pig sinew; they did not feel properly dressed without them. Soon each would be asking a favourite man if he would marry her.

'They've got the choice?' asked Art.

'Yes. Previously they had hardly any voice of their own. Now that they've been taught how to write they can send their own secret love notes.'

An old man was uprooting some tobacco plants, in case our guided tour headed in his direction. Sue laughed lightly. Smoking was tied up with spirit worship. You decided to uproot your tobacco patch when you let Christ into your life as your personal saviour.

23

On the next day, Sunday, an extra long grace preceded each meal, there was a prayer meeting during which my journey was blessed, and a service for converted Huplas, who were encouraged to wash in the perishing mountain streams each week before coming.

On Monday, Bundam Sole and Diam trotted up the valley at dawn. Mike got me out of bed and I raced down still in my underpants to find the two carriers crouched by the stove. Into action, I thought. I weighed the luggage which the three of us were to carry: seventy pounds each.

'You'll never make it,' said Mike.

'Yes, we will.'

'*They* will, *you* won't.'

Diam and Bundam raised and lowered the sacks dolefully.

'It's supplies for if I decide to go straight on from Sela, down into the lowland forests,' I explained to Mike, who was shaking his head as if to loosen a painfully crooked neck.

'I can easily pick up another carrier, if need be.'

Mike weighed my boots, which were wet from yesterday – three pounds each. 'You'll need a carrier just for these,' he said. 'And what . . . what is *that*?'

'That's my pocket Indonesian phrasebook.'

Big Diam turned to slender Bundam, blew air loudly through his short teeth and pouted.

'They want me to ask if you understand how hard this journey is. They think you don't understand.'

We heaved on our sacks and waved goodbye. Vi said she would radio to Ethel and Peter Nash, missionaries over at Ninia, to let them know I was coming that night. 'You're going to have to move yourself. It's gone ten o'clock.'

'Have a nice walk,' said Laura.

'Take care, okay?' said Kathy.

'Hope you know what you're doing,' said Mike.

Sue said, 'The headman wants to walk you to the edge of his village, as you are a friend.' The man, whose legs turned out to be not so good, took my pack, coughed, stared suspiciously at it and turned up the slippery path into moss-clad trees, ferns and silver lichens; the wet air maintained some stretches of path in a state of semi-permanent mire.

A harrier hawk poising and spiralling in the sky beneath us was lost as we were swept up in the first band of mist. The low sun, which a moment ago had been cradled by the notch of Soba's valley, was wiped from view too. Very soon I was licking the splashes that came from my sodden black felt hat, sucking in cool draughts of cloud. Short men with a few handfuls of flightless arrows stopped to stare, their bows planted

24

in the slushy earth, reaching to chin height. Girls scattered and splashed like scared ducks off our path and, bowed under their rain capes, waiting until we were gone, were as still and dripping as the crinkled trees.

So far so good: my ankles – damaged by the trauma of my previous Amazon expedition – were bearing up well, and if I kept them bandaged for marches I should not have to give them another thought. Before leaving home I had done my daily runs through the oak and beech woods of Selborne Common, my hundred press-ups before each bedtime, so what I was planning to do after this highland exercise should not be too suicidal.

Once out of the Kwik Valley, it was up through the passes of the 12,000-foot escarpment. The trees were pervaded not just by the winds and their loads of water, but by the eerie calm that was studded only by the crunch of our feet on the sandstones and distressed lone screams, light and strong, that I could only guess were coming from the beaks of kites, or some such bird that could traverse a valley in a moment's glide.

Next, it was down into the land of the Yalis, whose men wore yard upon yard of rattan hooped around their waists above their gourds. They had good trade with the Danis, who craved marsupial furs like opossum and bush kangaroo, bird of paradise plumes for headdresses, and fine wood for their bows. The exposed, severely rain-drenched slopes dictated that the Yalis had smaller huts than the Danis so that they could keep the warmth in. Pigs were allotted half of the living space in the women's huts, *homias*, and were breast-fed by the women if need be. Yalis built stone, not wood, walls around the hamlets.

Below, through the sleeves of moss and sheaths of cold bark, would be the Heluk, into whose white water and sharp rocks were once tossed those who angered the various *kembu* spirits (according to the missionary account).[6] The boys' initiation involved the passing on of the secret *wene melalek*, the commandments of the non-human spirits. Spirit men worshipped in the *kembuvam*, temple, which lay within the stone-walled *osuwa* garden and sacred pandanus grove. The main object of worship was a stone, where the god, Kembu himself, resided. If a woman heard the rituals, pigs were sacrificed, their blood rubbed in the offender's ears – or in her eyes if she had glimpsed anything. The other supernatural forces which kept the men preoccupied were the *dokwi*, spirits of those Yalis who had died in war. They constantly nagged you for revenge, and a sacred house, the *dokwivam*, contained the fetishes dedicated to them. This was Yali life twenty years ago, a world where the eating of enemy flesh gave you the strength of its life force, and where – perhaps because inbreeding was such a threat to the genes of the isolated Yalis – the *wene melalek* required that incest should be

25

punished by death, the convicted, or their offending parts, floating away down the Heluk.

Now, I guessed, there would be no temples. A woman I saw skipping with a gourd of water through the rain was not wearing the traditional garment – a thick, short bunch of stredded fibre front and back, tied with string – but a reed skirt, like a Dani maiden's. Her hair was cropped short in the Yali style, but not with the lengthier ball at the back. Men had the encircling rattan skirts, but few ornaments of the old days – high caps of fur, a charm, rolled like a cigarette and inserted through the earlobe, head bands studded with cowries.

We marched all day. I thought of the first strangers who came here. In the 1960s parts of West Papua were as they are now, remoter even than the Dark Continent. The missionaries Stan Dale from Australia and Bruno de Leeuw from Canada walked over the 10,000-foot Mugwi Pass from the direction of the Baliem Gorge in 1961 and into this unreached valley. Once the Ninia mission post was firmly established by the RBMU, the trails were widened, the Message spread. By 1968 Stan Dale had measured up the airstrip for Soba, west of the Yalis. Afterwards he planned his ill-fated walk right through the heart of the Yali country ahead of me.

Diam pivoted on his thick, gnarled legs, and pointed with his free hand to where the sun might have been. We stepped up our pace – dusk was imminent. The boy, Bundam, was far behind, looking like a hunchbacked spectre as he stumbled through the cloud, humping his load, kneading his spine when he could. Once I thought I heard whimpering, but it might have been any other of the mist's lost sounds. My mind had yet to change down even one gear, it was spinning in its Western mode. This highland walk above all else was for the purpose of emptying my mind of clutter. By the end I must be better able to absorb, sense cleanly. We saw the smooth slot on the hillside, knew that before long we might hear the battering that the rains were giving the metal roofs of Ninia. A generator started to life and was only a purr in the downpour. A light winked through the rain to us.

At daybreak we took two Yalis along. They had their gourd and hoop attire, but no language in common with us. Ethel Nash had given me a postcard of Loch Lomond to deliver to the Clark family at Lolat, the next mission two days away. Our sounds were the thumping bare feet, Diam's loose gumboots and my clumping stride, and our breath, in short light blasts. Their soles were white spongy pads with black cracks across the heels. They passed over the muds, shingles, bird droppings, beetles.

On each ridge, Diam called into the clouds, 'ARRK! ARRK! ARRK!', rousing Bundam to insert his own cry, which he did when he could spare

26

breath: 'Aa!' 'ARRK!', 'Aa!', 'ARRK!' It might have been a message to the villages obscured somewhere below to warn of our approach, but in Diam's tone there was exaltation. He was at peace with his mountain world.

Later, in the thickest mists, our sounds were sucked from us: even the biting noise of my artificial soles, even the calls of invisible birds which had sounded out like running brooks, with distant, fluid notes, could be heard no more. Drinking water was however scarce. I found it in the traps of pitcher plants, taking care to avoid the spiders, the scorpions and the ants. Higher, I dug my hands into the sphagnum beds and cupped them; cold water squirted from the sponge leaves, numbing where the moorland shrubbery had scored my palms.

The light began to weaken and we were still right up at 8000 feet in the murky summit forests of the Heluk and Upper Seng watershed.

'Where is the nearest village, Diam?'

He lifted his round fingers. Above his hand – flecks of bark sat suspended on the hairs, which were attracting mist droplets – a metallic green and grey butterfly wing spun on the end of a spider's wire. Diam was indicating a point high across the unseen valley at our feet.

We were going to have to spend a night out on the mountain and I did not like the idea. Above Diam's home, in Korupun, there was a *hwe waregon* at a spot such as this. A woman had snuggled into a rock crevice to get shelter, but the cranny was enough only to preserve her body, which was still there, a heap of bones bound in parchment-like skin. That was a *hwe waregon*. Her daughter had been with her; her life had been taken either by wild beasts or by spirits. As a Christian, Diam was not about to work any charms against ghouls, at least not in front of me. However, we kindled a fire with greybeard lichen, hoisted a shelter of leafy branches. We ate roasted pig fat and everyone tried my coffee, hating it but accepting it dutifully like codliver oil. Those who had clothes shed them. We nestled around, waiting for the chill to set in. There was no room to stretch out and it was too cold to leave the flames so we let them play between our splayed legs. Tomorrow, I thought, sleepily, we would tumble down through Wikboon into the Upper Seng

Wikboon was where the missionary Stan Dale met his end, coming the opposite way, back towards Ninia, the RBMU post in the Upper Heluk, a moderately sure foothold. With Bruno de Leeuw, Stan Dale had been venturing out further east. Then, after joining Dale for two months to finish off the airstrip, Phil Masters from Iowa went on an even further hike east with de Leeuw, right through the Yali country to a new people, the Kimyal, who were small and friendly. The two men settled down to building an airstrip and mission there, to be called Korupun, Diam's home.

Back at Ninia, the Yali spirit men were biding their time. Stan Dale, one Sunday night in May 1966, decided that the Lord now required a thorough purge of the fetishes from the more nominal of his Christians. As pagans stood by aghast, the sacred objects were brought out and jubilant hymns were sung as flames consumed them. Dale marched up and down the Heluk with his faithful followers, lighting up the bonfires, ignoring flying arrows. They ate the holy food from the *osuwa* gardens, to become living proof that nothing terrible would happen, barring indigestion.

All this was way out of order to the spirit-fearing Yalis. Two of Dale's teachers, Yekwara and Bengwok, were eliminated during an open-air Bible class. Dale called in an Indonesian patrol to find the bodies and received five arrows himself. One was through his diaphragm, one in his stomach, but though Dale was fifty years old he tottered through the night, 1,500 feet up, out of a gorge back towards Ninia. After several months, he recovered, but the Yalis did not. They wanted revenge on him, this man who had insulted their spirits. Some feared that his God had made him immortal, but they would be waiting for him anyway.

That was the setting in September 1968 as Masters and Dale marched from Korupun, along our present trail towards us and Ninia, putting trust in their God. They had had a cheerful lunch with their families, sung '*What A Friend We Have In Jesus*', and kissed their children goodbye. There were probably tears as they raised their packs and set off with three burly Dani carriers and a Yali. They strode happily up from the Erok river and Indal, climbed a thousand feet to Duram village and, still in Kimyal country, progressed through the evergreens which swathed the crests, to the rumbling Solo river. They forded those difficult waters and emerged from the severe valley. They were on the brink of the Yalis.

Their reception was as good as they might reasonably have hoped, and for a while they kept the hordes of rowdy men out of arrow-firing range by lobbing Chinese firecrackers at them. Some Yalis showed they were having nothing to do with the imminent massacre by accepting salt in exchange for sweet potatoes. With the high male cries echoing along the valley sides, the carriers stood incredulously as the two missionaries unwound their tape measures to assess the merits of possible airstrip sites. As they moved on into the Wikboon valley bowl the firecrackers began to worry the stalking Yalis less and less. They flocked in growing numbers down the vegetable-plot gardens; the clattering noise of their jiggling cane hoops penetrated everywhere. The women hidden indoors were heard by the missionaries sobbing at what was about to occur.

Behind the party, Yalis rubbed the offending boot prints from the soil, disgustedly. Those ahead raised bows but the intruders kept marching boldly and the Yalis found themselves walking backwards, confused by the nonchalant response to their warnings. The missionary party and company meandered from the east side of the river, beside Sohopma village, to 'Kibi' (Kybyanggenma, I guessed) over a spindly suspension bridge of poles borne on rattan. The carriers were all for chopping the bridge away – it would give them badly required time. The white men said no, it would be an act of hostility – it might save *them*, but the Yalis would definitely kill the next outsiders who came along. Besides, they had come in peace. The party made camp, tying a chart to a tree above their tent. It was an easy-to-understand picture depicting two roads: one to heaven, along a narrow but straight Christian trail, and the second to hellfire, down a broad but windy road. The Yalis were on the downhill route.

The Yali men jeered at the road map, either because they did not understand it or because they did not like being preached to. Rain dispersed the throng and through the night it bucketed down. At daybreak the party carried on up the Seng. They had only to go a few hundred yards further, and they could begin the climb to the safety of the forest above. But, on a beach of grey and white gravel, the first arrow was fired in earnest at Stan Dale, who was lagging behind. As the arrows grew thickly on him he lagged behind further, but to the attackers' horror he was almost casually plucking wickedly barbed blades out of his body, shouting at the four carriers to run ahead with Masters. By now the Yalis really thought their worst fears had been realised – the pale-skinned man called Dale *was* immortal. But after a while he did fall, and then it was Master's turn. He would not flee, Masters decided now. Stan had shown him how to face death, and he would try his best to emulate that courage. So, as the arrows slipped into his body, he accepted them. He stood, without uttering a single cry, and lasted much as long as Dale had, dropping to the pebbles only when he was already on his last couple of breaths. Kembu the Almighty had been satisfied.

The guides, nearby, could be fairly sure they would be the next targets. They dropped their packs and ran to the security of the pass, up to the clouds above. While they were scrambling, the Yalis down below gathered around the bodies and wondered what to do next. What action did the spirits desire? The Yalis stripped the men naked, and pondered. Eating human meat gave you power, strength, but what would be the effect of this insipid white skin? It looked neither tasty nor safely edible. And after all, the Christians practised cannibalism only symbolically: the bread and wine. What if the ghosts of these strangers haunted them? They cut off slithers of flesh and scattered them through the trees to forestall resurrection. It was hoped that if no such restoration had occurred by daybreak they might safely feast on the remaining hunks. These were left, and cooking pits laid in preparation.

The night passed; some men cursing at the folly of what they had done – what would be their fate at the hands of the white men's God now? Others simply thought it was a despicable thing to have done to any men of peace. At dawn there was relief – the body segments had not budged. To the annoyance of those who had been dreaming all night of sharing the life force of the two men, one man declared that their ancestors had never partaken of meat of such alien stock, and to depart from such custom would be an insult to their forebears. Though the audience muttered its irritation, no one could challenge the statement. Wood was lugged in for a funeral pyre, and Stan Dale and Phil Masters were gathered up and given a fine cremation.

That was September 1968, and somehow a message spread along the Yali grapevine to Ninia and Anguruk, the mission station directly north, that portions of the white men's fingers were being handed out and clans who accepted one were automatically committed to fighting off any more intruders. Enough was enough, the Indonesian powers thought. On 25 October, a month after the killings, a patrol left Ninia to 'pacify' the Seng Valley. Scattering with heavy bursts of gunfire the Yalis who blocked their way – the soldiers did not hit anyone, but the noise of the firearms was sufficient – the Indonesians said that if the Yalis refused to negotiate they would burn down the Wikboon hamlet of 'Kibi'. When the Yalis emerged from their retreats to negotiate, the Indonesians arrested eleven men at random. They would be kept hostage until the Yalis accepted outsiders peacefully. In the end, the Indonesians opted for burning buildings down after all, and the pacification patrol beat a sharpish retreat back to Ninia, with all but one of the captives having escaped or been shot.

Two months later, Wikboon stood empty. The Yalis were still hiding in the bleak forests above, wondering what the outside world was going to do to them next. Actually, what it did to them took everyone by surprise, not least the Christians around the world who were praying for the Word to spread through this now famous valley.

Of all the highlands, a MAF plane now chose Wikboon in which to crash. The weather was bad along the Snow Mountains but the pilot was flying a MAF accountant called Gene Newman, his wife and four young children up from the southern forests where they had been on holiday at a mission among the Asmat peoples. They came north to the cloud-barricaded mountain range, and spiralled down to look for what was the only way through – the huge Baliem Gorge up into the Grand Valley. The pilot finally saw what he thought was the Baliem, tumbling out of the highlands into the low forests. In fact it was the Seng, which emerges parallel to the Baliem. He headed up it – the white river waves seemed a breath away beneath, the cloud a low grey ceiling above. The valley narrowed, the river shrank faster towards its source than it should have, and instead of breaking out into the Grand Valley, it became the Wikboon bowl and an unforgiving wall. He tried to turn but was already too late.

Fire spread through the wreckage and over the occupants, starting with those in front. But, through a hole gashed in the tail, out squeezed a nine-year-old boy. Days later, when a helicopter came to pick up the corpses, one was missing – Paul. The poor child must have been eaten. But no. He had been adopted by a loving Yali and sheltered in his brand-new hut – new because the pacification patrol had burned his last one to the ground. To the Christians the sight of the boy holding hands with a warrior was a God-given miracle; to the Indonesians it was a sign that the Yalis were well on the way to being civilised.

That was years ago now, and even village fights were becoming rarer. During the 1970s the only direct Indonesian contact had been after earthquakes, or sorties to retrieve bodies of Bible teachers and so on.

We came out of the green twilit forest, mounted a ridge and were upon Wikboon, hamlets scattered on the carved slopes. Cloud clung to the escarpments above, but the valley was lit by a bold morning sun. The Seng river sounded only a soft hiss to us at this height. I thought I could make out Yendoal beach where Dale and Masters fell at the foot of the trail. Thatched with pandanus palm in the Yali style, the bigger huts no doubt were the men's, *yogwi*, the *homias* clustered around them. Each had a stick spire rising from the centre of the cone roof. Some groves of palm were in red fruit. The dark soil of the gardens far away was speckled yellow by the rattan hoops over men's barrel chests. There seemed to be rather a lot of them. Perhaps the men were only out in force to dig new gardens but I checked with the Yali carriers. Ethel Nash had written out phrases in my notebook. In response both men rubbed their scaly toes together, in a pigeon's stance. Their faces, seeming as darkly grained as their bow wood, turned from me to a lizard – rare, surely, up here – which had just snatched a fly.

'Oh well,' I thought, and meandered on down, passing three bearded men gazing stolidly, their heavily browed eyes a deeper brown than the soil tucked over the sweet potato tubers. A flock of women, though their tilling sticks doubled as spears, cavorted downslope, a child on the shoulders, stripey piglet in the nook of the arm. Behind me, Diam began to whistle, experimenting with notes he had heard from me yesterday. I had noted that this new game was one he played when uneasy.

Here it was that the Indonesian pacification patrol had made a mess of taking hostages. The hamlet was almost emptied out. Pigs were rubbing themselves on the inside of the short hut walls. I heard the snap of an open fire from a nearby hut, caught the smell of wood easing out through the small exit slot. It would not have been tactful to have stopped to chat about old times to the man who was hauling a duff leg along as if it were a chunk of firewood – nor to the ancient woman crouched under her eaves with flies bothering her dribbling nose. The sun began to fry us. The world was very silent, but dogs cried. They did not howl, or yap; their manner was to cry. Those were black-headed finches twitching in the sugar cane. Flame dragonflies dipped between the reeds of the brook.

Along the narrow descending paths it was hard for the watching men not to block our way. I squeezed by their black beards of coarse fur – the hair always removed from the upper lip – a single pig's tusk boldly arching from their nostrils, a dazzling show of teeth in a ring around the neck, men smelling of cooked pig fat. I offered a hand to anyone within reach – it was sometimes seized and squeezed lightly – and I wondered if the occasional sound of twittering swiftlets audible through the thatch came from the wives. But we never broke our pace and descended maybe a couple of thousand feet to discover that the bridge – previously a few poles extended from either bank and strapped with rattan – was no longer there. The Seng, a creamy foam between tumbled boulders, was trapped by a sheer gully as it blundered on south; so much cold water spilling into the forest warmth. Now, with the abnormal rain, the bridge had been brought down too.

We probed the Seng up and down, tracing shallows, staring forlornly at the river froth. At last Diam called us to him with excited, dog-like barks, we linked arms and, in a ring, skipped across. Squirming along loose cliffs, we picked our way through scree. A boulder was grooved in crescents, and might have served once as an axe-sharpening stone. The lighter cliff debris under our tread clicked like brittle pieces of crockery.

We ascended to a high forest jammed with ferns and chilling sphagnum. In dry nooks, blankets of spider-trap cotton collected dead leaves, sometimes the feathers of the agitated blue-beaked finches which clattered from the disorderly thickets around us. Here the drips on the leaves and bark had lost their pearly shine and were like beads of tar.

Bundam somehow spiked his nose on his parang. While we sat chewing groundnuts on boulder islands in the middle of a brook he moped with his head between his knees, watching each drip of blood splash into the water and stretch and twirl as it was drawn into the current. Soon the sight of that red ribbon entranced him. He slipped his hand under his nose and watched it trickle over his fingers. He was enjoying watching the crimson-dyed water dilute, combed clean by waving limbs of water plants. The Yalis sank into the same trance. Their distraction was disturbing. What were they seeing in that lifeblood ebbing away? Diam spat on a taro leaf and made a poultice for the boy, but Bundam was in his torpor and would not be stirred. Deciding to press on, I called them, but they ignored me, until the raindrops of the afternoon drummed so hard that our feet were almost invisible in exploding droplets, the track a riverlet.

Lolat was a lonely mission post with landing space for only a helicopter, and it seemed the Bernheisels had made use of it, because Art was standing there, hunched in the Clarks' front doorway. 'Well, what have we got here?' he said.

'Your postman,' I said, and handed him the soggy pulp which had been the postcard of Loch Lomond from Ninia.

'I'll get the stove water organised for a shower.' He shut the door in my face to keep the cold out.

The Yalis dropped their bags at my feet. I paid them off in salt and razor blades and they were led by a Bible teacher to a warm hut. I returned to tackle my bootlaces, which oozed peat water and decaying leather. Lolat children stood in the porch, crowding around, noses dribbling green drips, bodies pressing in so close they took the light, leaning against me. Their bare skin was not tight like mine from cold, but felt loose and warm even through my wringing shirt.

Peeling potatoes in the kitchen, Carol Clark said that the big earthquake had happened just after midnight on 20 January 1981, rattling their new house, and tugging ten villages straight off the mountains. The Klines were also shaken, right over at Sela, a mission established the previous year. Sitting around the Christmas tree, our feet among the presents, Kathy Bernheisel recounted a tale.

'This witchdoctor came out of his smoky hut and said, "Right, God, if you are so great, why don't you just show me your power" – this was in his own language you all realise, guys. Sorry I don't know if I know the story well enough.'

'Come on, Mom, that's great so far.'

'Okay. "Right, God, I offer you a challenge. You flex your muscle – prove you're really up there," he said, looking into the sky. "You do that and I'll forsake all my magic stones and tobacco and fetishes." He left it at that, went inside his hut, and, right on midnight, the earthquake came and—'

'Flattened his hut on top of him,' I suggested.

'Er, why no. Just showed him the error of his ways, and how real the Lord is.'

'That's real neat,' said Art Bernheisel.

'Yeah, just like the movies,' said Laura.

The man had burned his fetishes in a gigantic bonfire and dug up his tobacco patch; some thought he had been baptised.

'It's time for the morning sked,' said Carol Clark, during a late breakfast. 'Sked' was short for 'schedule' pronounced in the North American fashion. Now was the time when the RBMU missionaries exchanged messages on the radio to Sentani and up and down the Snow Mountains. At the moment it was Kathryn Kline, wife of Paul at Sela Valley, talking to Rosa at Holuwan, a station down the Baliem river, not too far from Soba.

'We'll be sending you our prayers, that you can be sure of, over.'

'That's appreciated, Sela. You're in our prayers also. Can you do with five tins of marge I've got spare, over?'

'Thanks, but negative, we've already gotten some, over.'

'Okay. Thanks.'

There was a second empty static, and I called up Sela Valley. Paul Kline said, 'We've been praying for you all the way – especially with this rain. Now you've got the hard part, Benedict, over.'

'Is the Dutchman, Jan Godschalk, there? I believe he's actually been through some of the earthquake zone, over.'

'I'll get him on the line. Wait a second.'

Then, 'Jan Godschalk speaking. Hello, you have two alternatives. A three-day route and a four-day route. I am supposing you're a good walker. The trouble is coming because the conditions are very changeable, ja? So, you talk to your guides of lots of landslides. Fresh ones. Beware for the overhead cliffs and stones. With all the raining, I think you are going to be very careful. The only slightly good route was the four-day one, and that is—'

'Sorry, I couldn't hear your last word, could you repeat, over.'

'Is no more, over.'

'No more *what*, please, over?'

'Is no more. It is not existing, over.'

'I see. Well, that's a pity. Have you heard of the route via Senokla, over?'

'That, I think, must be a variation on the four-day route I have heard of, though I am not entirely sure about that existing either now, ja? You will be the first to know, over.'

'Well, thank you,' I said, failing to sound unruffled. 'See you on time – Christmas Eve, over.'

'Do not rush along. And ja, good luck. Out.'

Diam and Bundam Sole stood around waiting for 'the off' the next day, pretending to look happy each time I came out to chat, but terrorised by the Lolat children, who found fun in Diam's gumboots, which burped rudely with each step. Kathy Bernheisel said the three Clark boys were 'real special'. Nathan, she thought it was, had saved the family from extermination by telling jokes to angry Yalis. He said them in English, and though the men did not understand a word, let alone the punchlines, they were charmed, and went away giggling, their bows undrawn.

And how was *I* taking to the RBMU message? The literal manner in which they extracted guidance from their Holy Book worried me: that acceptance of only one Way seemed a narrow conception of the spiritual world. To me, their Christianity satisfied spiritual needs in a humanitarian way, while not taking into account that humans sprang from nature. Yet the RBMUs were not intentionally cultural imperialists. They did not rush to cover over the Yali female breasts – soap for clothes was anyway scarce – and they appreciated the Yalis' own modesties: during baptism, the women's one fear during total immersion in deep cold water was that their reed skirt hems would float right up. And in the end the RBMU cause manifested itself in love. Even the missionary children acted as witnesses to their faith, bravely with their parents spreading compassion over the hostile Snow Mountains, bringing sound health and education practices. These outsiders were prepared to love the Yalis; the world at large, as and when it came, might not be so sympathetic.

Now, at prayer time, the prayers were for me.

'We pray, Lord, that you will be watching over Uncle Beean.'

'Lord, please keep danger from Uncle . . .'

'Lord, as Uncle Beean hikes out tomorrow . . .'

I was touched and strengthened. I could not let them down now by breaking my neck out there.

Chapter Three

In the Solo Valley, Kimyal country, the walls hung high above a sinuous river which tumbled with debris. The flow was slowed and frustrated as it worked on clearing rubble dumped by the earthquake four years before. All the soil seemed to have been sucked from the scree slopes – pioneering weeds were absent or in difficulty. The river – snowy from its unsorted load – was kicking against hillocks which had dropped whole from thousands of feet, with shrubs and humic soils transported from different misty climates of ridges overhead. Sometimes the braided channels preferred to plough under rather than over the mess. The sun rose and fired down on us walking the bleak valley, our shadows coal black at our feet, and even the hard soles of Diam, Bundam and two additional carriers were in trouble when pawing on the baking splintered boulders. I let the four curl up in the shade of some waning, willow-like saplings while I explored the fields of destruction a mile or two up the valley. The desert was awesome in its newness and violence, the waters churning so hard and loud. Life on the mountain sides was the occasional rolling dry clatter of rocks and boulders and chips scattering down; there were no stink bugs, metallic hesperid moths, tree lizards, nor even an ant in sight.

We traversed some flats smeared by a ferrous water, oily from decayed marsh plants, and crossed the lacey white river with its burden of rocks spinning like dice but invisible in the water's clouds; then we climbed out of the barren valley and up the chewed garden slopes. I was well ahead on approaching Senokla, which was lodged on a grim shelf. As their runny-nosed children fled uphill, dissolving into mist, the men accepted my hand, cuddling it affectionately. Invited into a hut of theirs, I sank back against the walls of vertical planks, with the fire in the centre and the wood-panelled ceiling of the sleeping loft only four feet from the floor.

For a while I relished eavesdropping on the unintelligible, sleepy chatter of children and women in their huts. Finally I keeled over and slept on a problem: how would the peoples of the forest below take to an intruder? In the way the Yalis had taken to Dale and Masters? I was pleased that I was taking things slowly. I could not afford a repeat of my previous expedition.

Old, tired memories floated into my mind from the Amazon: after my canoe's capsize, my bid to survive, confronted with pure nature, as embodied in tropical rainforest. I was alone, almost possessionless; it was just the life forces and I, facing one another . . . *Stumbling through horizonless dimness, thickets, lianas, day after confused dark day, scratches, hunger, ants biting, rotting skin, belly aches, leaves clattering with warm rain, isolation, solitude, thorns, fever, walking, my eyes not focusing; walking anyway, running towards false daylight, falling, bruising; more bottle-green days, lying in leaves and ant trails, the night cold, and mosquito pricks, and shelter of dizzily thrown-together branches, and meals of berries and roots and insects; and more walking, and more diarrhoea; a tormenting framework of curves, loops and knots – the only lines the vertical tree trunks, and close up those not straight either. Nothing true and straight in this non-human world – no crop lines, no road lines. Somewhere beyond all this – this pitiless, natural world – an openness, an end that would announce itself in unrestricted fresh air and daylight.*

So why did I want to go back, submerge myself in virgin forest? Because, even in those days when I had brushed with death, *especially* in those days, there I discovered for myself a new proximity to life. Stripped down, face to face with nature, for transitory moments I had experienced a feeling of supreme inner completeness.

The walk next day took us up and up above Senokla's gardens and along a crest that had been sharpened by landslides chiselling away either side, and leaving only the odd projecting knife-blade of a rock to break your fall down and down and down to the Solo Valley bottom. Bundam Sole and I went ahead to attempt a scaling of a face that was both a waterfall and a cliff fall. The base was firm enough, but it was only possible to gain height by crossing to the left, and up the slimy unstable scree of 200 feet, overhanging an almost sheer fall to the valley, whose river now was not the white slither it had been, but little more than a spider's loose thread in the mist. For moments, I was pressed to cliff rock that was perspiring from the bulk of water in the mountain behind.

At the top we sweated from the fear of what might have occurred. We had loosened the rocks only slightly, and the other three only slightly more. Diam came up last of all, his final step off the slide leaving the whole face critically poised. He had grinned at death, and now he grinned at me. 'Benedik, Benedik.'

From an open moorland peak of sandstone up above, I thought I

38

could see the forest that was my final target some twenty miles south, floating like duckweed on a pond; there I now saw a speck of bird drop into a deep, sun-hidden valley. We had still to cross the Duram region, then we had a short day's walk to Korupun and over the ridge to Sela Valley. I would spend Christmas there and fly back to Wamena, to plan the descent into that forest. This walk was not helping me to reconnoitre, but it was serving to cleanse my mind of the bustle of the consumer society, the distractions of Western life which distort our vision. I was better attuned now, ready to see the forest and those who lived as part of it. Which would be the most approachable people – Obinis, Wiminis or Indamains?

That night, at Duram village, Bundam murmured pitifully that he wanted to get it over with and walk on ahead to Sela; the two guides from Lolat said they wanted to go home. That left only Diam and myself. At dawn the next day we had a leisurely walk to Korupun, only a few hours away, coming to the mission houses standing empty in their gardens. This was Diam's Kimyal village and he convinced the house-boy of the Bible translator Elinor Young, who was away for Christmas, to let me stay in the house overnight.

That afternoon I read *Robinson Crusoe* in an armchair and stared out beyond the sink through the kitchen window. What must it have been like the day Masters and Dale left their families for that trek, fading along the wiggly trail? And then the days of waiting . . . It was Paul and Kathryn Kline who took over here from the widowed Phyliss Masters afterwards.

At twilight the generator came to life. When I tried the switch, the whole house erupted into music and flashing lights – an elaborate and expensive brand of North American burglar alarm, I thought. I'd soon fix it, and I gave the switch socket a sound bashing. Just before I did anything irreversible I saw that the lights were Christmas fairy bulbs, twined like rampant ivy around the living room. The horrible noise was some sort of choir at full volume, singing their version of 'God Rest Ye Merry Gentlemen'. 'Not just now, thanks,' I said, and pulled the plug.

I walked with Diam, up, over the ridge, to the cloud, occasionally taking Diam's bow and loosing an arrow after a bird, hearing the snap of wings as it escaped, and the skid and clatter of the arrow falling away through branches. I was now elated: Christianity had not yet succeeded in moving me spiritually, but these mountains had obvious power. This highland walk, a voyage through the mist waves, had been enough to confirm that in nature I would find my God, or myself, or both.

It was Christmas Eve 1984, 3.30 p.m., time for tea, when we made our curling path down out of the forests towards the roofs of the missionary homes. My hat was no longer able to withstand the rain, and its black dye leaked from the felt, colouring my face in streaks like blackberry juice. The lawns looked too smooth. I was used to the rough and tumble of the trail, and here I was, my size-twelve boots carving notches in the soft grass like the shoes of a shire horse.

Bundam, by Paul Kline's kitchen stove, must have sighted me, because Paul came sprinting out with an umbrella – was it for me or for him? I didn't need it – my clothes were as wet as the bark of the garden tree-shrubs. Paul saw that, and kept the brolly for himself.

'Hello, I'm Father Christmas,' I said. 'Lost my reindeer somewhere.' I turned to look for Diam.

'Father *who*?' said Paul, as if fearing that on the march I had been transformed into a Catholic priest. 'Oh, right – Santa Claus. Come on, follow me.'

In the kitchen doorway, Diam leaned over me, sadly watching the performance with my boots for the last time – the laces flying away, the socks peeling off, the bandages uncurling. We would have to part here. We hugged each other.

'Benedik, Benedik.'

'Diam, Diam.'

I sorted out some presents for him, adding some coffee, to which he had taken a liking, some oats, polythene bags and string. I sat with him as he chewed on a sweet potato, and hugged him again. We had an intuitive understanding, this sound, heavily structured man and I. He was noble as well as genial; his presence offered comfort and safety. I would miss him.

'Diam, Diam.'

'Benedik, Benedik.' He walked off with his little package, back up the trail.

'So you've made it,' Paul said. We were sitting round the kitchen table with his family, while they watched me sip the tea. 'I was going to go up the trail and meet you, but you've got here hours quicker than I expected.'

But now the two girls were dying to open their presents. Heather was fifteen, quiet, well mannered; Cheryl six, bouncy and already begging me to read her nursery rhymes and fairy tales.

'Uncle Benedict will read to you later, dear. Just you let him get settled in first. Have you taken your vitamin pills?'

Heather graciously led me down the grass landing-strip to the Godschalks'. Their kitchen was rattling with cooking for tomorrow's feast. There was no sign of Jan. I was whisked through smells of dough to a cloakroom. I had a quick shower, the hot water stinging my blue toes. The heat and the rich kitchen odour were things I had been without for days. The suddenness of this break in the rhythm of the hard march made me feel nauseated. I could not control my hands, and nicked my throat trying to shave off my stubble.

Back at the Klines, who were connected to the Godschalks by a field telephone which was on the blink, I was shown my room and a bed with sheets. I was about to collapse on it when I was called back to the kitchen where a special supper had been concocted. Then there would be a little prayer meeting and we would gather around the Christmas tree for the presents. It was becoming increasingly obvious from Cheryl's remarks that everyone had made an effort to produce a present for me, which was awkward because I had not done the same for them, and the word had spread that I had announced myself as Father Christmas. The oxtail soup arrived. Cheryl was on the edge of her seat, wanting to skip the meal and get on with unwrapping gifts. Kathryn was serving out the soup, Paul was asking me how I felt. I looked a bit rough. Heather was staring at my crimson finger nails.

'Well, Happy Christmas to one and all,' Paul said.

'Happy Christmas, Benedict,' Kathryn said. 'Good health.'

'Actually, I'm sorry, but I'm going to be sick,' I said, already accelerating into a dash. Against the odds, just in time I located a plastic washing bowl in my room, where it had been catching rain drips. Soon after that I was asleep under a wad of blankets.

Next morning I had presents on either side of me, and was admiring them while I ate toast and marmalade and the others their heaped vitamin tablets. The presents were Hi Karate aftershave from Paul, perfumed talc from Kathryn, more perfumed talc from Heather and a traditional net bag from the Godschalks. Jessie from Korupun gave me a tin of car sweets. Cheryl had made a creature with a strange woolly hat and buttons as eyes, on a loo roll. I fished in my supplies of trade items for something to give in return: battered boxes of matches? String, thread, razor blades? Hardly. In the end I settled for picture postcards of Eros in Piccadilly. 'Well, that sure is a remarkable piece of sculpturing,' said Paul.

We went outside and down the terrace, along the path which Paul patrolled often on his trail bike, and squatted on a bank for a Christmas Day service given by a Bible teacher. The preacher stood fighting to keep a grip on some paper scraps at which the breeze was tugging away. You could see daylight through his nose. I wondered how long ago he had abandoned the ornament which belonged there. It was a mistake to allow the congregation to have a view of the valley, dropping down to the white river 2000 feet below. Apart from being able to watch the weather get worse, everyone could see a heavy bird pitching and spinning on an uplift. The women, who formed the right-hand side of the crowd, found it sufficient to point out the bird to their babies as it zoomed nearer; a meal. But the men could not restrain themselves, and the preacher had to step aside to avoid the stampede as they rushed to fetch their arrows. 'Satan,' muttered the evangelist – was he joking? – and asked the women if they wanted to join him in a hymn. 'No,' they said frankly, seeing the rain coming up the valley and already tumbling their babies into their bags to leave.

Christmas lunch was a lavish meal around the table at the Godschalks – Dea and Jan and the two girls, Helen and Ingrid. Some ham had been boiled up, there were tomatoes and potatoes, cucumbers, the usual rabbit, and cranberry sauce had been brought in from somewhere. All the dishes steamed away, our plates were passed round having a bit of this and a bit of that added to each. Finally we were ready. 'Enjoy,' someone said, and we took up our knives and forks. The children had root beer. I looked around for something a bit stronger, like proper beer, saw nothing, and began to feel queasy confronted with so much richness after days of sweet potatoes. Jan Godschalk was sitting beside me. I blinked. Unless my eyes were deceiving me he was wobbling his front tooth forward and back with deft movements of his tongue.

'Many of our vegetables here are grown by the villagers – we are getting them to improve their diet with the vitamins and such. The climate here is remarkably hostile,' he remarked. 'That explains why parents are often doing away with the weak babies.' I nibbled gently at my rabbit. It was too strong. 'They practise this infanticide, you understand, because otherwise the foods will be wasted on the child, who will die anyway.'

'I see,' I said, lowering my rabbit back into the lake of gravy on my plate, and stabbing some ham instead. It looked as if it was tinned ham, not local pig's meat.

'This is being the only birth control here,' continued Jan. 'The infanticide. Could you now pass the cranberry juice, please?'

I put down the untested ham, not pursuing whether the Kimyals, much like the Danis, also abstained from sex in late pregnancy and during the child's early years. 'Thank you,' I said to Jessie, who had handed me the cranberry sauce. I suddenly recalled that it was a nurse called Jessie who was part of the medical team which tackled Stan Dale's first five arrow wounds, the ones from the ambush that failed to kill him down the Heluk Valley. Before I could confirm that she was the same Jessie, Jan had taken the cranberry sauce and was distracting me.

'Thank you,' he said, dolloping it on. My stomach lurched up, then settled down – for the time being. I plotted a possible escape route to the door. 'I have been doing many studies here you may wish to be aware of.

You may come to look at my office later. I am writing the language down, but also I work on their culture. You know what?'

'No, what?' I said.

'Polygamy is only practised on one in every ten cases.'

'Where do they practise?' I said, not listening properly.

'I *beg* your pardon?'

'Where do they get their stone axes and adzes from?' I said instead.

'There are two sorts, quartz and the more common "Andesit" – that is what the German geologists here call it. The Kimyals search the rivers, and take suitable stones. At Langda there is a good site, and they are trade items, of course, with cowrie shells and pigs.'[7]

I discovered that by confining the subject to stone implements, and by avoiding everything on my plate but the sweet potatoes, I could keep my nausea at bay. Outside in the drizzle, the length and breadth of the valley, pigs which had been roasted on beds of hot stones were being divided between family groups, as the converted and unconverted shared the holiday like the converted and unconverted almost world-wide: Sjovald Cunyngham-Brown back in Malaysia, my own village on a downland hill in Hampshire, with candles in St Mary's Church among the yew trees; also in southern England, Uncle Geoffrey and Auntie Joan with dollops of their tomato and apple chutney. But entirely untouched by this festival were the unknowing hidden peoples of the forests below, at my destination.

The Bernheisels were meant to join us. We heard the plane, but the mists were swirling up fast so the pilot gave it a miss.

The huts were roofed with grass here, not with palm. Paul said the grass was easier to handle – less prickly; the Kimyals had heard about the Dani grass perhaps from imported Bible teachers, and had adopted it.

'It's a kinda sad necessity,' said Paul, talking about the demise of the cowrie, pig- and dog-teeth necklaces, and the adoption by women of the all-round, self-conscious Dani maiden dress. 'It's like they associate them with their past. Now they want to become civilised and throw away all that.' He stopped. 'By the way, we're here to civilise them, not Westernise.' Paul had noticed that I hadn't prayed aloud in turn at Christmas Dinner. It was worrying him. By now we were washing naked together in a hidden brook, sharing a bar of soap. 'I'm free to talk about it whenever you want.' He sat up late in the kitchen, reading the Bible with a paraffin lamp overhead, patiently waiting for me to come.

But earlier in the evening he had said something interesting and I was busy absorbing it. He had spent a little time down at Sumo, a temporarily empty mission station, and the only one down in the jungle immediately below us. He had heard that a missionary at Langda had positioned on a sketch map the three remote lowland peoples of my destination:[8] the Obinis were 'friendly', the Indamains and Wiminis 'less so', he said casually. They were semi-nomadics — Asmat-related groups, he thought. Once the mission was in action again they would know more because they were going to be 'reached' soon.

Time was running out, I concluded. I had better get a move on.

'He'll never make it in,' said Kathryn next morning.

'He might,' said Paul. Then: 'It's Charlie Charlie.' Charlie Charlie was the pilot's call sign. We heard his approach on the radio transmitter, as he came for Jessie and myself. I had decided to fly back to Wamena and walk into the lowlands from there. The paths down were 'surer', Paul had heard from the Papuans.

'What's your visibility like, Sela, over?'

Paul said, 'The airstrip is clear as I speak, but the mists are expanding up the valley below, and are about to roll up the end. However, the ridges are open as yet, over.'

'Is the upper valley approach to the strip open, over?'

'That's a negative, over.'

'What do you suggest, over?'

'Well, that's the situation, Charlie Charlie. Worse by the second. You must make the decision and fast, over.'

'Well, I'm coming right on in to have a little scout around, over.'

'I don't like the sound of this one little bit, over,' I thought.

'Okay, come on then, over.'

Having a little scout around meant zig-zagging clouds and mountain peaks. We watched the lonely Cessna, which looked like a puny red and white fly that suspected someone was out to get it with a swatter.

We gathered on the airstrip.

'Is he coming in or not?'

'Rather him than me.'

'No, he couldn't.'

'He is.'

'Surely not. Well I'll be—'

The Cessna buzzed up the steep strip and swung round ready for a quick getaway.

Charlie Marvin looked as if he lifted half-ton weights for fun in his spare time. He had a spotless white cotton shirt with a discreet logo saying 'MAF', and thick forearms with golden hair. 'Hi there.' A crowd of Sela people mumbled and swayed on the boundary of the runway, keeping their distance. 'Right, no. time to chat. The two passengers, please.'

No time for goodbyes, only waves. Paul Kline rushed up and put something in my hand. It was a red pocket-sized copy of St John's

Gospel. 'This is for you. Read it. We're all goin' to be praying for you.'

'Thanks. I'll keep it with me.'

'You'd better hurry now, but just remember the Lord is ready to help anyone who searches.' Well, I was certainly searching for something.

We were strapped in by Charlie Marvin. He was keeping one eye on the strip, which seemed to run down to a precipice – already the mists had moved up so that the last third of the runway was invisible. It was up to the pilot to work out whether that was just a thin layer, so that, passing through it, we would have an adequate view of the valley and its sheer cliffs, or whether we could plough through that fleece and, if we never found a break, escape the cliffs blind.

Marvin freewheeled down the runway grass, braking at intervals as he stared out into the sheet. I could not see through it, and hoped we could turn back. Forward, stop, forward, stop, towards the invisible valley drop. Then a decision: we accelerated into the cloud; only whiteness as we closed in on the opposite valley wall.

'Come on, mist. Break! Break!' I thought, staring hopelessly at it.

And, of course, it broke; we saw the wall up ahead, and soared up and away from it. Jessie had been sick doing this once before; she said the plane had had to go up vertically like an elevator, and it hadn't wanted to. Down below the cloud had already covered the runway, and was moving over the roofs of the two houses. The question was, were we in time to get into Korupun, where Jessie lived?

'I'd rather we didn't try,' shouted Jessie.

The fogs were only patchy, but they were visibly progressing up the valley. We would have to be quick.

We approached the runway at Korupun rather more steeply than I had done anywhere before, but were soon bouncing comfortably enough along the turf. We had come down so quickly that crowds from the huts were still running up to look. We turned, the engine was kept idling, and Marvin told Jessie to 'get out'. 'Don't you move,' he added to me. I searched desperately for Diam's large, grinning face, but among the waving, jigging children there was no sign. Jessie's houseboys tugged her baggage and her away. They ran clear and covered their eyes in our airblast, as we sped away, escaping.

And so back to Wamena, over the route I had come. Over Duram, over the messy Solo Valley with fields of white rubble like those of a glacier, past Lolat, Ninia, Soba. And, finally, a clear view of the lowlands to the left.

Between the barren sharp peaks below were the lower red-hued ranges of trees and mosses, whose smooth curves sank down to the rich thick piled sward where all the rivers I had crossed, the Indal, the Solo and the Seng, slowed and curled through foothills, into the jungle. My mind had been cleared, flushed by the wet mountains, and I was ready.

Chapter Four

The main rooms of the MAF guesthouse were occupied by a desperate exiled Pole. He was desperate not because he was in exile, but because he had left his construction engineer job in the wastes of northern Canada, which was a 'goddam awful place', for the jungle near Merauke on the south coast. He had been thrilled at the prospect of this new job: coming to a 'nice warm climate' to start as head of his own company. What a break!

Now his dreams were gone. He was in Wamena recuperating. I was camped in the storeroom again, and he invited me in for a boiled egg one breakfast time to expound. His work was with the government Transmigration scheme. The Indonesians were flooding this 'empty' province with their own people. He said it was ostensibly to help the overcrowding problems, but it was also helping to swing the population here in Indonesia's favour. That would be most useful when they got round to having proper elections. 'You see,' he explained, 'I'm a cynic now. You know what occurred in the last election here? One thousand and twenty-five "representatives" of the province voted in favour of the Indonesians staying. That was 1969 and do you know how many voted against?'

'Er . . .'

'That's right: zero. I could forgive them that. "They'll sort themselves out one day," I said. "This island is underdeveloped, and if I take up this job it will be something worthwhile." You know – feather in my cap and all that dogshit. So, I signed up for it. Building roads. And hell – what do I find, when I drive up to my construction site, with my dear wife here?' He cast a finger at a woman in the kitchen. She was pretty, but overwrought, and just now had brown circles of loose skin around her eyes, which were very small. She curtsied.

'How do you do?' I said to her.

'I do very—'

'When I came I found nothing,' the man continued. 'I don't mean just jungle. And I was expecting the mosquitoes. But there was nothing else. Where was the workforce? Gone, that's where. They were natives and had got around to thinking that this project wasn't such a good idea, because the roads carve up their land, and – here's the nub of it, Benedict – bring in rice-gulping Indonesians. Anyway, I've got some roads built, ploughed up the forest. And what's happening now? I'll tell you if you like. The Indonesians are finding out that scratching a living from the jungle isn't as easy as the government promised. They are converting my project area into a desert. We'll have shitting camels soon.'

'I've heard the wood carvings along the south coast – the Asmats[9] and so on – are superb.'

'Where *I* was, the natives had orders not to make their drums out of ironwood any more. The government wants it for export.'

'I'm sure you're exaggerating slightly. It'll be fine when you're back there.'

'It's not the wood the Indonesians are on this island for.'

'There we *are* then.'

'It's because the province has that copper deposit. And the oil.'

While I was re-examining my fresh expedition supplies next door, I could hear the man strutting backwards and forwards, unburdening himself to his wife in Polish, and thumping the kitchen table with what was either a mallet or his fist.

The plan was taking shape. I would walk out of here, away from Wamena, along the Baliem river, which careered down the gorge, passing near Soba, then Holuwan, before spilling into the flat forests at Sumo, and winding a hundred miles to the sea. The empty mission at Sumo would be my base camp. From there I would walk east to Dekai and pick up guides to find the Obinis. I thought I would avoid the Wiminis and Indamains, the not-so-friendly villages. I was fighting fit, and everything looked set, except my maps. The airfields marked on them bore only a passing similarity to their true positions, sometimes not even that, and the missionary sketch maps flatly contradicted those of Mitton.[10] I would have to pause a few days to learn the true lie of the land from the pilots.

On New Year's Eve I went picnicking with the Pole and his wife. Many villages were holding gatherings; the warm breeze delivered smells of the dry fields, fires and roasted pig. In the shade of a withered rhododendron shrub, we watched Dani men crouched in the long grasses, near a growth of wild ginger, preparing their soot make-up; while children stalked each other blowing through whistles of snipped blossoms and pouncing on crickets and cicadas.

The women were not bothering much, but the men were thrusting pig-tusks through their noses, inserting gold quiffs of bird of paradise and glossy black sprays of cassowary feathers into and around their hair, often cocooned in string nets, painting clay lines with fingers or dusting their faces with charcoal, arranging brilliant white egret feather wands and adjusting the sheets of broken-backed cowries that hung down their fronts like chainmail bibs. The men never wore moustaches anyway but now they were plucking hair from their legs and chests with twig tweezers, letting their soot-blackened, greased skin shine through. The outlying hillocks looked like ant mounds, the black figures like ants grouping and dispersing. What looked like antennae were their spears; their burdens were slaughtered pigs strapped to poles between them. We drank thick Indonesian coffee – a gritty syrup – from a missionary thermos flask and chewed on bananas and tinned cheese, moving ourselves occasionally to keep in the speckled shade.

Most of the *kaio*, wooden watchtowers, which helped the defence of outlying gardens, had been pulled down, their political systems broken up, but though some Danis were organised by Indonesians to perform for tourists, they still had pride in their culture, enough to want to get on with it themselves. The fields where the Danis gathered were once battlefields but, like our picnic, battles had often been only a good-weather activity anyway. It was true that boys who once would have learned to use a bow by firing arrows through hoops of rattan tossed over the grasses now put pink myrtle flowers in their hair and did shy dance routines which would not have looked odd performed on stage by MKs. But all in all, we decided, the Danis had coped well with the interference of outsiders.

I said, 'What I don't understand is, how do those married women manage to keep their skirts high? They hang from their thighs, not hips.'

'Yes, they do, don't they. And have you seen any of them hitching them up?'

We decided we hadn't. They were made by the women's relations, orchid and fern fibres woven on strands in shiny reds and yellows, looping across the front and back. Weeks and weeks of work, we thought.

'The women are not having many of the fingers. They have fallen off,' the Pole's wife said, picking the one and only blossom from our rhododendron. 'They must of being many accidents.'

No, her husband said. The Danis expressed their grief at funerals by thumping a child's upper arm to numb the hand, then removing the two end joints of some fingers, or, with a bamboo knife, sculpturing away the top of their ears. It was done quickly and was not very painful to the Danis, judging by the casual way they accepted the removal of shallow arrows after battle.

'Not very painful? Surely it is painful?'

'Apparently not. And what more beautiful way to speak to the world of your love, than by a little discomfort, yes?' The man's English always deteriorated towards his wife's standard when he used it to speak to her. 'It is a little sacrifice, to ask . . . You see? Many of the womens have lost many fingers.'

'They have not smell.'

'I beg your pardon?' I said.

'This yellow tree bloom,' the wife said, 'it has no smelling.'

We were watching the Danis do mock charges at each other through the grasses, chucking spears to miss, and twanging their bows. Some gourds worn today soared extravagantly for a yard from the scrotum – which hung like an old black walnut – spewing out a feather or fur plume at the tip, near the wearer's Adam's apple.

'Do not many of the women find this hard to carry their little ones on their shoulders, holding them with so shortened fingers?'

'Well, the problem is finished now. The government has announced they may not make these signs of mournings any more times. Forget what the Danis think. Whether it is culture or not, to strangers the sights of a stone adze dropping on to fingers was too much and it is over.'

The men and women drew inwards for a victory dance, running round and round in a pack, the men wielding ten-foot spears, but managing not to jab anyone's bottom. A butterfly, with wings the violet of trumpeting sweet potato blooms, wove the skies above us.

Walking back from the picnic, his wife showing the first symptoms of sunburn, the Pole said that he was flying out by helicopter back to his goddam jungle camp. He would drop me at Sumo if I liked. Why not? It would save me worrying about my ankles on the week's trail down to the forest from here. I could start out from the empty mission, fresh. 'Let's hope someone down there speaks Indonesian,' I thought.

I flew back to Sentani, by the coast, to get my two-month visa extension; the official in Jayapura said he would give it to me in exchange for my camera, then he relented. At the hotel the palm which the owner's daughter had wounded by circumcising it with my name had been swished down the road in a flash flood. Scouting around for information in Abepura I found the Irian Jaya Rural Community Development Foundation, which tried to take an independent line on environmental issues; but I called too late. The office was closing for lunch and the man I had hoped to see had, some time ago, accidentally been shot by the authorities, they said.[11]

Flying back to Wamena the Twin Otter's two engines lost power over the swamps, and we had to return as best we could to Sentani. I spent a night with the Bernheisels and there was a church service with a MAF pilot recalling the day God had warned him not to land on an airstrip;

later it was learned that 'the natives had been working up an appetite' for him there. The pilot later said I would never get permission to enter my jungle; when he had hovered over the area 'not much further south' he had been threatened with arrows. They were the Cicak people, related to my Wiminis and Indamains. I decided I definitely would try the third group, the Obinis, first.

Back in Wamena and at the police headquarters I knew the system now and just asked to go to Soba again. The policeman who issued the permit had never been out of Wamena and did not mind admitting that there was 'trouble' along the border, and it was coming closer. 'Communists.' Actually, he meant the Free Papua Movement, *Organisasi Papua Merdeka*. The unlabelled wall map in the Police Office had shaded areas which coincided neatly with what I knew were problem sites or, in Indonesian, *Gerakan Pengacau Liar*, 'wild terrorist gangs'. I noted my forest stretch had no such shaded zones.

We lifted up from Wamena in the helicopter, hugging the mountain walls, chasing the Baliem river as it joggled down, its waters losing their energy, throwing away their silt along the banks and dividing in confusion as they met the level expanse of trees where logs were occasionally steaming upriver again, as if they were coffins intent on escaping some jungle purgatory. Eventually, there was a hole in the canopy cover below and in the hole a handful of huts with dull palm or sparkling metal roofs, a black figure in shorts up on one, fixing a bolt. The helicopter perched on a flat airstrip, beating the grasses horizontal. I tugged my supply sacks clear of the blast, shook the Pole's hand and ducked for cover. As the machine lifted away, I was wondering if I was doing the right thing. Too late now anyway . . .

Sumo was slow and sleepy, or seemed so after the violence of the helicopter. A few minutes before I had been in a mild upper valley; now I was here, in the swelter, the mountains like an upturned, irregular saw blade of blue steel, just visible above the trees, which hummed and crackled with birds and invertebrates. Parakeets, still flustering from the intrusion of the chopper, were squawking in wide circles in the morning haze. The air smelt rich, of orchard fruit. It was good to be here.

Faces tentatively closed in on me; one or two men in shorts and women in skirts of orange sago palm fibre. The Momwina people had cultural affinities both to the highlanders and to true coastal Asmats, but the three boys wearing gourds were Yalis from the mountains, I thought. Sure enough, they responded to my notebook Yali by making smiles of their full lips. The Momwinas in shorts frowned, the women grimacing. A child beat the ground agitatedly with a bent arrow. My Indonesian was practised now but it got this uncomprehending response from everyone, even the Yalis. That made my throat tight.

The man on the roof clambered down, laughing at the shy, angled heads. He did speak Indonesian; he was Hans, from the Sentani lakes, here as a Bible teacher with his wife, who wore her Papuan fuzz of hair stretched out, Westernised into two bunches with the help of numerous plastic bands and grips; she waved from the verandah of their house. Hans opened up the house of Les Henson, the missionary who was back home having a break, and piled my sacks in the kitchen, a ghostly room of dust and fly carcasses, a stained sink with seized-up taps, cupboards which had been ransacked long ago by four- and six-legged pests. Light scatterings of woodshavings lay where ants had broken through window frames and panels during raids. The wooden walls were peppered with insect holes, and the floor pitted by excavations. A calendar on the wall read May. The Hensons had exited in a hurry: on a sideboard lay a knife across a plate, now gummed down fast, and a dishcloth, which crumbled as I lifted it.

I sat with Hans on the steps and said I would pick up guides to go to Dekai, another well-contacted Momwina village, and from there travel east, to the Obinis. He did not think they had ever seen a white person, or anyone much other than the Momwinas. They were very quiet, but they would not mind me disturbing them – probably. I was wise to stay clear of the Wiminis. As for the Indamains, he was not sure they really existed.

'Did you hear about the Cicaks scaring the MAF helicopter away with arrows?' I asked, hoping it was the standard tale told to strangers to hurry them home.

'Yes.'

'And again those missionaries having an emergency evacuation, south of here?'

'Yes.'

'Well, are the Cicaks related to the Indamains, Wiminis and Obinis?'

'Who knows? Perhaps you can tell me on your return.'

The village's rectangular, stilted huts had been newly realigned so that they were in two rows of about eight each which backed on to a central alleyway. The new arrangement broke up the different clans, weakening traditional links, but it looked more orderly, and was civilised, the government said. The men half-heartedly wore shorts they had bought at the mission store with money acquired from scything the lawn and airstrip; a cluster of boys with red flowers in their tight wool hair plucked tobacco leaves from the tray of plants drawn up on a platform to keep off nosing pigs. A woman swung her legs from a doorway and, for her snoozing baby wrapped in bark cloth, she hummed as she sorted through a pile of white, squirming, finger-like sago grubs, taken for the evening meal.

No one could fathom Indonesian, but with Hans's help I picked out three guides to take me to Dekai, a short day's walk away. They would accept Indonesian currency. From Dekai he did not know what guides would accept. The two Dekai Bible teachers there should help me. They spoke just a little Indonesian. Very little.

One of my new guides had a muscular chest, eyes which were uncomfortably wild, and a semi-permanent smirk. The village idiot? The other two were Yalis — by definition not jungle people — with obstructive gourds and their build a frail assembly of poor-quality bone and gristle. They were the best three men Hans could come up with, and the Yalis looked pathetic.

I dozed on the verandah, munching pawpaw and enjoying the novelty of the whistling insects of the heated afternoon and the heavy forest air. At dusk fruit bats flopped through the tangerine sky like crows; fireflies sparked later and I lay on the floor next to a paraffin lamp with glass blackened by soot, reviewing my maps. They looked more hopeless than ever. But, with care, in a week or so I should be safely with the Obinis, immersing myself in their life.

I had told the three carriers to be ready at dawn, but was I truly ready? Supposing the Obinis did not like the sight of what might be their first white man — my height, or the brightness of my skin? Oh well, I still had plenty of time in which to have second thoughts. A good night's sleep, then full steam ahead. While I lay in a bug-ridden bed, soaking it with my dripping skin, I had a strange dream. It was so vivid I tossed away the clinging sheets and sprang to my feet to shake myself fully awake. Then I lit the paraffin lamp and captured it in my diary.

We, the expedition, are asleep around some dying embers on a great African plain. (I assume it is African because of the creatures that afterwards appear on this savannah stage, in the first dewy blue light before the sun is up.) A lame Thomson's gazelle stumbles into the camp and out through the damp spiked grass. After it ambles a lioness, taking her time in the knowledge that her meal is secure and that we are dozy and probably harmless. And then, from my position lying on roots and lumps of crusty elephant dung, beneath a sheet among the grass bugs, I see the gazelle make a dash for it. For life. I am aware that we have somehow distracted the lioness. Perhaps the gazelle saw it too — saw it as a last chance? The lioness gives no chase, confident that there would be other days for the kill. The same happens at dawn the next day: the gazelle hobbling past my sleeping companions, the lioness strolling after it, and returning.

That day I alert the carriers to be ready next dawn to help the gazelle, which we do, tempting it to feed on our scraps at a distance. The lioness does not appear. The gazelle lingers with us and over the days of our protection its fitness is restored. Each day it enjoys the shade of a lone baobab tree. Soon the delicate creature is confident enough to take crumbs from our fingers, black or white, and is no more wild than we are. Yet it begins to yearn to wander with the other gazelles of the great plain. We say a fond farewell and it bounds off and away into the insecurity of the grassy miles, where, before our eyes, it is struck down by the lioness, which for days now has been waiting, growing thinner all the while. The gazelle releases one weak scream and is silent. We see its carcass — or rather the dustcloud it makes, as it is dragged to the lioness's lair.

What could I make of it? I wrote: 'It seemed to mean something — but perhaps just reflects my neurosis.'

In the late chill, the night still black outside, I stumbled with a torch, dividing up packages. Then, the tropical sun rearing behind the trees, as the three naked shadows approached I crouched down to bind up my feet and don my boots.

Before we heaved the sacks on to our backs, Hans came out of his house bleary-eyed to say a prayer over us. Halfway through I scratched my neck and it dawned on me that I had not removed my hat. It felt more than impolite just now, and I could make a guess why — Hans's prayer for the expedition sounded to me like a funeral dirge. 'Amen,' Hans said, wished us Godspeed, and we walked off slowly through the garden of bananas. The leaves I parted were as yet damp and cool, though the sun, rising now above the tree-line, had already baked smaller creeper leaves stiff. We slipped into the forest shade — easy clear walking after the tangle of the garden's greasy logs and enmeshed vines. The leeches stretched and leaned out to us, judged our approach, waving, inching along to the centre of the path for a better position of attack.

A fat black-and-white chequered snake stuck its head up from a bush by my right boot. It shot it down again because of the heavy stick descending in the Momwina guide's two hands. The blows kept raining down, until its head was joined to its body only by a couple of torn sinews. With my parang, he divided the snake, lying there like a turn of dangerously frayed electric cord, into three equal portions and flicked them into a bush, an unhealthy sallow one, which a line of ants — though not the leaf cutters of the Amazon — nonetheless seemed to be dismantling.

Soon after was the Saki river, the result of contributions from the Seng, Solo and Indal, all of them unwinding fresh from the high northern horizon. The river was well over a hundred paces wide, but spliced into several channels. The mud was patterned with the footprints of the ostrich-like cassowary.

Along the shoreline were swaying phragmites reeds with wagtails twittering among them. A black cockatoo laughed overhead. Slate-blue, gluey rain clouds were sloping off the mountains – the water would rise soon with the downpour. The Saki was cool, only a day or so's travel from the mountains – the Clarks of Lolat, the Klines of Sela. We took it in turns to buoy each other up, reaching the far shingle among some plastic-leaved trees, losing a food sack in the flow, which was annoying but not yet serious.

Soon after dipping again into the jungle swelter, the rains broke, turning the track into an ooze with floating leaves. Palm fronds descended through the trees under the pelting rain. We could no longer step from root to root because they were submerged, so we just surged through the waters, regardless. Even the leeches looked as if they were retreating.

Eventually, through the dark of the rain-blackened forest barks showed a river, low on its banks, but maybe thirty yards wide. The guides yapped across the water to a break of river canes which swayed and parted. Two shoulder-height naked men yanked logs from the bank, and stood on them. Nearer, I saw the logs were simple, un-decorated dugout canoes, the men paddling standing upright, and through their noses a wood piece like a blunt pencil stub. Their skin was matt from infection and peeled away in curly intricate designs, their limbs textured like silver birch branches. A single soft green leaf was tied tight around each man's foreskin so that his penis was pushed back and concealed. They ferried us across, into a flock of children near a clutch of huts, where the only two Western-clothed people were the Bible teachers – obviously Danis by their thick torsos. I introduced myself as a toddling boy stared angrily into my eyes, his nostrils expanded open – two tunnels boring deep inside his creosote-coloured face – while he forgetfully wet the mud, chickens and my foot with a spout of urine. Taringgen, the more approachable Dani, by the look of one of his fingers had been in mourning for a relative as a boy, though it was usually girls who underwent the *iki palin* amputation ceremony.

I wanted some guides to visit the Obinis, I said. As Taringgen broke the news, everyone rapidly lost interest in this rare white visitor. They would not say why. Some girls looked scared, I thought. Men backed off and soon merged with the forest. Little girls gathered up their charges, crawling babies. Taringgen asked if I really needed to go. Had I a good reason? Yes, I said, and hitched up my boots on a tree stump.

Taringgen seemed to grow limp all over, standing there in a sky-blue baseball cap. It was as if his skin were suddenly three sizes too big; his chest slumped into baggy rolls. He said the Obinis were four days' walk away, two if you went direct, but I would have to sound them out at nearby settlements. Taringgen thought Swaai – my Momwina guide –

and the Yalis should accompany me, and told them so. Swaai rolled up the flesh of his slanting, grooved lips, and walked off. So did the other Bible teacher. I turned back to Taringgen. He had slunk indoors.

In Taringgen's hut I lay with my legs outstretched on the sago-bark floor. The central fire was placed in a clay basin within a box frame which rose to the groundnuts scattered for drying on the ceiling platform. Taringgen had his head tight between his knees. Only he understood Indonesian – the other Dani man had evaporated completely. Without Taringgen I had no means of communicating here. Unless I got him to come along, I would have to retreat. I undid my money belt: I would part with all I had in it if need be. The zip made a chirruping noise, and as it opened Taringgen's head began to inch up.

When at last he announced he would come along, the Dani's wife wept tears of fury. Five men also wanted to be signed on.

'*Hanya dua orang*. Only two men,' I said.

'*Lima orang, bapak*. Five men, sir.'

'Only two, please.'

'Yes, but they all want go, *bapak*.'

'No.'

'But maybe there is war, *bapak*.'

'*War*? When was the last *war*?'

'No war for many years. All is all right.'

'We are safe?'

'Yes, *bapak*.'

'No fighting now?'

'We safe, but they want friends come.'

After an hour or two, the carriers were whittled down to Meréné and Iuvea. Iuvea had brilliant black skin and a sickle-shaped scar curling under his left eye. He wore a necklace of blue beads, and he plucked off his leaf and put on a pair of withered underpants to impress me. 'Meréné is the one wearing only a leaf,' I wrote in my notebook. Both boys sat with us by the fire and I got Taringgen to teach them the Indonesian *awas* – 'watch out'. We checked that our hand signals meant the same thing – 'go away', 'come', 'quiet'.

Payment was half a sachet of salt a day each, my only possessions would be clothes – but no underpants – one jersey and spare shirt, a tarpaulin, mosquito net, rucksack, cooking tin, spoon, parang and sharpening stone, gifts, maps, medical kit, camera and film, diary, notebook and pens, hat, compass, matches, ankle bandages, socks, boots, and fourteen man-days of emergency food, but we would forage as we went along. No toothbrush, not even a waterbottle. As far as possible I wanted to rid myself of possessions, distracting reminders of

Western culture. Taringgen had a nail supply in a banana leaf kept balanced on a rafter and with his teeth he bent them through my boot soles as reinforcement.

We agreed to start off at first cockcrow.

On the third cockcrow, I groaned, rolled up my mosquito net and fumbled with strings and knots, tying up bags, jamming on my boots – to find out too late they had provided overnight accommodation for three orange caterpillars with black fur and apparently tender skins. They exploded soggily.

Taringgen chewed sugar cane and dribbled out the juice from his mouth on to a plate for three piglets to lick up. The light was grey and the sky grainy-textured. We took pawpaws from the gardens, waved goodbye at the Dekais who were ogling like gargoyles, and strode off into the dankness.

The arrow designed for fishing, with radiating wooden spikes, was also handy for trapping down frogs, lizards and the *kayay* – a creepy thing pretending to be a tree leaf but with sinister spikes. Taringgen, being a Dani highlander, was a bungler down here in the jungle. Iuvea, however, with his sleek, black vinyl skin as bright as a newly pressed record, heard the weak cries of a fledgling, snatched my bow and poked the bird from a nest, dropping it into his chamois-leather hand. The creature – bulbous blind eyes, trembling stumpy wings – was packaged in a leaf and unwrapped again at lunchtime. I stuck close to Iuvea, watching him tumble eggs from nests without cracking them, pulling berries, digging up roots like twisted squat parsnips. If creepers obstructed him he bit them through. When crossing swamp muds he tightroped invisible strands of vine. The white crisp meat of a palm, *ubyk*, he ate on the move. There was such beauty in his relationship with the forest: the harmony, the role in the natural struggle. For the two Momwinas nature was not something allowed out only in monocrops, or parcelled off, tamed in garden displays or allocated to parks. My heart rose as I watched their unbroken partnership with the forest, their acting as units of a living system. This present superficial intercourse with the forest, my nibbling of fern tip snacks on the march, was only a start; the Obinis, living in nature, would provide the chance of a true link up. We stopped while Meréné collected chubby grubs from the loose bark of a ropey tree – *bocani*, he said they were – and popped them into Iuvea's mouth raw and wriggling to the last.

Both Momwinas put a serrated leaf to their skin where the loads had rubbed. Meréné, carrying my rucksack, wedged bracket fungi under the shoulder straps to cushion the rasping factory fibre. In the afternoon, Iuvea left the trail and moments later came back holding his underpants and with only the leaf, secured with bark string, rolled up in its place. Wearing clothes was an affectation for these people, and ridiculous in the clammy forest. Later we bathed, disturbing a kingfisher sunning its green wings on a tree branch lit by shredded light. Taringgen, who was, I had begun to fear, a touch stupid, hung his baseball cap on a bough and covered his groin with his hand, in a modesty presumably gleaned while at Bible school. Before we took up our packs, Meréné bent to the water, stretching his lips to sip a drink, laughing at me for using my hands as cups.

We broke out into fresh dry air a couple of times at clearings occupied by single thatched huts, Muruku and then Taribu. The giant skin-cutting canes that had grown up in the sunlight could be breached by a walkway of fallen trees, ending with the plank-walled huts, raised just off the ground on stilts. These outlying Momwinas, just twenty to thirty in each settlement, had had most contact with the Obinis. Iuvea called, but they were shy and no one was prepared to come out through the slot which was the main exit.

'*Jalan?*' said Taringgen. 'Walk on?'

'Yeah, *jalan,*' I said, and we were sludging through the muds, which were thickening as yesterday's afternoon rain percolated away.

'No white man here before, maybe. Men scared, *bapak.*'

'What men scared?'

'Two men with us.'

'Iuvea and Meréné?'

'No, *bapak.*'

I twisted about and saw only Meréné and Iuvea.

'You wait see.'

We stood in the track, which was so thin it might have been a rat's short cut home. My ears were ringing from the insect noise. Finally, two small men crept up and stood behind some stringy saplings with their inturned feet looking warped, like tree roots.

'They with us.'

'Taringgen, I want a small number of men, the Obinis will get scared if we are *too many* men.'

'Iuvea and Meréné ask them come. They scared. You too think better they come, *bapak?*'

'No.'

'All right, they come, *bapak.*'

'*No,* I said.'

The arrows in our bows softly clattered against the striplings as we walked on with the two men, who were obviously coming along whether I liked it or not. I hoped I was not losing control. When would Meréné realise his load was entirely salt, the wages?

In the mid-afternoon, just beyond a stagnant pool with slumping waterlilies and rusty mud margins, was another hut. Barely off the ground, its vertical panels were shambolically slotted in and tied loosely. Structural poles stuck out everywhere like casual building-site scaffolding. 'This Kubooboo,' said Taringgen, motioning his hand with the two-thirds-missing finger. 'We sleep here.' Parcels of withered leaves hung over the narrow doorway — approached on a log bridging wood-shaving piles and charcoal of old fireplaces, and Taringgen thought they contained fetish objects, for instance to keep the dangerous spirits of the recently dead at bay.

Rather than retreating, the men of Kubooboo bore down on us from logs, hunting bows not drawn, but at hand, a line of five men. They had two, three or four turns of rattan about their waists. They spoke Momwina. I knew the greeting now, '*Coadré*', but their reaction to me was a none too passive silence. The men's groin leaves were supple, freshly picked, their skin was freckled with soot and tight as new shoe leather, their nose septums carried round, unobtrusive wood bars. Their flat nose flanges were pierced in various styles, bearing fine white bones (of a flying fox, I guessed), wooden studs and smooth sticks, some extending a long finger length. They had heavy upper armbands of rattan and their tightly sprung hair was twisted with dozens of yellow tassels of fibre. Usually their hair was crested, clipped short around the ears and riding high with the strings spiralling on top. The cowries and dog-teeth necklaces were as bright on that cork skin as the pearly whites of their eyes.

'I hope these men are your friends.'

'I am not come before,' said Taringgen. 'These are friends two men we bring, *bapak*.'

'Lucky we did bring them.'

He curled the fingers of his hand so that they were the length of the one which was a stump, and swept them along his brow, smearing away the sweat below the brim of his baseball cap. The five men had whooped greetings to our two new guides, but were indifferent to Meréné and Iuvea and extremely indifferent to Taringgen and myself.

'Why?' I asked.

'I do not know. Our clothes? They scare us. They want go away.'

I was growing concerned by the ambiguity of Taringgen's loose Indonesian. There was danger in it. I started decoupling my feet from the heavy boots and unwrapping the bandages. While I was immobilised like this on a log, the women came out from the hut's rear, which backed straight on to the forest. A clutch of whimpering children gingerly walked behind, holding each other fiercely, backing off when they sighted me, and climbing up their mothers' backs to their shoulders. They hung by the hut eaves, which protected a roughly hewn shelf stacked with firewood.

The six women had flighty, avoiding eyes which never came my way. Their children wanted to get back indoors and erupted in bellows of tears and tugged the women's rusted hair, their dental necklaces or their shaggy, clean sago-fibre skirts, which were mid-thigh length at the front, rising at the side and dipping at the rear. It looked as if they had no wooden pieces in their nostrils, though one had two very fine filaments which projected like starched whiskers six inches forward and out from the tip of her nose. She, like the rest, was too thin to be healthy, her skin not with the burnished look of my guides but shedding with scabies or some other infection. The only woman who was not thin was pregnant. Another had veins the size of mains electrical leads running over her dry loose chest to her nipples. Yet these women carried themselves well, their necks fine, their chins high.

I was fussed by tickly sweat bees licking my skin. To the Momwinas, who did not run with sweat like this and so were ignored by the bees, this spectacle was worth daring a closer look. Two little boys, clumps of cowries on neck strings, risked settling beside me but within arm's reach of an older man whose ear lobe had been extended to carry an inch disc, which he was not wearing today. He had a tickly cough and he coughed everywhere.

We were beckoned indoors to cook our frogs and insects. The forty-foot building was partitioned, the rear half for women and children. Food parcels were handed by slender female hands – joined to long wrists so coarse they were like vines – through two windows in the wooden divide. It was sago and bananas. Through the window I caught glimpses of figures around open fires, much as we were, but with children crawling over them.

Throughout the evening there was a murmur of men's voices on our side; a quavering, bee-droning noise from the women. The roof was black and sticky. From it, among the cobweb sheaths, hung pig jawbones and skeletons of lizards, opossums, turtles and rats.

On the march at daybreak, before the sweat bees were about, I asked: 'Why is there another man with us?'

'He is friend two men who friend Iuvea and Meréné.'

'I don't want one more man.'

'Yes,' Taringgen said, but I saw that his face was a mask and the decision had already been made.

The new man did not share in the carrying of luggage, he just eyed the forest for food, clutching a bow and half a dozen arrows – their bamboo blades, sharply spatulate or barbed with artistic, mean notches. We bagged two snakes, which seemed to be tying each other in wild knots of passion. Both were a pale lichenous brown, four foot long, and delicious.

Hours on was another garden, by a huge river of grey, which I took to be the Kolff, whose headwaters were east of Sela. To my surprise, there was hot argument about its true local name; probably it was the To-oo. We yelled through the banana grove, '*Coadré!*' The answering calls trilled with nervous tension. We waited.

'Trouble if these To-oo men not good,' said Taringgen, putting his luggage on a log which was a motorway for columns of ants. What did he mean by 'not good', *tidak biak*? Deceitful? Violent? Busy? Three boyish men materialised among the garden vine mats and, with quizzical smiles which bunched up their cheeks to their eyes, took up the packs. The building was very small, though housing twenty people, and open-ended at the men's six-foot-long section so you could sit on the floor platform and swing your legs in the smoke of the fire outside.

We threw a ball of sago into the embers to bake with the branches of both sweet and floury bananas. A boy was given tongs, a palm stick folded over, and employed to guard the roasting bananas from his pet cassowary chick – the size of a hen and with faint creamy stripes on its dark down like those of a wild piglet. The divided-off women cooed like pigeons, as they chattered among themselves, but we never saw them. A lean-to was attached to the side of the building above the river, and pigs rolled in the earthy holes there.

The trouble was, Taringgen was saying, as he ripped off one banana and blew its charcoal skin cool in my face, the people here, the To-oos, were not happy about the Obinis. 'This is all right, *bapak*. I'm no scare. To-oos like Obinis more than Wiminis.' The To-oos had stories of the Wiminis, a couple of days south-west, incorporating claims that the black slugs to be seen lying across the To-oos' skin were scars from Wimini arrows. I tried to establish genuine casualty figures of battles by drawing battalions of pinmen in my notebook. Finally, I had twenty-six representing the Wiminis, of which ten were scored out, killed. On the home side of forty-four – Momwinas? – five had died.

'Now, how much friendlier are the Obinis than the Wiminis?' I asked Taringgen, hopefully.

'Yes, *bapak*.'

'I said, "How much friendlier are the Obinis?" '

'Yes, how much? Interesting.'

'Oh, I give up. I'm off to bed.'

Chapter Five

We left the To-oos' hut and held hands in two circles to ford the river. There were ten of us now, because we had had to bring along three To-oo men to translate and guide. Iuvea and Meréné had more than got their way: our expedition was double the strength I had denied them at Dekai.

The river gushed by in a bed of cobbles, with low banks of grey silt stepping up into the jungle. Where the channel split there were islands with beached tree trunks, their roots washed clean of soil, the older trees washed clean of roots. The waters had not lost the sedimentary clouds of the highlands, but were darkening as they slowed through the forest system. At this early hour bats slowly flapped across the pink-scaled sky. in loose formations, and swooping along the forest walls were the spiky-beaked fishing birds. We raised a silver heron off its twig legs into heavy beating flight.

The trail now diminished and was muddled with the wild pig routes, which were expanses of excavated soil and beaten-up ground flora. Taringgen stumbled upon a green freckled cassowary egg, and kept the shell as a large drinking mug. We came upon a zone of wringing damp and droning mosquitoes, a continuous belt of sago. We thought we might see where the Obinis had felled the palms and beaten the pith of the trunk to wash out and collect the starch, but there was no sign. We talked less; the atmosphere was tightening with excitement. The head To-oo slotted a green leaf in his armband. He refused to say why.

We made camp; ten-foot palm fronds were bisected lengthways and laid on to a roof frame of stakes. In half an hour we had a shelter with a thatch three fronds deep and, by sawing a dry vine against a stick held between the toes, a fire. A cuscus's fur was singed off and portions of meat lobbed in to roast.

The smell of the guides – a pungent, sour ammonia – was strong through the chilly, damp night, and when I opened my eyes to do away with a particularly tiresome root working into my back, I found it was a Momwina hip. I did not sleep much. Instead I listened to the scampering of a rat and the insect throbs. I imagined the density of life around me –

the grubs snuggled in the sleeves of bark, scavenging beetles lifting leaves. Tomorrow we would reach the Abi river, at the Obinis.

At dawn we wound through stands of lithe poles, and across ground heaped with cherry-like fruit, through a dusty smell like that of roasted coffee beans. After the minor River Kweeki was the altogether bigger Abi. We heard it rumbling and much later saw its whiteness; seen through the vertical tree-trunk lines, it was an avalanche. We had reached it without encountering the Obinis, and this was their doorstep. Iuvea said we should set up camp, and wait while the To-oo leader crossed the river to make contact. There was no sign of a settlement – no banana stands, no dent in the forest crown, no spreads of the garden weed cane, no dog yaps or woodsmoke on the wind.

The water swirled in a lattice of racing channels, but the To-oo man, with the double-spiked nose, jumped quickly off the bank. The currents licked around him. He held one hand high – it clasped a packet of salt, a peace offering. We looked on until he made the far shingles and was swallowed up by the forest. Soon we had raised a palm shelter. I got out a dozen pawpaw pips for the Obinis to plant if they came. Meréné, out on a sand spit, began digging like a hound, and rushed up with a score of turtle eggs like ping-pong balls. Someone else brought in heaps of *keebaree*, rough pods like durian fruit the size of bowling balls, the green skins reminiscent of barnacled stones. Heaped on the fire they blackened and split to reveal seeds like broad beans. But for the sticky sweat bees and ascending fire smoke, the thick air was stationary. Periodically we stood up to look in the direction of the Obinis. With the water's roar I could hear nothing. I tried salt on the *keebaree* seeds and it was an improvement.

To distract us from this waiting, Taringgen launched into a cautionary tale of the Momwinas. Loosely translated from his bad Indonesian, it was this:

Two brothers were travelling *osawnia*, north, in a canoe. The sun was high. The air steamed. They were tired. They ate *kikébé*, or crayfish, caught in woven traps among the reeds. Suddenly there were two women approaching in another canoe. One had wrinkled, hanging breasts, chunky hands and the flabby neck of a *bowoo* (a turtle). The other was younger, and far more interesting. She was a girl newly arrived at physical maturity, her skin as beautiful as a snake's. She was slender and lithe. And whereas a smile danced lightly on her lips – she ducked her head now, with a becoming and quite appropriate modesty – the old woman glared at the brothers in an unbecoming and flagrantly rude stare. Quite independently, both boys knew they were stricken.

The woman uttered a sharp command – what a grating voice she had! – telling the girl not to turn her head to the men as they passed. The men had no intention of not turning to watch the girl go by. They viewed her eagerly as the sun bore down on her shoulders, which showed the soft curves of discreet muscle. The men's imagination ran riot. What was it about her? Women did not usually have this curious effect on them. It was very odd, and the mystery made them goggle even more. Had her skin ever felt the touch of a man's hand?

The two women were now out of sight down the river behind. The younger man wrestled with his conscience and it won. He regretfully concluded it wrong to waylay the maiden. The older man was thinking the same, but he said it could not be helped. As his brother refused to ferry him to the tree-crowded bank, he leapt overboard and swam ashore. He knew a path that would cut off the women, and he reached a spot downstream just in time to compose himself on a log. He greeted them both. 'Ladies, you shouldn't be paddling, let me take over. It is hot; there are no rain clouds to blunt the sun's rays.'

The older woman reluctantly agreed. 'Yo.' It was a great kindness. He could sit right at the stern, just behind the girl. Well, there was not much room in the canoe, and he had to squeeze in very tight, but scarcely had he sat down, his feet tucked in close to her soft sago skirt, when he was told to steer the dugout ashore. The girl nipped off to forage for wide leaves suitable for wrapping up sago grubs. All the way to their house, the man paddled only with the hag, while going and coming the girl was far too busy to think about the man, who dared not say a word to the beauty because he could not risk her guardian overhearing what he wanted to say. It was so frustrating that he was beginning to wish he had never come, and the sun was already low, hornbills crossing singly overhead to their perches, the little, insect-chasing bats twirling like light-dazzled moths.

Just as the sun glowed its last, the clouds dyed red, the man saw a house. Though he had been on the tributary before – last rainy season it was – he had never noticed this place standing among the river bank's grass rods. And that was rather unsettling – he was far from home. An old man was stepping from the forest. He had an axe. But he was cheerful enough and welcoming. He had been felling a tree for a new canoe, he said, but the blade was a poor stone, and needed a good regrind. What a day! It was very obvious that he was really pleased to see a guest. Not many men called in, he explained. He just had this pitiful bag and the idle girl for company. Laughing, relieved a little, the visitor turned and helpfully tied up the canoe with vine rope. He wondered if the girl was really idle. He was sure she was not. Behind his youthful sloped back, the aged man grinned broadly at the hag, and winked at the girl. He was so pleased they had brought someone back for him today rather than their usual stories of their troubles and aches; they were habitual moaners, real hypochondriacs. He took a big breath and swung the axe at the young man, whose head parted noisily from his body.

'You *are* in a good mood,' the old woman said grumpily. 'That's the first time you've lifted an axe for so many moons I can't remember. Why is it always left to me? That's what I want to know.'

'Stop moaning, woman. I killed the last one too.'

'Well, that was hardly the same. He was virtually female.'

'*And* the one before that,' piped in the girl.

'Shut up!' said the hag.'

'Yes, shut up,' said the man. 'You get your leaves and wrap up the man. You've left getting home so late, we've only got time to make a start on the head tonight. Typical.'

'Well, there was another man out there in a canoe,' the girl said, finding herself with a previously unknown courage. 'Tomorrow *you* can go and get him with mother. I'm no longer a child. *I* will stay home and finish roasting this one — you'll taste the difference. From now on things are going to be different.'[12]

Taringgen thought he saw a whiff of blue smoke. 'Perhaps, *bapak*, To-oo is lost, *bapak*.'

Lost? I thought. Lost his life? Lost his way?

There was a high-pitched yelping across the water. We were all on our feet. 'Taringgen?' Taringgen didn't know what to think. He looked to Iuvea; then to Meréné. Then we all looked to the To-oos. More yelps, as if from a pack of puppies.

'Obinis are happy,' Taringgen said.

'*Happy*, Taringgen?' You could have fooled me, I thought. Iuvea said it was all right; they would be on their way over. I paced; more waiting. I laid out leaves and spread salt on them.

We caught our first sight of the Obinis as they danced through the river, shouting and splashing; eight or nine men, only two with bows. They looked not much different from our To-oo guides, all with plaited hair strings, armbands of fine weave or of twisted rattan. Two wore a bare cassowary quill which looped from earlobe to shoulder; nose septums bore sticks, nose flanges were spiked with half a dozen radiating wooden pegs and fine bones. They got across the river kicking with the current, apparently carelessly; youths with broad, full smiles and healthy teeth and gums. Perhaps this was like a dare for them, I thought.

Taringgen extended a hand; but as if we were invisible they ran past, clustering around the fire, stealing sideways glances, fidgeting with the raffia-like braid in their hair, a rattan looped in a figure of eight over the head and under the arms, or a stick like a slim pencil across the face from one nostril. There was no talking except the mutters of the Obinis who stood there as awkwardly as early guests at a sherry party. Spotting the salt, they squatted to lick it from the leaves – the taste seemed to mesmerise them – and, before I could gently intervene, a youth chewed a pawpaw seed, made humming noises and passed the packet round.

The Obinis heaved up the sacks and steered us through the waters. In mid-river, standing in the creamy mud among the logs which lay strewn like washed-up whale-bones, was a clutch of five older men and a boy with clear skin, who seized my hand. It might have been to give me balance as we cut through to the shore, but he held it possessively as if I were his captive, pulling me into the forest, along logs, over a ditch of black water, into an opening. There, through faint blue smoky air, rose up steeply a long roof of foxy brown thatch; around it banana palms, pigs running loose, tobacco – not off the ground on trays as in Momwina settlements – a couple of huts raised ten feet on stilts and two or three tumble-down shacks being engulfed by out-of-hand creepers. No chickens, no groundnuts, no pawpaw and I could see no sugar cane. I tried, and failed, to loosen the boy's fingers. A man eased out of a high shack with a bow, but its band was slack against the arrow. We had arrived.

The hundred-foot main building had open ends, with ragged side walls of loose, feather-shaped palm leaves up to Obini head height. The floor on the right-hand side was left as bare earth, pounded smooth by feet. Why? I wondered. Fireplaces, encircled by seated women, were dotted along the left half. They were hunched, heads down, shivering. With fear? In their hair at the back they wore smooth, woven orange and white cords which bobbed on their necks as they began to whisper among themselves. Above them were slung folds of bark cloth, spare sago skirts. From the centre posts bristled arrows, spears – with a foot's worth of double-sided barbs – and bows; no Asmat-type lizard-skin hand drums but on the left wall was a six-foot shield carved with red and white painted geometric designs. Male toddlers with toy bows and arrows crowded around me, but my boy fought them off, and began to pick away my leeches. He had a spiked rod through his nose, new and not entirely comfortable yet, and occasionally he spun the wood in its home with his fingers as if rolling a cigarette. I brewed up coffee for everyone, but they wanted only to stroke my boots and hat and to peep inside them.

As the forest shadow stretched over the clearing, women with string head bags came back from gathering produce – birds, roots, pink sago in damp, fresh clods, and long tubes of bamboo (which were water vessels). They took the long way round to avoid us.

Seated around the fires we put our mouths to tobacco pipes: the filter was a foot of prettily cross-hatched bamboo stuffed with sago fibre, and this was held to a tube with a plug of the smouldering leaf mounted at the end. The ritual of exchanging the pipes broke the barriers, which were as yet very tangible, and even the evangelist Taringgen partook, drawing in the blue fumes, wincing at the painful thought, 'Allah does not like.' Up above dangled skeletons of kangaroos, monitor lizards, flat white blocks of bone – pig jaws – and leaf packages. I thought I would work out later what everything was and signified. There would be ample time. I was here; at the end of my road.

The night stole by. We decided to stay up – better safe than sorry. These people had been welcoming but the welcome was incomplete. Their minds were all but closed to us, a defensive move. Building trust would be slow and precarious. The women sometimes slipped sago to the Obini men, but only slyly gave us glances and always sat in circles of their own. Tomorrow maybe all the guides could leave me, I suggested to Taringgen. We agreed we would see how the day went.

'*Weeteé*,' Iuvea said in the morning. 'Cassowary.' Three Obinis fingered our arrows and beckoned us to join in a hunt for a local, elusive bird. Two To-oos and I thought we would; the rest said they would rather not. The boy wanted to tag along with me.

We all fanned out to unravel the criss-crossing cassowary prints, scouring the ground for fresh scratchings. The tracks said the bird was a lone adult, and we began to thump the tree buttresses in an extended line, the Obinis flanking the To-oos and myself, to herd the bird on to the open river shingle. I hoped the cassowary was not going to get too upset. I could not stop thinking of an ostrich creature thumping the ground with its feet and charging head down, beak forward through this morass of sago palms – that was apparently what they did when cornered.

The hunt was becoming a muddle. Was that a To-oo man to my right, the cassowary, or an Obini thinking I was a cassowary and levelling an arrow? The To-oos were calling to each other in a warbling high pitch, from my left and right. Their voices were as tight as drawn bow strings. Why? Were we all sharing the same concern? The thought dispersed as I heard a smash and fluster ahead: the bird, surely. Soon we would break out into the open, trapping the cassowary against the river. That was the theory, but somewhere ahead there were high urgent shrieks, and soon a terrified scream of pain. Suddenly I wondered where the boy was. I winced, then scanned the foliage for a chink and clear view. All was ferns, showers of emerald leaves, cascades of jade shoots. I discovered myself running forward, on towards the river, knowing the To-oos were doing the same. A final hack through the last of it, squeezing under a log, and I was out, my boots rattling the riverside stones.

There was no threshing, arrow-stabbed boy, no trotting cassowary jerking its head this way and that for an escape route; only a pebble-dashed shore and a black mound of feathers weakly kicking, the boy's hands blooded as he grappled with the bare, gristly toes. He had killed the bird almost alone: he stood to attention by it so that I would realise, his eyes lit like buffed diamonds as I saw that the bird was transfixed by a single arrow.

Yet the atmosphere was wrong. The To-oo men were snarling at the Obinis, talking sourly. The Obinis were smiling. I took the To-oos aside – I could not have them upsetting the Obinis like this. Soon, however, their hand signals – fingers shooting through the air brushing my nose – told me differently. Their claims were that during the cassowary chase one arrow had been fired right along our line, passed one To-oo, then myself, then the other To-oo. The arrow had planted itself in a log. Its flat blade was bamboo-leaf shaped, only with chunks cut out for barbs, a type suitable for lodging in pig, or cassowary, or human.

An accident? A joke? A warning? Meréné and Iuvea said they would stay a day or two longer, if I liked. Yes, please. That night we chopped up the bird and roasted most of it. The thigh bones – *bo*, the Momwinas called them – were saved for carving into daggers, to be slipped into their upper armbands. I handed round fishing hooks, whose point was lost on the Obinis, but they liked the neatness of the sleek barbs. Experimenting, the Obini boy snagged the ball of his thumb and the whole hook had to be drawn through; a messy business.

The next morning the stray arrow incident was forgotten.

Chapter Six

On the third day we were at ease sufficiently to sit in the same circles around the fires, though if we veered close to the clumps of women, they shot off, pulling babies behind. To the men we used their greeting, '*Kesiné*,' rather than our own, and each time the Obinis grinned. A father presented his sick baby to me and I dabbed antiseptic on his reeking yellow sores.

But I was far from content. What was this fierce excitement in the eyes of the Obini boy? He was smoothing his fingers over the bright red paper around a sardine tin which he had unearthed from our stores. Bigger Obinis, as bewitched, wrestled it from him. There were tears. I had to produce another can for the boy quickly; then one more, and another; yet the Obinis would not stop bickering over the tins, whether full or empty, and they licked round the serrated edges, saving the containers as drinking cups. Then they frantically scraped around for anything else, swiping a ball of green polythene string and knotting it in bangles around their wrists.

The Obinis had already obtained a taste of the outside world before I came along – a pair of boxer shorts which might have been red once, and which the men took turns to wear; one metal axe (blunt) traded from the To-oos; and a mouth organ which had been sat on too many times and now only offered an asthmatic wheeze. My tin cans and plastic string were only the latest arrivals. The reality was that I was only in the vanguard of the inevitable future. I shouldn't feel guilty. 'We're here to civilise them,' the voice of the future had said in the highlands.

For the moment, I told myself, I must be content to understand the present: the Obinis had their bows, stone tools, arrows, spears, shields, houses, pigs, dogs, armbands, feathers and shells; they had sacred ancestor skulls like the Asmats for all I knew; certainly they had holy objects hidden away; they had their few crops; and they had themselves and their forest – nothing else that I could immediately think of. Here I was with people who had had no distraction from nature, except a stray axe, disintegrating shorts, a mangled mouth organ gummed up with mud, and stories from the To-oos. They must have seen the missionary Cessnas traversing the sky, stopped to marvel at their buzz. The oldest might have remembered other aircraft, the Second World War going on outside. Now there was us.

The next people along would be quite different. Unknown to the Obinis, their land had not only been claimed by the Indonesians; it also happened to be the territory of the Netherlands Reformed Church – that is, if they established it before the Regions Beyond Missionary Union.

No, there was an immense amount for me to learn and I might as well get on with it. I wondered if the skeletons of the dead were propped in the nooks of fig trees, revered skulls kept as pillows as I had heard they were by southerly tribes.

And Hans, at Sumo, had heard the Obinis were on the Kolff river, but the Momwinas insisted that the nearby river was the Abi, which had to be the one marked on the maps as the Steenboom. It was all very confusing, but I was not here to position the village for the world at large; so, instead, on the fourth day I started putting down the names of the Obini men.

That very simple act, the opening of a red notebook, seemed to trigger some deep associations in the Obinis' minds. I suddenly wondered if a Bible teacher had called here. They sprang away. I might as well have exploded a flash bulb. The men were immediately pacing up and down as if each was afflicted by a grumbling gut pain. They got up from their fires and squatted down again. They swapped places. They went out to pick more tobacco leaves; they took lighted sticks and went to stoke embers which were in no danger of going out. By last light I was alarmed. 'What is happening?'

'*Tidak apa-apa*. Doesn't matter,' Taringgen said. 'Have mosquitoes maybe.' But if anything there were fewer mosquitoes that evening than there had been before. Iuvea shrugged. He wasn't sure. Meréné frowned. He didn't know. After a few minutes, the evening frogs twanging and popping like bedsprings along the marsh outside, the Momwinas, like the Obinis, became as restless as livestock before an electric storm. I would not use my mosquito net tonight, I thought. I would sit up.

So, I was seated with two To-oos, sticking close, dragging on the pipe. The sick Obini baby was screaming among the women, but that did not cover their bleak silence. A dirt-coated dog prowled, shifting up and down the hut, infected by the behaviour of the men. Taringgen was outside, presumably with Meréné and Iuvea, humming while urinating noisily in the bushes.

A woman stretched out her long, narrow fingers, in them a crust of sago for the lead To-oo with the spiny nose. Should he take it? This was the first intimacy we had had with the women, and this surely was not the right moment to start forming relationships. '*Avené.* Not yet,' the To-oo said, reasonably enough. The girl, who wore blonde, plaited strings in her hair, and a disc almost the diameter of a cotton reel in one earlobe, was not to be put off. She hastily placed the chunk of pancake in his lap and looked away, sharply. Would the men be offended if he did not express some sort of gratitude?

'*Kesiné*,' I said, meaning 'Thanks,' but the word made no sound. It was lost as, at that instant, the world we had known here was eclipsed by a new one.

We were all on our feet – every woman and child, every Momwina; and no one was standing around, everyone knew the time had come. The women were vanishing into the night, babes flying in the air after them, some Momwinas or To-oos running out behind and the Obini men trying to come in the opposite direction. Each man whirled a hunk of firewood or an arrow. I was being backed against the wall, next to the shield. The Obinis, a wall of fifteen, banged the sticks in our faces, clattering the arrows in the semi-darkness. I say 'our faces' assuming the To-oos were by my side, but who could tell? A hard object slammed against my nose, and I tasted blood on my tongue.

There was shouting, and all of it was coming my way. There was no room indoors for fighting – we, or I, would stay put, I thought. With the screaming and jumping, and firelight stolen by the shadows, there was too much muddle for anything hasty, I hoped. I remember, despite all this, a pang of sadness: the Obini jumping up and down highest was the little boy. And typical that Taringgen had gone to the loo at this moment. Where on earth *was* he? Looking at shooting stars or something?

A couple of Obinis peeled away. It looked as if a younger one was in pain; he had walked over the bed of a fireplace maybe. He hopped up and down, almost dancing. Then I realised he *was* dancing. '*Ee-ye-ar, ee-ye-ar wani-wanimo!*' he screamed in a contralto voice. Maybe ten men turned to him and roared, '*Wah! Wah!*' Their attention was not on us any more, but on this song. I now understood how useful it was to keep one half of the building length clear of fires or other obstacles: the men panted heavily as they hopped, up, then back down, up . . . and down, a spear or flaming torch in one hand, the other splayed over the groin. I hoped this was not a sexual taunt, but it rather looked like one. The gang went bounding up and down the building, each man taking his turn to lead the high-pitched line: '*Ee-ye-ar, ee-ye-ar wani-wanimo!*' And each time the chorus mob shouted '*Wah! Wah!*' louder than ever in return. They were working themselves up into greater heights of frenzy.

I tried to listen for sounds outside – Taringgen, the other Momwinas, or the women, but the thumping feet alone masked all but the dancing chant. Even the sizzling night insects seemed to have fled. There was not much to be said to Taringgen, when he finally tiptoed in, except: where were the others?

'They wait in forest, *bapak*.'

'Tell them to come.'

'They tell "You come. We go," *bapak*.'

I shook my head. I was not going to tramp off into the forest night with this lot after us; not with their blood up.

'*Pergi*,' repeated Taringgen. 'Go.'

'*Tidak*,' I said. 'No.'

I got Iuvea and Meréné to sit down with me. Taringgen reluctantly brought out all the presents and food, spreading them. The men were dancing on – '*Wah! Wah!*' – but they could not help but be curious: curious about us, not the gifts. Perhaps they were wondering why we were not retreating. Taringgen from time to time tugged my arm. '*Pergi! Go!*' Meréné and Iuvea were playing with their fingers. We were waiting for the Obinis' energy to dissipate – there must be a limit to how many two-footed hops a human could do. However, the Obinis were a strong lot, and they managed to bob about fifty lengths of the long house before wearing down. I do mean fifty; we counted most of them, and by then it was nearing dawn.

I pointed out the gifts, all our possessions; the Obinis went straight to their fireplaces, forming closed circles. The pipes came out. They were not offered to us. Notwithstanding, Meréné, Iuvea and Taringgen tossed back their heads, chuckling with released tension. Soon after, the To-oos and our Momwinas slipped back in to be with us, and first light revealed that the women too were back.

I dozed off and blinked open my eyes to see that our luggage – only my blue rucksack now – had been made ready for departure. Iuvea hissed disapproval as he rubbed his fingers over a slit in the pack, a gaping wound from the ripping barbs of an Obini spear the previous night. He swung the rucksack up on to his back, to hurry me along. But no, I was determined to stay if possible. After all, if these were the Obinis, a 'friendly' people of two hundred, what would the 'not so friendly' Wiminis and Indamains be like?

I kept the guides occupied brewing coffee and strolled about memorising the shield motif, the Obini facial character, the arrow styles, while the Obinis were rummaging through the blades, rice bags and hooks. Had we been over-generous? We had saved enough salt to pay guides and had nothing else. With a To-oo man for company Iuvea went searching for *ma*, the big dull brown eggs which jungle fowl placed in mounds of leaf compost – to hatch if the lizards did not get them.

The Obinis, bored with the gifts, were already sorting through their weapons again for favourites. I squatted down to watch the dance as its racket started up again. This act smacked of neither bravery nor foolishness. This time, tension was absent. We had proved ourselves no challenge; this was like a victory dance. I snapped a few photos, but the flashlight relit their fears – I was again a threat. The Momwinas strutted about outside, waiting for me.

The dance was clear enough now. They were hopping like bush kangaroos, a hand holding a spear, heads back, and spear and pelvis jerking forward at the cry 'Wah! Wah!' The atmosphere was getting hotter, the message stronger – that jab of the spear matched with the stab in the air with the penis. The rattan curls around their wrists flew and, as the men thrust, the single-leaf garments were loosening off each man. The sound of breathing, in wheezy pants, was louder than the hard feet beating the compacted dust. A man holding a bunch of bird of paradise feathers on his head, a wave of gold, led the group. The women looked uninterested.

It really was time we were going. Even I saw that. I was stretching the endurance of the Momwinas, whose hackles were beginning to rise at the jeering, taunting, now leafless, flapping sexual organs.

'Pergia,' said Taringgen, wanting to tie my laces for me. I pushed his hands away. By dashing off we might only be encouraging the Obinis to a chase, for which they should be all warmed up.

Now I was ready, but where was Iuvea? And the To-oo man?

The Obini chant beating on our eardrums, louder by the minute, was becoming too much.

'Jalan, bapak?' said Taringgen.

'Yeah, jalan,' I said, but our Momwinas were already into the trees and out of sight.

I yelled the salutation 'Kesiné!' The Obini boy, hands on his narrow hips as he caught his breath, looked up, surprised. There was no hostility in his face. He touched his sharp nose bar, adjusted it from side to side using the splayed fingers of the left hand, his eyes on mine, staring quizzically as if trying to recall something he had meant to ask me. Responding to an abrupt call from indoors, he turned on his heels, uninterestedly strolling into the deep hut shadow, out of sight.

Iuvea and his companion were sitting by the river, the sandy shore disturbed around their feet where their toes had been ploughing at it nervously. They had not been looking for ma at all. Our fear, the fear of a silent arrow speeding towards our backs, was not an imagined one. Even once beyond the Abi river we trotted rather than walked back to Momwina land. I let my boots crash through the mushy pulp of rotted logs and kicked through the ground creepers, carrying my compass, medicines, mosquito net and parang, in case I was separated from the others. We waded the Kweeki, and were soon on the Yakee, both as smooth as stretched polythene.

Iuvea mocked the Obini chant in a girlish voice, holding his groin like the Obinis, but in agony, as if his leaf had withered dry and been caught by a stray firespark. Along the bank the To-oo river canes swayed with a light breeze, and their pallid brown flower clusters – which said that this was the dry season – drooped and darkened in the first raindrops of the afternoon.

After a night's hard sleep at To-oo, we took a direct trail homeward via Bookosooboo, where a new house was going up on twelve-foot stilts, ready for the rainy season. One member of the six-man work crew had two shiny black horns, like those of a rhinoceros beetle, rearing from his nose. The man stroked me with both hands in wonder.

Only Iuvea, Meréné and Taringgen continued for the final leg on to Dekai. Our pace quickened as the light changed from the rich greens of daytime to the dirty grey–green of dusk. The noise of insects changed tone to a dull fizz in the lowering light. When the first evening cicadas took up their scratching noise, we would have less than an hour before the path was lost in the dark, and the frog chorus would be on us, with the night and its cold. We ran on and on, until the whoops of Meréné and Iuvea were picked up by Dekai women returning home, humping firewood. Iuvea stopped and produced his crumpled underpants, which smelt of the dank stale air you get in cave chambers. We were out of the forest. They were home. The sharp profile of Dekai's roofs broke above the tree line into a sky smirched with ochre cloud.

'I thought you said the Obinis were friendly' were the first words I said to Hans, at Sumo.

'Hello! What? Er yes, I thought they were,' he said. 'Perhaps you called on a bad day.'

In the house I dried out with Taringgen, by the stove.

'What you do now, *bapak*?'

'*Saya tidak tahu*. I don't know. I just do not know.'

Taringgen looked as depressed as I felt. He said it was because he had a cut foot, but the cut in reality was not worth wasting iodine on. 'Allah isn't with the Obinis yet,' he said. He spoke it so fluently that I suspected he used the phrase regularly of his Dekai flock.

'You needn't lose sleep over that. He soon will be.' I said I would see Taringgen off in the morning, but he left as the others had without saying goodbye.

I stayed on in the mission house, wondering what I should do. Should

I try to visit the Wiminis? The Indamains? The ants, I noticed, had re-routed their roadways in order to get at the goodies in the sacks which I had left behind. Now I was going through my supplies again, and they were having to reorganise their food lines. No, I would leave for 'easier' Papua New Guinea. I was tired of the forest just now, and that, on top of the dubious Wiminis and perhaps non-existent Indamains, might be dangerous. PNG would provide time to rethink. Those Papuans were colourful, there was a large assortment of them, and even now their land retained many secrets. It might well offer up something of importance to my journey. I would delve around. Flicking through Paul Kline's Gospel had not been of service, so far, but somehow this island might yet help loose me from what the writer Peter Matthiessen had tagged 'the fatal spell of the mystical search'.

Finding guides and carriers at Sumo, for the journey into the mountains towards Wamena, was almost impossible. Word had spread that I liked to gallop through the forest and now had abnormally heavy loads. Anyway, it was always a disagreeable prospect to leave the comforts afforded by the mission. Finally, I left with three reluctant guides – Biaricoo, Darius and Tarkoo – who, from the start, were more interested in hunting. They soon trapped an *oh*, a grey lizard an arm long, between the buttresses of a tree. The Baliem bellowed on our left, here only just released from the heights. By dusk, high in the foothills, the guides were raising the payment by two extra razor blades each, and claimed to have lost the path to Uu-am, the first stop.

In the night under a lean-to of fronds, I was woken by the feathery touch of long black ants. They bit and clung as I tried to shake them off in the dark, and got into my scalp and between my thighs, where, trapped, they chewed to get free. At dawn I discovered that my ankle bandages, which the guides were meant to be watching as they dried, had 'burned away' in the camp fire.

The Sumo boys made it clear, even though they spoke in Momwina, that they were not going a step further. Of course, I could go on alone if I liked . . . They moved to get at my stores. Before the mutiny could get any further I kicked the sacks away. The three guides stepped back, unsure. I piled on to my back all the stores I could – about seventy unbalanced pounds – and turned around to Sumo. After five hours I met a squad of Momwinas who were levelling a tree to get at a colony of birds, doomed fledglings in the nest balls screaming for help from their distraught, flapping parents.

At Sumo I plugged in the radio set, waiting for a break in trans-mission. A Papuan child had been bitten by a death adder. The mission had broken the news of the offspring's demise to the mother, whose reaction just now had been to jump into a ravine; the mission was mortified, but it was agreed that it was nobody's fault. At last I spoke to Paul Kline, telling him about my personnel problem.

'Yeah, lowland people aren't so used to hard hikes. Tell you what, there's a plane flying to your locality with a heap of petrol cans, why don't you take a flight out, over?'

'Well . . .'

'Good, I'll hand you over to Kathryn. She's fixing the flight schedule for next week.'

'Hi, Benedict. Glad you're getting out now. That way you'll live longer, over.'

'Well there is that, I suppose . . .'

The MAF pilot was David Marfleet, who had conquered his malaria and had just arrived from England. 'Well, have you found whatever it was you were looking for here?' he asked.

'Nope.'

'What are you? I can't remember. A biologist? Geologist? Or just someone having a good time?'

I thought back to what had seemed like an imminent massacre at the Obinis, scratching at the ant bites which were going septic in my hair. 'I don't know. Yeah, maybe just someone having a good time.'

But I was not finished yet. In the highlands I had prepared myself, cleared my senses, and in the lowland forests I had used those senses, come close to knowing, for fleeting seconds, what it is to move with the natural forces, rather than against them. Now I would find a means of slipping inside those forces, of flowing along within.

Chapter Seven

I touched down at Wewak, Papua New Guinea, on 13 February in a plane which was empty except for a man, with a red beard like a soiled bath mat, and his wife, who had been an anthropologist in her prime and had met Margaret Mead (Mead had studied, among other peoples, the Manus Islanders).[13] The air hostess, serving cooled orange juice and coconut biscuits, had endearing tattoos like flowering daisies on her cheeks, and she had danced for Mead on a nostalgic return visit there. Only a child, she had twined lemon-yellow petals in her hair and, as she performed, a soft grass skirt flew around her legs – she had been scared that everyone would see they were bandy.

That night I stayed at the guesthouse which is perched, together with Wewak's radio mast, on a crest overlooking the bay beside the road to the Sepik. Ralf, who runs it, is a German. The story goes that he chose to settle down with a Sepik girl, thus terminating his calling as a Catholic missionary. But only a few months before my arrival, she had died suddenly, I think in labour with her third child.

While he bottle-fed the baby next to an Australian backpacker who had slumped through the doorway, deadbeat from a venture around Hagen in the highlands, Ralf mentioned the name Jeff Liversidge. He was, I understood, a man of Australian origin who lived on the Sepik riverside. By night he hunted crocodiles, by day he carved chess pieces and, a lapsed Seventh Day Adventist, he was fond of a stiff tipple. He might know of a forest retreat for me, way upriver. Some of the tributaries, like the August and May, were off the beaten track; and the Sepik's upper, mountain reaches towards the Fly river[14] wandered through West Papua, not a hundred miles from the Obinis. As for the nearby middle-water stretches, they were easily navigable and had been subject to almost continued contact since the German days, when Angoram was established as a post towards the end of the last century.

Turn left from the guesthouse and you are soon on Wewak's sea front, with women in the waves, bobbing on car-tyre inner tubes, whipping the air with bamboo fishing rods, and ships manoeuvring into port behind. Turn right and you roll down to the Sepik Plains. I wanted to go right – this Jeff Liversidge sounded promising – but first I went on a shopping spree.

Wewak was an easy-going town after Jayapura, and here there were no morning exercises for government employees. Also noticeably absent were fried rice smells, accompanying chillis, sweet, ground coffee, flashy rings on fingers, cheeky calls of peanut-butter-skinned children assailing foreigners, straight hair parted so cleanly it might have been done with a sharp knife. However, as in West Papua the most smartly dressed people were not the indigenous New Guineans but administering foreigners.[15] There were no Indonesians here but Australians with white pulled-up socks and nuns in habits. Tourists and locals wandered around in thongs and bare feet. The single main commercial street began with the post office, where the population of expats, dwindling since Independence, inspect their mail boxes. The street's trees were laden with staghorn ferns. Youths leaned against the stores, kicking their large dusty feet, below signs in Pidgin English: 'Sori tru. Nogat wok'.[16] Very sorry. No jobs. By night the more disillusioned became 'rascals' and the capital, Moresby, became downright dangerous.

Bearing a sackful of rice bags and mackerel tins and a leaf of airmail paper on which was scrawled the name of a Catholic priest who might or might not offer sleeping space that night, I waved down a white government jeep-like car with Department of Primary Industry (DPI) markings. The driver was a squat man with a gold-capped tooth and he told me to trap one of the SP beers rolling around the gear box. Then he bit off the lid. We shared the bottle and sat in the ditch together drinking the remaining six, in between efforts to change the tyre. He spoke English, like all the young who had properly attended school. His government work along the Sepik was mainly the rearing of crocodiles for the skin market, and in the bush it was rubber and coffee – rural employment to stop the young wasting their lives lounging around the streets.

We resumed our journey, and it began to rain. The red road was soon sluiced by the downpour, the vehicle sliding along through the coastal scrub hills as the drink loosened the driver's grip on the steering wheel. We dropped down to the grassy plains. It might have been the dry season for the Obinis, but here it was definitely the wet. The buildings were modest palm-roofed houses; occasionally there were explosive flashes of light as metal roofs caught the sun – a school, a church or a trade store. Once I saw towering huts with a forward-leaning triangular façade. The shape reminded me of a photograph I had once seen of a spirit house at Maprik, off the road to the Sepik west of here. The front had displayed dozens of painted faces with eyes ringed concentrically in

80

pink, black and white; in the dry season the harvesting of the staple food, yams, was accompanied, the picture book said, by 'bright fertility rituals'.

Children dashed to the roadside waving betelnut branches, coconuts and almost spherical cucumbers, hoping to sell them. We forded a river with women in full clothing dipping themselves in to wash. Girls walked the dirt road with their cotton dresses hitched up to carry earthy root crops; men stepped out of clumps of coconut palms with shotguns broken over their shoulders. Ahead I could see the foothills of the island's central buckled spine of mountains, a continuation west from the series that hung above the forests of the Obinis. Through the plains, rolling fields had been burned that week and only cooked earth and charcoal bristles remained.

We were drawing close to the Sepik now; the DPI man said it flowed quietly through the pitpit – that was the Pidgin for cane – ahead of us along the horizon. Some of the anthills in the grasses were moving. Looking closer, I saw that they were hunched black birds of prey waiting to catch lagging chicks. A few tight-skinned cattle with mud-clogged hooves gazed at us.

'Oh Bennyjiks, Bennyjiks, the beer is all over.'

'It was good though, wasn't it?'

'Oh Bennyjiks, yes. Anyway, we are here now at Timbunke. I will take you into the mission compound. Can you see grass where I can pass water?'

'Pass *what*? Here? Just leave me by the roadside,' I said, looking at the mission compound. It was so well kept it was formidable. It had an apparently rust-free wire fence, an immaculate lawn, a perimeter of delicate flowers with no deadheads, and a tidy outshed with insulated wires gushing from the eaves – a generator house? We edged up to the compound.

'Well, I'll unload.'

'Oh Bennyjiks, we drank well together. I'll drive you right to the door.'

'No, please don't bother. I'm worried about the Father's beautiful lawn.'

'It's no trouble.'

'No, please . . .'

Between a stark white church of wood to the left and the residence on the right, we trundled across the lawn, biting into the turf.

'Oh dear . . .' I could see through the ground-floor mosquito netting a pink face coming up to the window. She was a Sister and her jaw dropped.

'There you are,' the DPI man said. 'And that's the Sepik.' The lawn stopped ten yards beyond us, and then fell away to muddy banks and a silent river of dreary flat water and twirling weed. The driver did an untidy sweeping, sliding curve across the lawn, stopped to engage in four-wheel drive, the wheels chewed deeper, and then he was off on his DPI duties.

Father Michael, from Ireland, winced a bit when he saw the dissection of the turf, but said he didn't mind too much. The grass was kept short only so the mosquitoes could not lurk there.

'You have come at a bad time.'

'Oh, I am sorry. I'll—'

'No, no, I mean you have come at a bad time for mozzies.'

'I rather thought I had.'

'Come and take a seat.'

'Thank you.'

'You've a yellow sort of colour on your face. You've been roughing it in the bush, I think.'

I was surprised he had called my face yellow, with all its dappled pink ant bites. 'That's right. I was with forest people called the Obinis, trying to understand their life. But they got bored with me.'

'Good, you must tell me all about it. But now I've got to go to prepare Mass. You can be resting here. Be reading some *National Geographics* if you like. Last year's, I'm sorry to tell you.'

After Mass, Father Michael, sipping instant coffee with me, patiently answered my questions. The DPI man had said that even the combined might of the Catholics, Assembly of God and Seventh Day Adventists, who had invited themselves to stay along much of the middle Sepik, had not entirely suppressed dabbling with the spirits. Indeed, the shamans and other spirit priests claimed to meet with exactly the same success as Christian priests, praying for rain to come or go elsewhere.

'You know, I'm a good deal fond of traditions and old goings-on here. Will you look at that?' His eyes were on a sculpture of Christ in caramel-coloured wood on the white wall. He was being crucified and had a phallic nose and a distorted, stretched jaw. 'That is the style of the middle Sepik.'

The Sepiks, I already knew, are famous for their carving. As with the Asmats of West Papua, it is regarded at a man's job, because the pieces have a spiritual role and, in common with most religions worldwide, the men permit only themselves to conduct the rituals. Hung over a house entrance, a glowering face mask with a frill of sago fibre will help guard it from bad spirits, as will the miniature protective figures with sea-shell eyes and fibre aprons hung from rafters as food hangers.

'You see, our Lord has been carved with the initiation markings. I think that is nice.'

Father Michael was right, the patterns looked splendid on Jesus. The initiation markings were stipples working up either side of the breast, down the upper arms and down the back. They were an imitation of the crocodile skin. The animal was held in such reverence that the prows of canoes were even carved in the shape of its head, with cowries for eyes. The men paddled standing up, so that they could punt, and the blades were webbed, like an amphibian's claws. I could see them tomorrow, the Father said, but Timbunke spirit house was now merely a men's social club, and the carvings inside had price tags on – a first bidding price and a final offer.

It was time the generator was switched off and I was shown a guest bed above which was a naked bulb with orbiting moths. The generator clanked to a halt and the light flickered out. In the sudden dark, the moths continued drumming on the hot bulb.

Ralf had said the river plain was so lacking in boulders that the Sepik people used to hump them back home from far excursions and treat them as sacred. Timbunke, I saw, had its own cluster, standing like gravestones of long-forgotten relatives by the spirit house. These *haus tambarans* were not like the small round temple huts of the West Papuan highlands. They were barn-like buildings with palm roofs sloping to an apex at either end, where lurked a large leering face mask – often with a mouth the size of a rugger ball – under its own protective apron. I was not interested in looking inside; instead I discovered that Timbunke had a modern hospital, a brilliantly painted white-panel and silver-metal affair with a wire perimeter fence, proper staff in long white coats and an open ambulance boat serving this portion of the river. That day the ambulance was going to Kaningara, on the Blackwater Lakes. Did I want a lift?

The map showed that the lakes had interesting shapes, so I postponed my visit to Jeff Liversidge, the crocodile hunter, and hopped aboard. We turned off the Sepik up the Korosameri, which drains the Blackwater region, adding peaty water to the Sepik near Mindimbit. That was how I came to the Blackwater Lakes, a place that held me for a month. The hub of the lakes is Kaningara; there, on a hill which is said to be a giant cassowary print from ancestral times, stands an immodest Catholic church. As well as the school there is a health clinic, with pickled poisonous creatures to help identification. They are especially proud of their death adder. It was the children who paddled me from village to village, through drifting weed and grass islands, they who taught me the basics of the three 'language groups' that composed the lake population. They also expounded the different fishing traditions which the three lots of ancestors had brought with them; nets made from bark string, their mouths stiffened by cane, traps which men built from a single bamboo, split many times lengthways and interwoven with canes that spiralled around. This gave me a feel for Sepik life. Govmas village had a cunning one-way fish trap called the *taswuesh*; bags for sago were *hollees*.

The need to know such details became an obsession. It was a route, I thought, to the soul of a people bound to nature. So I filled my red notebook with the assistance of pipe-smoking dear old ladies, who introduced me to the nailfish – with its brown flesh, dorsal spine and armour-plated head – while we were bent in the shade gutting them. Children played marbles with *yarungoka* seeds at our feet, the girls with rings of tortoiseshell through their earlobes, teenagers with tattooed initials, squiggly worms or arrows to their eyes. They did not wear pig tusks in their noses like their fathers, or hang 'Tears of Job' seeds from their upper ears; they only wore sago skirts for dances and longed to become nurses and rock stars. But the past was not all embarrassment. There were stories of the Japanese: their army put a match to Sevenbuk's spirit house but a potent sacred stone, now looking like nothing so much as a flaky baguette, had picked itself up and tottered from the inferno to the safety of the bush.

At Govmas was a larger spirit house, a heavy two-storey structure: downstairs a gallery of tourist carvings waiting on the cold mud, upstairs a floor where initiates could be secluded. At Kubriman two widows had been covered in ghostly paint; a string passed through their noses and trailed to the bark floor. They were in seclusion until it was considered decent for the husband they had shared. The mud that was cracking over most of their nakedness was washed clean away by water from their red eyes. These were the slackening bonds of the past. Others required you to agree to a cross-marriage arranged on your behalf – perhaps you took the girl, and her brother married your sister. A Kraimbit man who had speared his first pig was led, adorned in a cavalcade, round and round the spirit house to happy tears and the clunking of slit gongs. It was exciting, stimulating, but by the time the fires were low at dawn I knew I would not find the end of my journey here. The stained Western garb – sweat bands, hole-riddled bras – strapped proudly on among the flicking headdress feathers, the swinging painted limbs and crescent kina shells was slightly pathetic.

In the morning the elders confided that this new spirit house had not yet been ritually dedicated to the spirits or gods. Worse, a helicopter had dropped in with a camera crew to film 'an initiation ceremony' with the building in this unholy state. The man whose night it had been, and who had had the bravery to strike down a pig, had not been given the initiation markings. He had been afraid he would stand out from his police colleagues on the beat in New Britain, the small island across the Bismarck Sea.

No, I had to move on. The grubby bras tugging awkwardly around the women, the itchy polyester shorts under sago skirts, were only symptomatic. Here the fear of the spirits in the young had been replaced by a fear of being fined two kina; here the young had their own independent aspirations and wanted to break their ties with the material poverty which went with an unbroken partnership with nature. That was reasonable. Maybe this individualism was something to be encouraged. I wasn't sure, but I *did* know that seeing it would provide no answers for me.

On the Friday the white ambulance boat sped towards us, breaking the tranquil lake waters to tell the clinic nurse that a relation had collapsed and they were to take her to the funeral right away. It was all right, the nurse excitedly told me, she hadn't seen the relation in question before; this would be her first chance. She would arrange for me to be dropped off at Mindimbit, where I might seek out Jeff Liversidge, 'Master Jack'. We wound through the lake grasses, a male nurse potting off two sitting ducks and three crested pigeons whose plumes he would adapt for a headdress. We raced on and on through the spray, our lips dry and cracking, and came out of the backwaters, down the Korosameri, dashing past milky green walls of pitpit and low shelves of grey or tan silt. The water was just around its highest today.

Nearing the Sepik and Mindimbit, the nurse gave me a run-down on Jeff, all hearsay or harmless gossip. 'Master Jack' crossed over from Australia in his youth, seeking his fortune here and there, eventually here. Now he had a string of tawny-skinned children by his wife, a local. The Mindimbits had taken him to their hearts, though Jeff lived slightly upriver and saw them infrequently. His firstborn, seventeen-year-old Jeffrey, saw them more often. One of those he saw was a girl, who was pretty and now expecting. Jeff had wrongly assumed that his son's weekly outing to Mindimbit arose out of an interest in the Seventh Day Adventist Church, which was as strong as gambling in the village. No one had bothered to ask. And no one had noticed anything until the girl began to put on weight. Jeff was now bracing himself for demands for a brideprice.

Dropped off at Mindimbit, I found the villagers concentrated around their meek hut of a spirit house. Edging through the crowds I saw men engaged in a shuffling dance, back and forth, back and forth, across a stretch of riverbank mud. They were togged up – cowrie shells clapping like castanets on their ankles and below the knees, faces and chests which were blackened, headdresses of charcoal cassowary feathers, bare feet thumping to the beat of hand drums and a slit gong. A boy at my elbow pointed out a woman whose richly black skin was all the more intense for her spanking new yellow blouse. 'Meri bilong Master Jack.' Jeff's wife.

Jenny said Jeff would be pleased to see me. 'You know,' she said in Pidgin, 'he's as white as *you* are, but I suppose we Mindimbits still love him!' Her laugh was hoarse from talking above the dance noise but there was no alcohol on her breath. If I could hang on until the end of the singsing she would give me a lift upriver to Jeff. She didn't want to miss the dance ending. Good gracious, no one but no one should miss out on that. I had been a month on the river and I had picked up a great deal concerning the custom of these Iatmul people. I knew that a boy should never strike an older brother nor tease a friend he respects. The boy's father disciplines him; his maternal uncle, wau, acts as a gentle guardian. This dance I was watching was one the wau might arrange every now and then for his *laua*, prodigy. I suppose anthropologists[17] would say the *naven* ritual reinforces the special relationship between the wau and the child and it occurs throughout his youth, marking various achievements from incising patterns on a lime gourd, having his nose or ears bored, to killing a first crocodile – or, in the old days, a first enemy. For a girl it might be scratching her first sago from a palm. Through life the ties are close, and waus will definitely give you solace through the trials of your initiation (though now the only thing you can be initiated into at Mindimbit is the Seventh Day Adventist Church).

Over many hours the dance subtly intensifies as women and all relations join the throng; feathers wave in the air, sago-skirted hips swing, and the dance evolves from a squad marching back and forward into a circling whirlpool, the *lauas* being drawn into the swirling vortex. The *laua* is raised in the air above the bobbing headdresses, then lowered on to the bare, damp shoulders of his wau, who has covered himself in clay as mourning women do and wears tattered girl's sago skirts: he is acting as the boy's wife. Other men may take the weight of the child for a while as the pace intensifies, but he is transferred without his foot touching the ground. Quite suddenly, each is dropped to the flattened mud and made to stand as straight as a sentry. The wau drops his loin cloth and smears the cleft of his buttocks down the boy's legs – *mogul nggelok-ka*, anus grooving. There could be no more palpable way for the wau to demonstrate publicly their mutual bonds, and the villagers relish the spectacle, screaming with the drama.

The boarding of Jenny's canoe was delayed by a punch-up. Mindimbits who had been hired to help an oil company which had sponsored a seismic survey of the river basin were all for kidnapping the dynamite, for which the ransom would be a pay rise. Others did not think it such a good idea. Jenny said that striking oil on their land was just the shot in the arm the Mindimbits needed, because the Sepik had cruelly chosen to take a short cut, so more or less bypassing the village. Now most of the river traffic and the tourists gave them a miss completely. At this time saleable carvings had been stacking up, ageing nicely, and the next art dealer who chanced by would hit the jackpot.

Upriver, once the dogs were in hand, Jeff welcomed me with open arms. 'But where's your Union Jack?'

'My what?'

'Aren't you from that Royal Geographical Society, come to discover me? No, guess not. Well, you stay as long as you like, Benedict. Just as long as you like. Boys, grab his bags.' I saw that his half dozen or so children were mainly boys with loosely spiralling tobacco-brown locks, and catapults. 'Don't think there's much entertainment for you here, though,' Jeff added, as we walked through the clearing between the river pitpit and the forest. The house was the sort Wewak carpenters would knock up for a missionary. 'Mind them or they'll have your leg off,' he said pointing at the wobbly steps up. 'And the hounds will if they don't.'

Jeff did not ask why I had come to stay. If he had I would have said I wanted advice about the least travelled upper Sepik tributaries, but I was intrigued as well by the niche he had carved for himself here, holding the West at arm's length. We spent days just chatting together while he scratched at his tool bench, in only his shorts, his freckled back slumped deep in the bare chair foam. His hair, straight and greying, was kept raked back over his crown, down his neck. His beard was clipped short, his blue eyes brilliant but shy and tucked close to his straight, lean nose. He could walk on forest thorns in bare feet, and his flesh, though not obviously muscular, was certainly in trim.

He had a workshop with a bleak metal door labelled 'KEEP OUT' in dribbling white gloss. Inside he carved, not chess pieces as Ralf supposed, but crocodile teeth. His clientele were often the frail tourists on board the *Melanesian Explorer*, which takes cruises up the river and which he himself captained some years ago, before, I surmise, the blue-rinse life almost drove him to drink. At a glimpse of the delicately stalking egrets etched on his necklaces, tourists would tuck away their Instamatics and reach for their purses. If they needed further induce-ment, he would reveal a lovely ebony figurine of a nude girl. Once they had been cajoled into trying her on and had seen the little black creature lie so snugly in their white cleavages, they always fell in love: she was either 'darling' or 'cute' or 'sweet', depending on the wearer's national-ity, and as Jeff once said, 'There's something about her curves all right.' The girl was an enchantress, though it was odd that her charm worked best on females, and that old grannies tended to snap her up first.

There was a rule that the workshop was out of bounds unless the boys were being productive, cutting up tortoiseshell. 'Coming in to fiddle is a no-no, fellas. I'll wire your hands behind your back if I catch you in here again.' The workshop was screened off with sheaths of palm bark, along the top of which snaked a black flex to a naked bulb. Six cylinders, chunks of bamboo, house glues, knife blades and nails.

Jeff always said the coffee I made was no better than the Papuan stuff. 'Know how to brew "Papuan coffee"? Take a mug, fill it with hot water. Put a teaspoon of sugar over a candle flame until the spoon is black with soot, then stir the spoon in the water. Finished.' His first real disturbance for years happened the week before I came when an English university graduate and his team dropped in on a quest for the elusive Sepik oil. He had been left a copy of the *Daily Telegraph*. News of the old England's state was depressing, so much so that Jeff was thinking of writing to tell the editor how lousy his newspaper was for rolling cigarettes.

Outside the workshop on the floor of well-tailored boards, his wife's *wantoks*, relations, sat from time to time. 'They used to come in herds, as hungry as bush pigs, hoping to get a meal off me. Now they don't bother. It's dawned on them I'm poorer than they are.' Those who did come were given standard compensation of two kina for each dog bite.

One caller was Cursacaik.

He looked normal enough at first sight: stomach a little tight, skin the bluey-black of a hornbill, fingernails large on skinny, shiny fingers. But the younger of the boys stayed well clear of him, and Jeff said why. 'Knows a trick or two this man. Talks to the spirits. He's a sangriman – witchdoctor.' Jeff asked Cursacaik in Pidgin whether he minded me knowing that.

'Em i – orait. It's all right,' Cursacaik said, though he had been staring into space.

Is he ill? I wondered, wanting to click my fingers in his face. This was the first I saw of his eerie manner: always apparently not listening, always listening. Spiritmen are not the bone-rattling, curse-wailing, creepy individuals that you would expect. Nor are they the cauldron-stirring wizards in dank caves of Europe's fairy stories. But Cursacaik looked as if he were trying hard to be both. I sat in a chair, Cursacaik squatted, and Jeff talked from behind the workshop screen.

'What tricks then?'

'You name it, he can do it. Healing; shooting about faster than the speed of light. Says he won't murder though. Goes against his scruples. He's more like Superman really.'

'And who believes him?'

'Every Mindimbit, for a start. I think he was out with the spirits last night,' Jeff said with a twinkle, 'because he's got bags under his eyes. I'll ask him.'

Cursacaik answered yes, actually, he was out last night – as it happened, underwater with the river spirits, asking them not to hassle the white men, because if they struck oil the Mindimbits would become as rich as white men. I was intrigued, not by the man equating white skin with wealth, but by his continued stone wall of a face while he spoke what most Westerners would call mumbo-jumbo.

'Rob, come and tell Benedict your story about the flaming torch and Cursacaik.'

'No,' came a small voice from near the meths stove in the kitchen.

'My boys are scared frigid of Cursacaik.'

'No, we're not!'

'Jeffrey! It's storytime.'

'I'm feeding Arrk.' Arrk is a tame hornbill whose idea of an outing is to fly down the river to Mindimbit where he scrounges scraps of food by impressing children with his ability to orientate his six-inch bill and never miss a lobbed tit-bit. Jeff is sure they will lure him into a cooking pot one day.

'Well, we went out one night, my Jeffrey and I, hunting pukpuks – crocodiles. We left Cursacaik quietly on the floor as per usual like a Buddha contemplating his navel. Just as we were leaving, clambering slowly down the loose steps in the dark, he said "I'll see you upriver." We laughed at him. You know what he's like. That straight mask he puts on, like now. "No, I mean it," he said, "I'll get along there before you, and be doing a jig, waving a torch from the bank." "Huh!" we said, and trotted out laughing loose our underwear. You can imagine.

'We baled rainwater from the canoe, cast off into this night. Not a star in the sky. Black as your bowler hats. We scanned the canes with a torch beam to pick out the red eyes of pukpuks. Nothing though. Nothing was out there at all except us and the frogs. Until we saw that torch burst alight, then caught the crackling as the flames waved to us out of the night. Just like Cursacaik said! Jeffrey turned lard-like and I wasn't too brave either. Couldn't work our paddles homeward fast enough. Ran indoors, panting, and slammed the door. And there was Cursacaik sitting as we'd left him, but with a smacking grin over his face . . . That's Cursacaik for you.'

Cursacaik got up at this stage and optimistically headed for the kitchen. 'So he does eat and drink like us then,' I said, straining to listen for the boys scuttling out of Cursacaik's view. 'What's your conclusion? He's genuine?'

'Don't know. But if he ambles into my workshop in five minutes, says he needs a rooster for sacrifice to keep a spirit off my back, he'll get it. I'll tell you, when the oilmen first came in their clean overalls they had hernias laughing. A local bloke had insisted they hired a magicman to keep the rain off. Then they went along with it anyway. They claim it's all good PR.'

Cursacaik re-entered now, ruminating on a betelnut. I wondered how he would react to my asking if I could pick his brains about the spirits – nothing special.

'Worth a try.'

Cursacaik, insisting on speaking through Jeff although my Pidgin English was already reasonable, answered that he would see me in private at Mindimbit. Why not? He would happily talk. I should not expect much else though. Mindimbits would pay a lot for the secret of his power. But of course I was a white man, so I would not let myself believe easily. I should know about his special stone.

'Oh, that thing. He's got this lump which he dug out from under a mountain, he says.' Jeff raised his voice in tone and pitch. 'You've seen it, Wally, haven't you?'

'What?'

'That dirty stone Cursacaik's got. Glows in the dark. Turns it off and on like a bedlamp when he wants.'

'No. Not me.'

'Anyway, that's a good offer, Benedict. Take it up, I should. And see what else you can pick up from old Cursacaik.'

'Tenkyu tru,' I said to Cursacaik. 'Thank you very much. Me kam long ples bilong yu tumora.'

Cursacaik sniffed. 'Good.' He spoke again to me via Jeff.

'Well, you heard that. He said to prove his power – to get you in the right mood, so to speak – he's going to visit you in the night, and make you have a very bad dream.'

'Thanks.'

As it was, after Cursacaik paddled off home, Jeff and I were up talking most of the night.

'When he's not thinking of doing spells I treat him with all the due respect and deference expected by my wife's relations.'

'What's that?'

'Ignore him.'

Jeff worked on, the generator softly coughing under the house among the snoring dogs.

Slipping under my mosquito net I had already decided I would be damned if I was going to let Cursacaik ruin my night's sleep with scary visitations, and I put Paul Kline's little red St John's Gospel firmly in my right hand before drifting off. That would do the trick, I thought; and it did.

Next morning, taking the scrawny mutt of a dog called Musky – a name which sounded suspiciously like the Pidgin expression for 'doesn't matter' – little Robert and I paddled downriver. Leaving the canoe high and dry in the pitpit behind Mindimbit, we hit a trail which had been cut up by the trotters of pigs and emerged prickly with pitpit fur beside the nursing clinic, adjacent to Annie's house. Annie, one of Jenny's sisters, had a bad eye always covered by a scarf of Parisian glamour, and she was still as beautiful as her restless nymph of a daughter – the result, perhaps fifteen years before, of a white man who had been and gone. The daughter often played hopscotch on the mud paths, a teak-coloured girl among a dozen ebonies.

Annie sat me down in her house with a bowl of bananas in hot coconut milk, and told Robert the news. Margaret, another sister, had written from Wewak saying she was having a marvellous time and could she have some more cash. Oh, and some drama: her own daughter had woken to see a snake greedily swinging from the rafters the other night. It had been tempted by the pet kittens, of course. (They, by the way, were doing just fine, even the runt.) The girl had screamed blue murder, but when a posse of youths came to the rescue, expecting to land their sticks on the back of a rapist, they found the child standing over the python, which she had hacked into lots and lots of little pieces. They were shared round first thing the next day.

'What a girl!' said Annie, taking my empty bowl, and I had to agree.

Annie was not keen on my mixing with Cursacaik. Then she declared her hand: she was an enthusiast of the Seventh Day Adventists and, so to speak, a rival to Cursacaik.

Cursacaik's extensive home was, I found, a most inconvenient place for getting to know the man, let alone his secrets. His relations did not keep their distance the way Jeff's children did, and had to be pointed to the exit regularly. We sat facing each other on wooden stools, mid-floor. His house was gloomy and had a whiff of dampness, and other things besides, from the pond. This pond featured a community of billowing dragonflies and a quizzical adolescent pet cassowary. Nearby stood two lavatory shacks with attendant starving dogs whose unsettling habit it was to eat up everything, but everything, deposited in either.

Jeff had said I must be sure to ask Cursacaik the obvious question. 'And what's that?'

'Well, to disappear in front of your eyes. Tell him, *then* you will believe him, all right. If he's a conman, that'll sort him out.'

I didn't want to rub Cursacaik up the wrong way, and I put this suggestion out of my head. To Cursacaik I was already an enigma. I was a white man, a 'master'. I belonged to the world which had undermined the Old Ways through the lures of its Church and of Wewak, both of which captured the hearts of the young — if only because both were associated with the West's material wealth. What did I want from *him*, stalwart of past religion? I guessed Cursacaik would play along with me for a day or two, work out the answer to that question, achieving great reverence among the Mindimbits for being a white man's guru — even vague friendship with a master gains you kudos on the Sepik — then, bored with all my confusing doubts, would drop me. If he was a conman he would drop me all the same, but sooner.

Cursacaik dipped into his woven shoulder bag. It had drawings in black ink on the outside which might have been magic symbols and certainly must have helped ward off the stray hands of children.

Cursacaik brought out a human jaw, yellow and missing a few molars. He put it in my hands. It was light. He said it was his father's, and it gave him strength. Next was a tight roll of bark. He had to chew it to clear his mind before making spells. I smelt it. Cinnamon? Almost certainly. Cursacaik asked me to bite a piece. I did. It was as you would expect cinnamon bark to taste: slightly hot and interesting but no more than that. I would not tell anyone his secrets, he said. He was not requesting me, or ordering, but just stating a fact.

My expectations rose, but the secrets he was prepared to give up were light, uninteresting, and came in dribs and drabs, always at night under the fidgety light of the fire embers. Cursacaik refused point-blank to raise his voice above a whisper lest the children under their mosquito nets were feigning sleep. If they turned on their rush mats, he would shut up like a threatened water clam for a good thirty seconds. I was having to be very patient; Cursacaik seemed to want to kill my attention with boredom. I clung on.

Once we tried to eliminate eavesdroppers by promenading the river path but, nearing the third hut along, two normally stone-deaf dogs caused a fracas. In the daytime the eyes of the villagers regarded me darkly. They were jealous of Cursacaik, convinced he was sharing his most secret of secrets — which he certainly was not with me. In particular there was a man whose child had been whisked away by the spirits — no body had ever been found — who wanted Cursacaik's exclusive help to please the spirits before it happened again.

The second morning, Cursacaik woke on his wood headrest with the last flakes of decorative paint on his face. He said he had been off to Maprik. There was a good singsing there just before dawn.

'Maprik's a day's ride at least,' I said.

'Nogat. No,' he said, and unfurled a leaf package. Inside was a fistful of chalky powder.

I thought, Now we're getting down to business. Cursacaik was beginning to open up.

It was a potion and, even better, a chief ingredient was human bones – to be specific, the remains of Clements, a famous sangriman. Rubbing the powder over both eyelids at bedtime enabled you to float from your sleeping body to wherever you dreamed of. But there were safety rules – the stuff was potent, and I must never be drunk. Afterwards I should always rise before dawn and scrub my eyes and hands clean, and not in a popular bathing spot, because one taste was enough to kill a healthy pikinini, child. My natural scepticism was qualified by my own memories of Cursacaik washing quietly but excessively before the village was awake, days before. Or had he meant me to see him?

'Just that white dust? No spells, no rituals?'

'Nogat,' Cursacaik said.

After going to bed late, but well before cockcrow, I would lie on my back wondering just what went on in Cursacaik's head, behind those heavy eyes, below that disorderly nest of black hair. This was a man who claimed to have a potion, made from human dried kidneys, which, blown into the air, hid your presence. One day he would have the power to control a man by mixing a scrap of his clothing up in a compound, so drawing the victim's spirit out of his body. Failing that Cursacaik could plant a spell on a stick, and lay it in the victim's path. When the victim came by, the stick would soften and writhe, transforming itself into a snake; then it would revert back into wood when the man had been bitten and was himself writhing.

Yet such doings Cursacaik disdained. He had the means to be transported unseen at night – bypassing the hazardous dogs – to lie with girls without them knowing; but he had been given his powers on trust. More up his street was detecting murderers, with bamboo poles. He said that at night you would stand over a grave, naked, or, in my case, wearing black clothes, so that interfering spirits would not see you, and you would ask the ghost of a corpse to point the stick in the direction of his killer.

I had no proof of this man's powers – only stacks of yarns along the lines of the one about Jeff's flaming torch. If Jeff was not convinced, how could I be? Here and in the Ramu district, he had had lots of experience of 'glasmen' (a term used mainly to describe lower-powered diviners). My direct challenges – Could I try your magic powder tonight, just a dab? – were always fenced with his favourite word, 'bihain', later. It was that or his other stock answer, 'nogat'. Procrastination was his byword. Perhaps some mentor of his had once lent him advice: 'By all means *offer* to share your secrets, but never get *round* to it, Cursacaik. Procrastination is the thief of time, but also the embezzler of knowledge.' So I would not, he said, use the dust, which he now gave me (and which I have still), until I had accompanied him to a kind of spiritual get-together in over a month's time, out on the road from Pagwi to Wewak. It was a simple catch: I saw he had never intended to tell me anything of substance at Mindimbit, but I had been enticed enough to want to hang on. I did not know that substantial road in those days, and in my mind's eye I saw a rutted track, lost in wilder stretches to jungle creepers.

The meeting was strictly secret but Cursacaik would get me squeezed in all right. I visualised types more weird by far than Cursacaik – withered, spitting, detestable codgers with bad breath. Cursacaik said they would bare their arms before the chief sangriman, who would nick a vein and smell their blood. If it had a bad whiff – like cabbage water, I imagined – that man had been guilty of using his power for wickedness. Cursacaik's was a benevolent sect, it appeared. The meeting would by no means be sombre. There were three days of feasting, animal sacrificing and dancing. You should bring your own bottles.

Now, I guessed, I had passed the acid test. He was prepared to entrust his secrets to me. The spirits, he said, had told him it was 'orait', absolutely fine by them. They were also telling him something else. 'Em i-bikpela.' It was big, this something. With normal people you would have known that by tracing a furtive look in the speaker's eye, his restless fingers, his playing with his fingernails, or his trying hard not to do these things. With Cursacaik you could only learn if he told you. I think I can say his body never betrayed his thoughts to me. He helped see to that by holding our conversations at night; if there was light, it was on my face, not his. Most mystics, the cynic would say, have a weakness for atmospherics, and his face, black, silhouetted against a halo of firelight, provided them.

Well, spill the beans, I thought. And he did.

Again he was the stereotype wizard of fairy stories. He had a 'feeling in the blood', he said; the spirits were 'speaking' to him; he could 'see it now'. All the clichés. What he was 'seeing' was me being initiated just like a Sepik boy to the secrets of the spirit house. 'What?' It would take place at the culmination of his lessons. 'No, it won't.' He was happy for me. 'I said it won't.' He envied me because he had never had the chance himself. The Church would not allow it here. But me? I had no ties with any village. I could go anywhere for this ceremony. I should choose the most respectable of villages and tell them to prepare an initiation for me immediately. Any objections – and, understandably, there would be plenty – would be overcome by the spirits, whose will it was for me to do this. He had seen the future, and it would happen one way or another.

'No,' I said, and laughed at myself for having played along with Cursacaik so patiently up to now: to be flogged and knocked about with a load of crying boys until considered tough enough to share a group of old men's redundant secrets? To what end – to become a *human crocodile*? That was how they traditionally saw themselves. I said, overtly sardonic, that his spirits had forgotten to mention I was leaving this country before taim bilong biksan. That is the dry season, then only three months or so away. We dropped the subject, but that was my future mapped out in Cursacaik's eyes, and from day to day he reminded me of it, each time making it more likely by conditioning my mind to the extraordinary idea. Eventually, it came to seem not so obviously absurd. If I wanted to learn, to get to grips with whatever it was inside me that drew me away from home, I should do it properly; strip myself down to my bare essentials alongside New Guinean youth. Cursacaik's spells were all very interesting but they were not leading me anywhere.

One day, a sentence once quoted fleetingly to me sprang to mind. It came from Saul Bellow's *Henderson the Rain King*. My memory had stored the words intact, and something had decided that it would be useful for me to be reminded of them: 'mankind as a whole . . . is tired of itself and needs a shot in the arm from animal nature.' Wasn't this my quest? And didn't transforming yourself into a human crocodile amount to getting a shot in the arm from animal nature? The act would be a statement of personal commitment to life forces in general, and it was a commitment that I felt I needed.

I saw little of village life, but I could not miss Willi, the Kansol, an elected post now introduced by government for village representation. He was as tall as a fishing spear, with a skeleton of long cumbersome bones articulated by an inadequate allowance of muscle. During my stay he had a hobbling gait, but this might have been a temporary limp from injury. We somehow developed a mutual distrust, and once he curled his lip in my direction like a bone-guarding dog.

Annie sometimes fed me boiled bananas and offered words of advice; for instance, she warned me that Cursacaik was exceptionally fond of alcohol, including meths, which had just claimed another two of his drinking companions. She confirmed that he *did* disappear for a month every so often, and yes, apparently for witchdoctor refresher courses. He always came back with a spring in his stride. Annie tried again to dissuade me from going 'too far' with Cursacaik. If he got *spak*, drunk, he became unpredictable.

After four nights and three days at Mindimbit Cursacaik became distracted by other business. A child was seriously ill and needed his help. Timbunke hospital had said they could do nothing more and as usual the case had been left in the hands of the village witchdoctor. Cursacaik said he would have to nurse the patient all night. He would get back to me later. Then there was the noisy arrival of an art dealer who, as the man lucky enough to stumble on the jackpot of carvings, simply refused to believe his eyes.

Tai was the dealer's name. He had been collecting for the US market for almost eight years and he looked forward to his annual jaunt. He always went down well with the locals, not just because he brought in money, taking care to buy from each of the clans, but because he came scattering trinkets from the States – sweat shirts, baseball caps, stickers with garish slogans and weak puns, and other tasteless promotional junk collected free over the last year. For Sepik children he was like the funfair come to town. Back in the US, Tai had a rock band – the Sharks. His business card had bite marks out of it; I once came across one left at the reception desk of the Windjammer Motel, where Ralf the German got waste kitchen scraps for his dogs (and, as the expats joked, for his guesthouse menus).

Tai occasionally played the mouth organ to round off business sessions, hypnotising children and adults alike before moving on in a canoe rendered unstable by the stock of artifacts. He always put his popularity down not to his money, his gifts or his musical renditions, but to his hard-nosed bargaining. 'I don't take any bullshit, and they know it.' He could spot a bad carving at ten paces. 'Trash,' he would say and the villagers, having learned the word from previous visits, would disown the piece with grave tutting noises, and would bring it out again only for tourists. Generally, his theory went, tourists could not spot boot polish when it was used to darken wood, and just wanted something archaic-looking to hang above the mantelpiece – nothing too dusty or too heavy, 'paying excess baggage is such a bind' – something that would not crack under the strains of central heating. The solution was for carvings to be divided between those intended for tourists – mass-produced things of a light, easy-to-carve wood, aged a bit by being hung over the fire while perhaps fish was being smoked – and those genuinely used for spiritual purposes. The central posts of the best spirit houses were owned by collectors of 'tribal art', and the more portable pieces, such as skulls housing ancestral spirits venerated over decades, were already safely behind glass in galleries around the world.

After Tai's brisk business at Mindimbit, the carvers struck on the idea of spending their takings at Timbunke, where the Seventh Day Adventists weren't around to ban beer. Cursacaik muttered something about having put the sick child back on its feet and wanting to go along for the ride. He might have gone for the ride but he came back legless, only his burps announcing he was conscious. Tai meanwhile commandeered helpless Cursacaik's house as a storage depot. He invited me along on a jaunt, back to the Blackwater Lakes. We shared his tinned pears and frankfurters, and Kansol Leo from Govmas presented me with a carving of a forest spirit on a section of old canoe. Though the spirit had the face of a grimy gnome, it was so unusually ancient that, when Tai inspected it, his firm business jaw betrayed a weak shudder.

Cursacaik was going to be out for the count for a few days. I paid Jeff a call.

'À propos of nothing much, Jeff, what's the likelihood of there being a Sepik initiation ceremony soon? Like next month?'

'A big fat zero,' said Jeff. 'Not a hope in hell. Or heaven for that matter,' he said. 'Want a dozen reasons? For a start, it's the wet season.' He was not thinking of the bore of teeming mosquitoes and rain either. The ritual burned up almost every ounce of village energy, day-to-day life came to a 'snivelling standstill', and fish were in short supply now – the high water. Then it had to be carried out strictly to custom or the spirits would be livid. Many villagers had given up risking their wrath and had gone over to Christianity, which for one thing certainly looked as if it had done the white men no financial harm.

Jeff, however, recalled Kandengai from his time working on the *Melanesian Explorer*. Up a backwater, this village's traditions[18] were just about standing firm, against the odds. As far south and north as Kraimbit and Maprik, women were allowed to wear crocodile initiation markings on their skin without going through the boy's ceremony; at Kandengai this did not happen or if it did the elders apparently ordered a pig to be sacrificed to appease the spirits. It was Kandengai which had been chosen to carve the yellow posts outside the Banking Corporation in Wewak – the erect male nudes. You could see the crocodile patterns like lace falling down the youths' straight wooden chests. But, it had to be faced, Kandengai was a non-starter. No boys had been shown the secrets of the spirit house for years, and their elders would be scared that they had forgotten all the correct procedures. What was more, fishing was bad because of the pesky salvinia weed. The one hope was that there were recent indications of a revival of old customs along the Sepik. At one village the ceremony had been resurrected after decades and even ageing men went through with it. Elsewhere even a white girl had been involved, though superficially.

I pondered and pondered while Jeff notched up another crocodile-tooth engraving. I had lived for long enough in the Amazon, removed from the West, to be able to resist the false romantic glamour of exotic ritual. Getting mixed up in alien culture would be a complication, not an attraction. The challenge of pulling through an ordeal designed for another society did not interest me much either. I did not see a need to prove myself. And I had already been initiated into the Christian faith at baptism – though the Church of England had fallen short for me somewhere along the line. Moreover, to be very pessimistic about it, my involvement in the ceremony might attract a lot of undue attention that could easily cheapen the personal quest, as it had the Amazon journey. Missionaries, with their own interests, might be furious at my encouragement of paganism, anthropologists fume at a layman 'meddling' in their domain, expatriates turn green at a visitor dabbling in *theirs*. Back home in the West many would inevitably view the spectacle with only morbid curiosity. Would it be worth it – taking on all this, and the ceremony itself – just to satisfy an inner 'back to nature' urge which was no doubt shared by so many of my culture, somewhere in their hearts? I was a Westerner and stuck with it, but I did require a top-up from nature. And to open my soul so that it could obtain that top-up, I would need to take drastic measures – so drastic that a thorough initiation into a crocodile cult might not even be enough.

Cursacaik's suggestion was anyway so ludicrous a long shot that it was hardly worth contemplating. Why should Kandengai village come to a 'snivelling standstill', at my request? Wasn't the initiation worth a try? Not really, with those odds.

Yet I packed my rucksack for Kandengai.

Chapter Eight

What was I searching for that day as I sped upriver towards Kandengai, the Sepik spray washing my face? A community which would agree to come to a grinding halt and grant an eccentric favour to a white man. Why eccentric? Because by requesting that I share their old spiritual secrets I was stating that I valued something in their world – at a time when those Sepiks of my own age had discovered a greater attraction in *my* world. Ever since the previous generation of men had stepped into their very first pairs of shorts, and had kept them on longer than just to please a transient fashion, most communities here had strode along the Westward path with hardly a glance back. Only by an accident of geography did Kandengai, up a backwater, seem to be dragging its feet.

You can branch off the Sepik to Kandengai up any one of three channels, but in March there is an even chance that each will be blocked by floating grass and weed. The first is adjacent to Kaminabit, beyond the lonely shack of a murderer. The driver could not recall whether he had served time or not, but we waved merrily as we caught him in the shallows having his back scrubbed by a wrinkled woman up to her knees in grey soap suds, her dress drawing water up from its hem. We tried to nose our dugout through the grasses, but they were firm. The driver stood up in the prow, spat a curse, urinated overboard and reversed us out. We slept at Kaminabit, where the men blow tunes through plastic drainpipes, in place of the less robust bamboo flutes.

The second channel at Suapmeri was going to be a dead failure; we could see that without having to slow down, which was just as well – the afternoon breeze was already plucking at the river surface. We had stopped too long at Kanganaman, whose spirit house is higher than the coconut palms, and Yentchan with its two woven crocodile dancing masks. Now we were jogging, not skating, upriver.

Our last chance was the channel which meanders off the Sepik through the forest, leading almost to the doorstep of Kandengai. We curved into the channel entrance. The water slowed and darkened, the waves died, trees bowed over us, and flies spun in the thick, trapped air. Signs of nearby habitation were rotted ribs of fish traps abandoned in the riverbank silt. I saw an adult footprint, a day or two old, pitted by rain drops and half lost in the channel wash.

My mind was rattled. How would I put it to the Kandengais? Damn! I had wasted a whole day wondering whether what I was doing was sensible and had totally forgotten how I would address the elders to bring about this miracle. Now already we were clearing the silent waters of the forest, and the engine speed was picking up a notch. The channel opened out. I had only a few seconds more to think. My Pidgin was not brilliant; I knew only a dozen words of Kandengai's language – a dozen inconsequential words learned while at Mindimbit – and here I was an unexpected and uninvited visitor with a certain little request to put! And no money, no barter, nothing but tears and sweat in it for them. What a long shot! I must be mad – stark raving. Had I even thought of bringing a gift? No.

A closely forested river spread ahead, and in a while, on the right, was a modest settlement. My first sight of Kandengai arrested me. The dimming yellow light of the sun was low and soft on the dark-green bank; trees and auburn-coloured huts stood beyond the waterlilies. It was just as well the sight was fine. If it had been a heap of crotchety old sheds and mud paths, strewn with discarded blue-and-yellow polythene Spear tobacco sachets, I would have asked the driver to turn the dugout round there and then. As it was, with this soft ball of sun behind the village, I was enchanted. Some of the smoother black branches in the trees were naked children. They were hurling themselves to the water in ones and twos, limbs kicking the air as they fell. As each child broke the surface, he let out a scream. Water was streaming from the bodies of those who skimmed up branches for another turn and, in that clean light, it fell away like delicate sheets of tin foil.

The view gave me confidence; there was beauty here. Whatever else happened I could always remember that Kandengai was beautiful.

The children ran along the bank with us, and pointed to a convenient mooring place. The man I later knew as Johnny – heavier, with cooler manners – had been handling an axe. The air was sweet with the sap of a tree. It was that same old dugout he would be working on when I next came into the village. But at this moment there was a very different atmosphere – I was just a 'white man', maybe I was lost, maybe I would buy a carving or two. However, visitors here were rare enough to be a major distraction and to entice children from even the more pleasant household tasks.

Johnny put my blue pack into the dripping arms of three naked boy swimmers, who fought for holds on the straps and finally folded up under the weight of it. 'Me laikim toktok liklik wantaim ol bigman bilong Kandengai,' I said in my version of Pidgin. Saying I wanted to talk a 'little' with the elders was a distortion which would only delay the breaking of the awesome truth. The cheek of my fast-approaching request was beginning to unsettle my stomach. I wondered where the loo was. The driver was tapping his foot. As I paid him, Johnny edged a pace nearer to gauge my wealth or generosity. Miserly, the driver seemed to think, judging by the noisy manner he sorted the coins in his palm.

We watched the canoe returning to the narrow channel out of sight, swerving to avoid the shifting grasses. He would get through but a single floating clump now pursuing him would jam the bottleneck as securely as a cork. Shooing away the children, Johnny and a lighter-muscled, quiet man called Andrew took me for a wash and brush-up before my visit to the spirit house. I guessed their real motive was to find out what I was going to ask the elders, before the news was on general release. White men did not appear from nowhere just to come and chat to old men about the weather. Andrew held my clothes as I pattered in the water, enmeshing my toes in the weed. It was the only time I came to this spot to wash; it was a sump of a ditch where all white strangers were automatically conducted, I learned later.

'So you want to have talks with the bigmen,' said Andrew, in English. His ability to speak my tongue was a disappointment. It showed that many young must have attended school, and I had already noted that they had abandoned their village names for biblical ones. If this was a measure of Westernisation then the new generation of Kandengais would already be very much immersed in it.

'Yes, that's right. With your elders. Could you pass my jacket? It's what I use as a towel. Thanks.'

'No towel?' said Johnny. 'For a white man, you are poor.'

Before I had finished drying, Andrew rather tentatively sloshed his feet in the water, then backed out. 'I think I am clean enough.' Then, looking at the film of sweat over his chest, he shook his head and splashed himself, borrowing my judo jacket and rubbing himself dry. Running up his chest and down his back, arms and legs were delicate ridges like those of a crocodile hide. This pattern revealed that he was an initiated man from the Niowra tribe of villages.

Andrew said, 'The young girls love the men with the pukpuk marks, Benedix. The young girls say they look pretty.'

'Yes. It's the initiation I want to ask the elders about.'

'And they like to feel their hands on them.'

'Andrew,' said Johnny. 'Let Benedix tell. He has a problem.'

But when I confided it, both men refused to believe me. There was some misunderstanding, they thought. Kandengai was the best village on the Sepik, I ought to realise. The bigmen hurt their boys, spilled their young blood until they were the strongest of men. Then they told them 'secret stories'. They could not treat an outsider like that. And I could not learn any other way. The elders would lie, as they had before to white people.

'But you have a little influence?' I said.

'That is true, little,' said Johnny. 'And what you can want is too much.'

'Can you help me try to persuade the elders, though? Please?'

'Yes, we can. But it is silly time-wasting, you see,' said Andrew.

They agreed to give it a go.

'Where are your presents?' asked Johnny.

'Presents?'

'Presents to bigmen to help them make up their minds.'

'I'm afraid I haven't brought any. I'm short of cash as well.'

I could afford to buy a pig to sacrifice if they insisted. Johnny said at least we would not waste much time debating. It would be over in a blink.

So I walked to the spirit house with Andrew and Johnny. The sun was all but down. Clouds lay like giant grey slugs along the tree tops. I had not gone more than ten paces when Johnny's young brother Elijah screamed out something to the village. Immediately, it seemed every woman and child was running alongside. Although he had been given strict instructions not to, he had revealed why I had come. I was aware of the villagers' clean skin and health and of a lithe girl with hair smelling of fireplace smoke, and above all that every face was white-eyed in the dusk light and looking up into mine. Good God, I thought. When I slink away from this Kandengai place tomorrow, having failed, every fish in the Sepik is going to know what I was requesting.

Children were taking short cuts to get to me, between the stilts under the family houses, rectangular buildings whose floors were at head height. We wove between these, and after some two hundred paces the grass opened out behind the village to the forest. But before the huge shadow of that forest was the principal spirit house, half obscured by palms.

It was hardly grandiose, though some forty yards long, and that for a second disappointed me. Yet a couple of strides on I was aware that the structure had what you might call 'presence'. From the long high roof, which lifted to an apex at both ends, flew a fish eagle, shaped from wood and apparently in the act of rising through the green palm fronds. The building wore no paint coat, no awesome mask had been positioned to glare down at those who approached and it was the very drabness of the house which loudly spoke its character. Here was something sombre, intimidating perhaps, and though not hostile it took itself seriously. The heavy architecture was boldly simple and suggested masculinity. The thatch dropped down to four feet from the ground at the sides, beneath which it was open, apart from structural posts. The ends of the building were likewise unwalled below this height; above, leaf tiling ascended towards the apexes. Views to within were limited only by the peculiarly severe shadow masking the interior, and with the addition of thin skirt screens (of what looked like grasses) over the gaps created for entrances.

As we came up, the women and their young fell back from the building, inspiring Andrew to dither on the threshold at the right-hand end, recounting the tale of the Sepik girl who came within the bounds of a previous spirit house – the first female to have done so. She had accidentally survived a bloody ambush on her settlement, and survival wasn't necessarily a good idea. The ambushers, men from this village, had not really wanted to be lumbered with prisoners, but she was female, and young, and the hot-blooded men must have thought of a use for her because she was brought back to Kandengai to be incarcerated in their spirit house. Her experiences were much as she might have forecast, but there was one compensation: she saw more of the men's rituals than any other woman. Sworn to secrecy, she was allowed to live on and ended up exiled far away from Kandengai and, the men say, happily married.

The women turned back with children hanging on their skirt hems, as I fell within the spirit house's block of cool shadow, glimpsing two human skulls of wood lodged in the end wall, overhead, facing the outside world. I parted the screens, ducked and entered.

The smooth mud floor was refreshing to the dry soles of my feet, but mosquitoes perpetually stirred the damper air just above the ground. The men were flat on their backs on high, wide benches along both sides. Overhead the rafters were blackened with smoke; light was coming in low from the ends and below the benches. Tilting my head back I found I was looking straight up between the open legs of someone naked with a roughly cut lanky physique, a work so clothed in webs that I could not distinguish its gender. Occupying considerable space in the centre of the floor were two mighty slit gongs. They were not just musical instruments or bush telephones, they had individual personalities: the far ends were crocodile heads. Though crumbling from the bore-holes of insects, and other workers of time, they had been cared for, and painted with pink and grey clays.

'Meet Yo-anga-mook and N'iangandoo,' said Andrew. He was smiling at the waist-high crocodile slit gongs. I wanted to say 'How do you do?' but they were facing away from me into the distance, where, as at this end, there were two half-dead fires with radiating ashen logs. Anyway, this was no time for flippancy – the murmuring sounds of the score of men were petering out. I bowed as faces turned to have a good look. Most men did not bother – they would have had an inspection as I approached the building. Some dozen faces wore joyless expressions – had they heard already? – two looked on pleasantly. None revealed inquisitiveness. A slender youth in football shorts said he was Jimmi and shook my hand; Andrew said Jimmi's wives would cook me up some sago afterwards.

It had been a mixed reception, barely more than half-hearted considering I had been delivered to the very bounds of the spirit house by a loud entourage of villagers, who had been fussing not just because I was a 'master' with the usual pink skin of sunset clouds. No bench space was free, given the manner in which the men stretched themselves around. Johnny forced open a gap on the left and was sworn at. He laughed and beckoned me up with Andrew. Johnny started the talking, and his Pidgin accelerated until I could no longer fathom it. I tapped my fingers irregularly on my tanned knees, offering polite smiles as the men of the spirit house really sat up and took notice now. The intelligent ones were soon correctly guessing what Johnny was trying to lead up to, not fooled by his matter-of-fact tone, appropriate to an everyday request.

'Fugging skulboi [schoolboy]!' That was the first pronouncement on my insolence, and it was approximately what I should have expected. Voices blurted out short words, shouts were exchanged back and forth across the benches; some men wanted Johnny to have his say. But the voices were as hard as gunshots. Johnny's age gave him low status and he was inevitably outfired. The exchanges across the floor were replaced by those up and down benches, presumably between conferring members of the same clans. The argument seemed finished.

But Andrew said we were waiting for the headman of the spirit house to come along, and soon we were all watching as this man announced a debate by taking up a heavy wooden club and drumming a tattoo. The slit gong boomed out, echoing way up between the beams and the dusty, dry cobwebs. The men stretched, the old headman threw the club into the mouth of the slit gong and picked up a baton of grasses. He then began a spiel which paid no attention to diction or clarity, a curl of smoke ascending from his crumpled pen-length cigarette. I guessed that if no one took pains to listen properly, tough luck for them. Regarding spirit-house matters, *he* was the man in control.

The ranks of wizened faces along the benches nodded – not in agreement but with the chewing of betelnut. Men with insufficient teeth used rusty pliers to crack the husks, which were lobbed to a sheath of palm on the floor; then the gums chewed on the acid nut with pepper leaves and ground shell lime from gourd containers – *ya-boo*, Andrew called them – held tight under their arms. The oldest men exerted their privilege to rattle the cassowary bone dipsticks, *tak*. These used to have *tambanja* swinging from them – tassels which reminded onlookers of how many enemy heads the holder had taken.

From now on, the headman muttered, the debate would proceed in an orderly manner. Those who wanted to express their opinions would speak from the floor. One by one the men did so, using the baton to express their curses even more explicitly – an enthusiastic flourish, a rude thrust. What debate though? Who would be on my side?

As evening came, men drifted in from the river and from their forest gardens through the four entrances – those at the ends, and the other two midway along the sides, which divided the benches into two halves. By the time the fires were being stoked to shed better light we had the full complement of available men. 'Godfrey is still not come,' Andrew said across me to Johnny, in English. Johnny said nothing, but gave a nod of comprehension, and maybe – in the dimness and floating ash I did think so – was smiling. Whoever Godfrey was, his absence was good for me, and more than that, Johnny was taken aback, pleasantly, with the composition of the male turn-out. Johnny was out of the discussion now, and I could assume it was because someone more senior thought our proposal was worth an airing, and had taken up the cause.

'This is too lucky,' Johnny told me. 'Many bigmen are come from their houses. I couldn't expect it. Some are little alive.'

'That's good, is it?'

'Yes, of course. One bigman from our second village called Timbun is by luck here, and he wants the banis, initiation. It is ages from the last. He has gathered bigmen from their homes to tell the headman he cannot listen to other talk.'

I was beginning to see what I had stumbled upon here at this village. A fight was in progress between two factions, which could be broadly labelled Traditional and Alien–Modern. I had called when a revered elder happened to be around, and when a man called Godfrey – against the traditional stance and *for* Western change – was not. The elders wanted any chance to reinforce the Old Ways – Jeff had said there had not been an initiation here for years – and my arrival provided that chance.

The debaters were again raving and ranting; they had slipped out of Pidgin and into their own language. The darkly ancient men were doddering, bickering, spitting. Who was this old man of high station, the one apparently hurling all his power on my side? I could not hear or see. Veined, wasted arms waved, catching firelight. So did those thick with muscle, firm in youth. The Traditional and Modern fought what was to be the first of many fights during my time in Kandengai – bare limbs gleaming with perspiration.

It was soon mid-evening. Moths were dancing around the flames getting singed when a lobbed coconut shell caused the embers to flare.

'Well, how are things going, Johnny? They certainly seem to be talking enough. And I can't understand a word.'

'Kandengai village is broken.'

'What's that?'

'Broken into two bits. I am Christian – headman of the Catholics of Kandengai. Most of the youngs are Christians here; the olds are not. But I can help you because I want the old customs also. I was learned the bigmen's [initiation] stories. Also, Andrew and Jimmi was. But we are Christian. *Different* Christian men want to stop the customs. Such a man is gone, in Wewak today. If he was here he can want to stop talk of the banis. He is Kansol. You came to Kandengai when he is at the Garamut goods store: it's special-offer week. The bigmen are fast taking this chance. No time-wasting. They are so pleased: a white man chooses Kandengai, and tell them this village custom is best. If the master can want the custom, so can the Kandengai childs be made to want the custom. Finished.'

'That's it? But I haven't spoken a word yet – let alone understood what's been going on here.' And help, I thought, all this politics! What have I got myself involved in? 'Don't they understand I can't give any money? Only enough to buy a medium pig.'

'That is okay. I will feed you.' Bringing my white skin along here, I saw, was payment enough for the elders . . .

A cluster of less decrepit, huffy men – the defeated camp – walked out into the black village. The remaining figures slouched back on to the benches, joking or muttering. The headman got down, touched his cigarette to the fire embers and pottered over. I was pleased. I wanted to thank him. I slid from the bench to my feet, not knowing quite how to express my appreciation or respect. He extended his hand and it had an incandescent layer of orange from the firelight. I saw that his lips were loose, no longer propped up by teeth. I put my own hand out to his, and he gave me a smile that was fond, but wary. Yet he had not come here to stand around shaking hands. His palm had bypassed mine and was journeying along the inside of my forearm, slipping so gradually up that I stiffened – his feel was so intimate. His eyes were fixed on the spot where he had now grasped my arm. He lifted it firmly into the flickering light. I was surprised rather than alarmed as he curled his thumb, claw-like, and dug a thick yet sharp nail into my skin, meanwhile smoothly drawing his hand back to his ribby chest, so scoring a straight line up to my wrist. There was no blood, but even in this light he could see the line quickly rise in a fat ridge. I felt slightly indignant at the man satisfying his curiosity about a white skin, but this was an experiment to be

The earthquake-torn Solo Valley.

Talking in sign language at the men's side of the To-oo building.

An Obini shield.

An Obini inspects his arrows.

ABOVE: An uneasy welcome: an Obini emerges from his hut with a drawn bow.

LEFT: Danis assembling for mock battle.

A spirit house similar to that at Kandengai. The covered stairway leads to the upper storey where the initiates are secluded.

Inside the Kandengai spirit house. This was my view to the right of my usual space near the Niamé end exit. Pinga and Warbee are making initiates' skirts; Saun is below their bench.

'Wunjumboo spirit'.

ABOVE: Dancing in the nest prior to the second initiation.

LEFT: Fears of the spirits' anger mount: wigs worn as a precaution against the initiates being seen by women and children.

repeated by teasing elders several times before the initiation. (One bright morning in the spirit house I was stood naked, my shorts rolled around one ankle, as old fingers ploughed over me, wondering how the thinner, more delicate skin would take to patterning. 'Scarification', the word used in the West to describe the skin-carving, is inappropriate insofar as it implies ugly disfigurement.)

I dwelt on the immensity of what was going to happen. An ancient village of many hundreds of people, split into six major clans, was about to enter a new chapter in its history. But for the moment I was to know only about as much as the women and other boys knew. Quite simply, I was uninitiated, *koonongoo*. I would be marched with other chosen boys through the fence to be built around the spirit house. Inside the fence we would be dirt under the feet of the elders. We would count for nothing – we would be beaten, spat on and trodden on according to their whims, until we were considered strong enough to be men – or rather crocodiles, because the tradition was that we were baby crocodiles being brought up in a parent crocodile's nest. Then we would come out and be *waarkvarinango*, knowing secrets kept for centuries.

I left the village after a week, with the promise that I would return for the ceremony at the month's end, when the community would be fully steeled, and all urgent chores out of the way. The boys who would probably be initiated with me had agreed we would get on like brothers.

'Whenever you choose to come,' one named Martin said, 'the village will be waiting. When your canoe is seen boys can be happy, the women crying with too wet tears.'

'Chicken shit,' said Jeff, on my return downriver, trying to guess the ingredients of the potion which Cursacaik had given me weeks before. He dipped his finger in the white powder and licked again. 'And porridge.'

'Cursacaik said that's poisonous,' I said.

'You don't believe everything he says, do you?'

We demolished a crate of SP beer over two evenings while Aark the hornbill perched indoors on the back of a varnished wicker chair. He was relieved to get away from the mosquitoes attacking his black shiny toes – black shiny toes which the boys said were like Cursacaik's horns.

'How much longer are you waiting for him?' Jeff asked.

Cursacaik was meant to be turning up to take me to the witchdoctor's conference.

'I'll give him two more days.'

Left much to their own devices, the children liked to scramble up vines in the forest and pluck the fleshy white and purple buds of the *laulau*, which they slotted into bamboo sticks with plungers; with those popguns they warred with each other until one or other burst into tears. Once, we saw a mother hen flustering, scuffing the grass, calling her brood in. I was already jumping for a stick, while Robert grabbed the pronged fishing spear. He made a direct hit first, piercing the ground through the grasses until he struck on the snake. 'Death adder,' I said.

Jeff stood leaning in the doorway and said slowly, 'Give him a minute and he'll be dead.' He meant the chick that was running in giddy circles. His son Jeffrey plucked a few feathers and found traces of blood. 'Had a dog who went that way. But that was two hours,' Jeff said, dragging on one of the Benson & Hedges I had bought him. 'I'll be going for a bath now. Seems a good idea as I smell like a bloody Afghan hound's kennel.' The boys tucked the chick under its mother's wing. After lobbing the snake into the Sepik, Robert ran back to nurse the victim. It was warm, but quite lifeless.

The boys reckoned that the chick had saved my life by walking along the track which I had worn to the river. I laughed and kept to the route until the day after when a black hen lay sprawled across it, gazing up at the morning sky and blinking. Its life was seeping away, death spreading from two incisions a thumb nail apart either side of its ear. It was another of those adders, but before we could put the bird out of its misery Cursacaik paddled in, his breath reeking of meths, and staggered up the dangerous steps saying the bird would not die. Strangely enough, it didn't. Jeff said the snake must have already run dry of venom.

I sat over Cursacaik, who had collapsed on Jeff's floor after imparting the news that the tourist houseboat, part rival of the *Melanesian Explorer*, had all but sunk at Timbunke. So the Timbunke men, who like the Mindimbits know how to spot a bargain, had boarded the listing vessel with axes at night, leaving very little that was immediately portable by the time dawn was clearing.

When our cooking smells reached Cursacaik he woke with a jolt, blinked at me, then stiffly sat up. He wanted a 'pispis', he said; he ambled out of the door and fell off the rickety steps.

In the afternoon Cursacaik spoke to me through Jeff, whose Pidgin was more precise than mine. ' "You see me sitting here calmly," he said, "but under my skin my heart is pounding and quaking. I'm worried you will misuse the powers I have given and will give you." ' Jeff managed, with no smirk but obvious strain, to keep delivery of these words straight.

'Why?'

' "You are a white man. A white man needs clothes, and his women need rings. So you'll feel an urge to burst Wewak's bank doors open with your powers. Money is your food garden." '

Outside, Jenny began singing to her two daughters. They were all Seventh Day Adventists, and had almost learned to harmonise. The sound drifted down the boarded passage in the close afternoon air. It sounded like:

Jesus says we must love away,
Love away,
Love away.
Jesus says we must love away,
And what He says we do.

However, Cursacaik was prepared to risk me going to the spiritual conference. I should meet him at Wingei village. I would be given the *kwara* plant, and a drink that, in Jeff's translation, was like 'stale instant coffee and Alaskan wine in a bad year all shaken up'. Also I would have some *ibika*, which was grown where there was no risk of boys spraying their pispis accidentally on to it. After that, like him, I would know in my blood when the time was right to return to the bush to meet with other spirit men, and to be taught spells.

'What does he think of British spirits?' I asked Jeff.

'They are too sophisticated. He doesn't understand them,' Jeff said. 'Ask for direct proof of his powers once and for all.'

Cursacaik wet his cracked lower lip with his tongue, and said we should watch through the screen netting. The breadfruit tree out there would burst into flames at ten o'clock.

'Well, he really has stuck his neck out this time,' Jeff said after Cursacaik had gone home with a tummy full of boiled rice. 'By bedtime we'll know for sure if he's a fraud.'

Jeff and I sat in the workshop. It was 9.45 p.m. and all dark outside. We had already had our eyes peeled for half an hour.

'If he comes up here with a can of petrol, the dog'll sniff him out, and that'll be the end of him.'

Wally and Robert were hiding under a sheet together, close beside the workshop. At five to ten Jeff and I were stolidly looking at the forest which was obscured by the night out there, the generator deadening the trilling insect sounds. The glows of fireflies blinked and flipped, sparking brightly against the black. The generator gave a pained hump, and fell silent. The lights were out.

'He's come,' said Jeff, but there was a chuckle in his voice and he went off with a torch saying the generator had guzzled all the petrol. While it was being tanked up, I could hear the bugs and moths beating their heads and drumming their wings against the window netting. Jeff was clanging a petrol can, and slapping mosquitoes on his bare legs and back. I heard a rustle in the trees.

109

It was coming from where the breadfruit tree stood against the sky. With no light in the house, I thought I could see its skeletal silhouette against a smear of charcoal cloud. Something *was* happening out there. The generator came to life again; Jeff looked through the netting beside me. 'Yeah, it's coming all right,' he said.

Now I could smell it in the wind: rain.

It was a downpour that would have extinguished any burning tree and we went to bed none the wiser about Cursacaik.

In the morning a pink lady with three chins roared up in a shaded river truck from the Ambunti Lodge guesthouse driven by a Sepik friend of Jeff's with polished sunglasses clinging to his forehead. The woman was an orchid collector who had heard of Jeff, and knew he was 'the right man' to find a 'Sepik blue' for her. Wally, Robert and I waded through the marshes, boarded an island of vegetation – slashing our legs on grasses like extended razor blades – and came back with two sorts, a puce one and liverish yellow flower head. The latter she said was probably dead and both were common. She agreed to swap them for the nuts and raisins she had in her handbag, which was padded out with dozens of calling cards from her 'orchid restaurant' in Moresby.

'Well, you'll see something very out of the ordinary,' said Jeff, as I left for Wewak and my rendezvous with Cursacaik for the witchdoctors' meeting. It was to be held in about a week's time. He paused. 'What'll you do once you've finished that?'

'Who knows?' I said vaguely, wondering how many Sepiks did know Kandengai was waiting for me with bated breath. I was due in a fortnight and the news must be working its way downriver. Perhaps today it would arrive here.

In the depths of the forest stood a solitary shack where a dozen men of the spirit powers were to gather, bringing with them empty bamboo tubes to fill up with fresh blends for their rituals and practices. Perhaps one of the younger men would be stammering with guilt, worried that an act of atrocity would be discovered by the head sangriman. Sweat might be betraying him on his brow. The sangriman would be black-toothed, cross-legged, his eyes distant, fixed on the licking tongues of the fire. The young witchdoctors, Cursacaik included, would be hanging on his every word.

That was the image Cursacaik had put into my mind, but I was dropped off by a truck on a road, not a rutted track, and though dead snakes and dogs featured along some portions, this was a highway with regular PMVs, the free-enterprise bus trucks. Our rendezvous point, Wingei, was not a collection of huts; much of it was a school with a football pitch, and a flamboyant church on a hill peak, biting into an otherwise gentle skyline. Cursacaik had said he would meet me there by the roadside at eleven. I sat on my rucksack in the road dust, under my black hat. It was ten past.

The sun rose, the heat rose, my temperature rose. My hopes did not: he would meet me here by the roadside, he had said; without fail. 'Me toki-tru,' he said. He would bring a bottle of SP. Before long, it was the school breaktime. I had imagined this a wilderness and here was the school population, 380 uniformed little boys and girls, giggling at me from the rucking grass behind the goal post.

'Hello, master.'

'Hello.'

'What are you doing under the heat, master?'

The headmaster scattered the children and invited me into the school complex for a shower and pineapple. He said only one sangriman had been to Wingei lately. It was to cure a young man. He had charged a fortune and the man, who had been healthy apart from a very slight chest infection, had died. 'Most of these magic men are crooks. Undesirables.'

'I know,' I said. Yet my faith in the Kandengai rituals was undisturbed – the men were not witchdoctors who conjured 'magic'. I had seen that, to the elders themselves, these spiritual doings were real. Theirs was a true religion, guided by shamans, priests.

No other engagements now stood between me and Kandengai, which lies not far from Pagwi. Although a week early, I decided I would proceed straight to the village. After a night on the staff common-room floor, I caught a lift towards the road end, feeling uneasy excitement flitting in my stomach. After a half hour on the road, the feeling of anticipation had become so strong it was unpleasant.

The truck stopped at Brurui village to drop some planks off at the health centre, which was having an extension built. The doctor was late, and a glasman was profitably dispensing spiritual cures to the queue. A woman with a throbbing pain in her chest took off her dress top and the old man snuggled his lips between her swollen, young mother's breasts and sucked out what the spirits had put there to cause her pain – gravel chips: three grey, one quartz.

Dr Brown from England, with a Norman nose, fair curls and a stethoscope waggling around his neck, arrived from Mapnik, just off the Wewak–Pagwi road. His most distinguished patient today was a bigman who had not in the least enjoyed leaving the village for foreign cures, although he looked at the white coat of the doctor as a dog looks at its master's face. His jaw was opened. A wooden spatula felt around and about his gums. The doctor said he should hit him in the ribs when he felt pain. The patient nodded his head obediently, but this white man was his hope, and how could he? Yet the point came when he could not hold himself back – there had been one prod of the spatula too many.

The man's eyes sparked. His knuckles jabbed deep into the doctor, and his jaw slammed shut as the white coat and spatula flew away.

'Papa, yu smok paip [pipe]?' Dr Brown said, finding his feet.

'Me smok pepa [roll-ups], master.'

'Brus [homegrown tobacco]?'

'Brus, master.'

'Papa, yu sik.' The old man looked into the clear blue depths of the doctor's eyes. 'Yu gat cancer. Yu save [savvy] cancer?' The man shook his head, but guessed that this meant he must return to his village. He walked limply out of sight. 'Poor old Papuans,' the Englishman said to me, coiling up his stethoscope. 'They see the white man as having everything, and think we can give it.'

Up the road was Pagwi market, and the Sepik. We were within calling distance of Kandengai's slit gongs. The news had already come by word of mouth: Master Benedict was at Brurui, and heading this way. Even back there I had seen the realisation of who I was in the coy, secretive smiles of women and the questioning frowns of men.

I was unloaded from the truck with a swarm of Brurui women who had come to market with bags of sago for villagers, including the Kandengais, who wanted to exchange it for their fish. The Kandengai women were physically indistinguishable from the dozens who sat with fish for sale. But it was clear who they were. Their neighbours were being tapped and grabbed and I was being pointed out from a dozen angles among the crowds. Theirs were proud faces. I was their Master Benedix, and I had turned up as promised. Nicholas was the only Kandengai boy here, and I had never met him before. He carried my pack and walked behind me, like a serf, swaying his immense, square shoulders. I brought some brus for the elders, and soon registered that my premature arrival had produced an excitement verging on panic.

Down by the water's edge, Nicholas commandeered a dugout and a man to paddle in the prow. He said that at Kandengai the slit gongs would be beaten to announce my return and to call a meeting of all the men. Untying the mooring line, we set the canoe into the current.

The sound which signalled my return was enough to send shivers of apprehension through the village. We pressed our dripping paddles to the grey wood of the dugout to listen. From where we were across the water, we watched as even the oldest women were drawn from the dark of their huts. They merged with the agitated figures rushing to wait for us on the river bank. Sprinting behind were half-naked children with hands up to their faces and maybe tears in their eyes – it was difficult to tell from so far away. We lifted our paddles again and the gap between us and them continued to shrink.

Chapter Nine

At last I was ashore, enveloped by the riverside crowd. For a second, standing there without the slit gong drumming on the ears, despite a hundred jabbering and murmuring voices, all seemed to be silence. I searched for familiar faces, said the local greeting 'Apman gramboo!'

'Apman gramboo!' 'Apman gramboo!' – my shoulder tendons were almost torn in the race to shake my hands. The crowd gave way, sighing, and followed as I went with Nicholas straight through the village towards Wumbunavan, the central spirit house to which I had come last time, the big one of the three, shared by four of the six principal village clans. Maree-ruman and Aurimbit, the spirit houses either side of Wumbunavan, in comparison looked small and lowly. Johnny – I recognised his unusually pale brown skin – was bent over, giving the finishing touches to his dugout. He was unimpressed by the fuss, but looked genuinely pleased that I was back, throwing down his adze, brushing the wood chips from his arms and calling for little Elijah to run back for my baggage.

The gaigo, spirit house, was as impressive to me as it had been a month before. It evoked mystery, standing half-concealed by the mounds with old palms marking out its territory, and shrouded by its thick, thatched roof, from either end that gowi of hardwood, wings outreaching, soaring from each end. Indoors, waiting, were the men, and in their midst, the two crocodiles Yo-anga-mook and N'iangandoo.

I sat up on a bench with Andrew and Johnny as before. But this time the uninitiated boy called Martin had been permitted entrance to act as my companion and he sat on my right. There was another change: the spirit house held a very different composition of men. Though the weather was good – a veil of cloud lessened the sun – spritely men who might have been out working were gathered here instead. Such a one was Godfrey, who wore a fairly new white shirt, as was his usual habit, and long, but not long enough, blue trousers. He had the height and comfortable build of a town-reared man. His English was smooth, fluent, his manner with me the most comfortable of all the Kandengais I was to meet. I had learned last time that he was the Christian with the most evangelical tendencies, and as he got up to give my hand a firm shake, and my eyes a direct challenge, I wondered if he thought I was a traitor to that faith. But what was *he* doing in the grounds of the spirit house?

Rom was the name of the little dusty headman with the green wrap loose around his hips. He had already called a debate and proclaimed that while white tourists were sometimes allowed to see initiations going on (but not to learn the great secrets), this white man was going to be treated like a Kandengai boy. It was the way I wanted it, and he said, heavily, that, as I had insisted, that was just the way I was going to get it. Now he was proposing a sacrifice for the Niamé half of the spirit house: one fat pig, to keep the spirits' goodwill during the initiation ceremony.

According to what Andrew had told me outside, a man representing the Niowi end should now say that they too would offer a sacrificial pig. But something was going wrong. Cheered on by a couple of men in the Niowi half, Koma – a town man, just in – was working himself into a hot lather, thrashing the baton so vigorously against the slit gong during his speech that green spews of plant juice flipped up through the air with his sweat. The spirits appeared not to exist any more. Only Jesus. Why waste a pig? He was not going to co-operate, he said with a whirl of the shredded baton, chucking it into our fire-ashes. The matter was put aside while names of other candidates for initiation were put forward and discussed.

'Tell me,' I asked, 'do you want to go into the "crocodile nest"? Go in and be kicked around and carved up, Martin? Really and truly?'

'Of course!' His face tightened. 'I may be small but I'm nearly *sixteen*, you know.'

'So you're not worried?'

He brushed a finger across the soft moustache that curled around his small, serious mouth. 'Well, a little, little. All boys are. It is a scary business.'

'The others don't look it.'

'But they are. And now with this hot talk they'll scare even more, because the bigmen say the spirits can be angry. If they become angry the spirits can punish us.'

'So *why* do you want to go into the nest?'

'Why? To show we do not scare, of course. Our mothers are sad but they are proud also.'

Johnny handed along a coconut from the left; the milk was cool and fizzy. Some relations were having second thoughts about letting boys be put in the 'nest' – the gaigo and the surrounding grass to be enclosed by a fence. Proceeding with the initiation with the spirits out of favour used to be risky in the old days – perhaps it would be the same even now, when fewer took them seriously.

114

'Do not fear. I'm coming to the nest with you,' Martin said. His wau had made up his mind. 'He's sitting over there,' Martin said, jabbing an arm out through the steam twisting up from the crumpled baton on the fire.

Many men were opting to give up only one son, just in case. The plan was to start the initiation of a certain number of boys, and if all went according to plan, after a week or two a second batch would be sent into the nest to join us.

'It seems ridiculous,' I told Martin. 'The last time a boy died was decades ago.' The victim had been buried under the gaigo and the loss kept secret from outside the fence. When a number of his fellow initiates were let out temporarily to perform dances in front of the women and children, the bigmen checked the boys' eyes for tell-tale tears, so the uninitiated's suspicions were not aroused. Much later, when the initiates were about to be released as men, as *waarkvarinango*, the boy's skull was dug up, brushed down, his features modelled in clay, given a healthy lick of paint and decorated prettily before being handed over, like the other boys, as a man to his family.

I felt myself in the grip of a forceful stare, and looked to its origin well up the building on the other side. The man was old, and probably older than he looked – a tough body like that would resist the punishment of the years well. He was giving me a look over, and he made no attempt to avoid eye contact. His eyes were vigorous, the more so for being the youngest part of his face, the most agile, changeable feature. Now he had one of them screwed up, as if he were levelling gun sights to shoot me down. These eyes would express changes in mood simply, vividly, and fast, I guessed. I could imagine them being open and soft for a toddling boy, blue–grey in hard staring anger at a wife's slothfulness, red and fiery in the quick rage of men's argument, or plain and uninterested, as his emotions distanced themselves from acts of cruelty. I had seen this tall, brisk figure forcing its old legs to keep up as he strode through the village, and even Rom stepped sharply out of his path. Wasn't he the man who Martin said had thirteen wives? Perhaps not, but this man could definitely keep a good many people on their toes at any one time, that was for sure.

'Who's that man over there, Martin, the tough old man with the regal graces?'

'Yes, he is Martias of Timbun. The bigman who made the nest come for you.'

With the count at ten boys, the men were interrupted by a shriek from a mother, outside, rolling in the long grass at the feet of her husband, who had his hands on his hips and looked bored. Martin said she could have guessed her son was to be placed inside the nest ages ago. 'And what is more, he's more old than me.'

'What's her bundle of clothes for?'

'She is going onward to her brother's home – she's saying, "I am protesting."'

The debate was going on all night. I decided to go for a stroll. Martin stayed on, hoping the bigmen would forget he was there and let slip a secret or two about what went on in the nest. Really, as boys we should not have been allowed in the gaigo, and it was such lapses that the traditionalists feared might move the spirits to anger at the initiation. Outside, the woman had attracted an audience, and, judging by the clothing scattered around, the husband had decided to help his wife move out, and she had decided it wasn't such a good idea. The boy they squabbled over was nowhere to be seen. Probably he was swimming among the river grasses, content in the knowledge that his mother would not win the argument, and that he would soon be proving his manhood in the traditional way. Like the rest of us, he was no doubt living in the hope that the stories put about were exaggerated – the time in the nest would not be as bad as all that. 'It can't be, can it? Is it true that any cuts you get from beatings are rubbed with the husks of coconuts?' Best to ignore the rumours or to laugh quietly at them, and certainly to avoid speculation.

I walked through the thin shadows of palm stems and hut stilts. The shadows were stretching fast, and the first fleet of fishing women would be drawing up soon. 'Do you want a bath?' asked Andrew, who had been stalking behind.

'I'd love one.'

'I'll meet you by the waters and guard you.'

There seemed little point to me: crocodile attacks were so very rare; though this *was* around the first anniversary of the afternoon when a little boy stopped for a dip in the river on his way back through the forest from school. They found only his pencil, exercise book and leg. And two years before that there was the girl who was out fishing. They didn't salvage anything of her – only the canoe, containing a paddle and two fish.

I skipped up the back ladder of Johnny's house – I had already made a mental note not to call these structures 'huts'. As usual Johnny had wasted no time in tearing me off a strip: 'You white men talk of our homes like they are dirty sheds.' Inside was just the usual big bare communal room. Johnny's two warm-hearted sisters were laying sticks in the clay firebase ready to smoke the daily fish catch when it came. Hanging from the rafters with the empty sago baskets on a *chambung*, a wooden figurine hook and home of a protective spirit, was my judo jacket, the one which served as a towel. I waited for Andrew, enjoying the algal smell of the riverside breeze.

Girls who were not out fishing lost spare energy by punting a deflated football back and forth over a dumpy child on the brink of tears – she already had grazed knees, and dust was clinging to the damp patches on her frock.

As I swam, Andrew guarded; crocodile heads were sighted nosing through the water, the dusk sun picking up their white artificial eyes. Fishy smoke was still wafting behind some of these dugouts on which the working women had cooked up midday snacks. The catches from the fish traps they had been emptying were poor, the sun had been harsh, and, to cap it all, they had heard the slit gong bellowing from the village. Some women tied up the canoes slowly, playing with rope knots, cautiously eyeing me. Most were just intent on getting indoors to put their feet up for a second. What a day! The poor women. They would have to work themselves to the bone to catch us food while we were in the crocodile nest and be ashamed if they could not keep up with demand. It would not be *our* demand, but that of the bigmen. Putting two and two together, Martin considered we were to be force-fed. In the past, however weedy boys had been when they entered the nest, they came out again round-tummied – as with crocodiles, you could not see the ribs.

'Is that why they're sad – because they'll have to work so hard?' I had asked Martin.

'No. It is all right, they are only sad for us.'

'Ah.'

Andrew's voice cut into my thoughts. 'Come on, keep moving, the mosquitoes are horrible here.'

The two of us walked the length of the village, along the water front, from the Smaarks, through the Yaark, then Posago clan territories – in the soft light, through woodsmoke and the steamy smells of boiling fish.

Still by the river bank, beyond the Posagos, where some palms grew, marking the clan boundary between the next clans, the Yargoons and Gamas, a waist-high sea of children yelled at us to look up. There in the top fronds of a bush was a treefrog grimly gripping a broad leaf, its marble eyes almost out of their sockets. It shuddered as one of its rear legs, which was in the mouth of a sleek metallic black and yellow snake, like a rat, plastic-insulated electric cord, was yanked backwards. We joined in, waving our hands to the frog, offering it advice. The emerald treefrog was at a loss to know what to do; it hung on to the leaf with its feet suckers. Fortunately, because it was the rainy season and the leaf had been washed free of dust, it could cling well. But the snake was as tough as a yard of mooring rope, and had only to bide its time. The time never came. An imp of a boy triumphantly smacked the snake across the back with a cane kept handy for bringing pawpaws down. Both

117

creatures tumbled to our feet and lay bewildered, joint losers – doomed to spend the rest of their days as pets, or to end as food for people, ants or birds.

We returned, wandering inland, through the Niowras (the only other major clan).

Martin sat with me on the palm-skin floor in Johnny's house, while at our feet Elijah used a whisk to concuss mosquitoes. We poked tentatively at the boiled fish brought by Johnny's sisters. 'What are these?' they asked in Pidgin. Martin handed over a sachet of mixed herbs ('de Provence'), five mushed Oxo cubes and one damp tea bag. They were left, apparently, by 'Father George' on a pastoral visit. Martin did not take in my explanation about these Western goods. He apologised. His mind was elsewhere, and he unburdened himself: the men were bound to beat him ruthlessly inside the crocodile nest, he said quietly, it was what was expected. All because his father was hard to boys when he was a bigman. 'You see, now those boys are grown into men. They want revenges on my family. That is me. Me! This is so unjust!'

'There's not much I can do about that, I'm afraid.'

'And also you have problems. The bigmen are saying they'll also stick you badly; extra badly, and I believe it. Otherwise you can tell the whole world Kandengai village no longer makes their boys into men as strong as the crocodile, and we are no longer the best on the Sepik.'

I warmed to the pride he had in his village, and was conscious of it now in myself. I noticed something else: I was losing my sense of objectivity. I was slipping into that same anxious, self-absorbed state of mind as the other boys.

'Do you want my fish?' Martin said, 'I'm not hungry for it.'

'No, thanks. You can have mine if you like.'

Johnny's sisters said they had lost their appetites as well.

Chapter Ten

It was the day the 'crocodile nest' was to be constructed.

I made my way between the houses before the damp chill was off the grass and was surprised to smell the air so sweet, to see the greenness of the village so intense, the browns darkened. I had somehow slept through a night of rain. The gaigo was on an island, with ducks circling the surrounding pool.

The slit gong was beaten, and other boys came to the gaigo in ones and twos. Slumped on a *t'gurt*, a low stool carved from a single block, was Rom, in his green wrap. His old man's baggy chest rose as he sat up to smear charcoal on the foreheads of each of us, our blackened faces announcing to the spirits and anyone else that we were playing a part in constructing the nest fence, the *waarkdumba*. Once the working men had also been marked, Martin asked, 'Would you like to look at a completely dried out man of one hundred and twenty years old?'

'A mummy? That sounds interesting.'

'He is not a mummy. He's a daddy.'

'Oh. Where's he buried?'

'They cannot plant him yet.'

'Why not?'

'They wait until he is dead, of course.'

Martin showed me a lean man with a wheeze and with skin which, rather than slackening with age, seemed to be tightening. He was Saun, the senior man of the Smaark clan. He mouthed '*Apman gun*. Good night.' It was mid-morning. Using us as crutches, he made it to the gaigo, where he was installed to proffer advice on customs. From now on headman Rom should eat no fish or greasy food, just bananas, taro and so on, otherwise, Martin said, the spirits would consider him 'dirty'.

We paddled the river waters to the far bank's forest, and, knowing the youngsters were watching us with awe, tried our best to be all *puaabur* and *taaung*, chest and shoulder, not *yaark*, tummy, as we hauled fence poles with men's help. All day the forests cracked and moaned as trees were felled. The ducks retreated.

'What will happen if it rains?' I asked Martin.

'Rain? It can not rain. Rom can make a spirit prayer and it can not rain the day we walk into the nest.'

Adding further to the medley of village noises were some Korogos, who turned up uninvited for a gambling session. Today they had come equipped with meths, beer and card packs to win their money back – Lamin, the dreamy-eyed brother of headman Rom and quite a different kettle of fish from Lamin Wogoo, an efficient, tireless man who was to be a prominent disciplinarian at the initiation, won 375 kina the last week, and the Korogos, although they were from a brother village, were still fuming. They said they passed by a white man picking his way along the muddy forest path towards us. He must be a carving dealer; either the Australian 'Head', or his brother 'Kriss', described as having legs like an egret's, leg joints like rope knots.

The gambling got under way; it was the game called 'Lukee', the size of your luck often dependent on who is cheating. Later, a broad crescent of moon rose. The Korogos returned home skipping out of sight along the path that curves away through the trees. They clutched thick bunches of cash, leaving behind the drained bottles, and Lamin hugging his head. The Korogos had been avenged.

What of the carving dealer? Perhaps the Korogos would bump into him still stumbling along the path.

It was Sunday morning. The egret legs were Head's, not Kriss's. 'Well, blow me . . .' He stopped in his tracks when he saw me. 'You can say it's a relief to see another white face, all right.' Sweat was creeping from his armpits over his khaki jacket, and trickles of blood from his shins were being soaked up by his once cream-coloured socks. 'If you want the truth,' he said, 'I'm knackered.' We were about to discuss the mishap he had had while climbing out of a dugout – it had not been moored quite tightly enough – when he was swept away by a wave of enthusiastic carvers.

'See you later,' I said.

'Got yer,' he said, drowning in an ocean of children's hands. Pretending to swat mosquitoes, they kneaded his bare legs and arms, inspecting him.

'They do not do this thing to you,' said Martin, startling me from behind. 'They respect you.'

The village had not done very well so far in keeping the Sabbath holy, what with the selling of carvings and the continuous sighing of falling trees for the distinctly pagan fence. For Kandengai the issue has luckily been clouded by the Seventh Day Adventists. Their evangelists have only to point to the written word of God: Saturday, not Sunday, is the

Sabbath. Though the churches represented here, the Catholics and Assembly of God, justify their own stance, the confusion allows useful leeway for hectic occasions like this. The Kandengai flock, I discovered, had been wayward some years, very wayward others. Godfrey, the bush-bearded man, had loudly prayed with his bass voice that this year Christianity would tip the balance against past customs. Everything was staked on the non-Christian initiation: how it acted on the young candidates ...

The Catholic slit gong sounded light and homely — not unlike a woodpecker drilling a hollow tree — compared to the roar of the gaigo's wood crocodiles. I joined the Catholic congregation, a move that swelled that Church's normal attendance figures and shrank the Assembly of God's in proportion. All the men were away seducing the carving dealer, but this was a chance for the women to satisfy any lingering curiosity over me.

Fresh palm fronds arched over the church doorway. It was Palm Sunday. The theme of sacrifice was particularly apt, with the sufferings of the initiation on the horizon, and, even before we set foot inside, anxious tears were being rubbed away. It was a simple, cool building — thatched, and walled with tree stems splashed in pink clay paint, quite new, one of Rome's latest investments. The door was of woven cane sheets splashed with a cross in black charcoal or paint.

The women entered first, and they bobbed inexpertly to the end wall, where you might have expected an altar, but where there were only seams of dusty light. The women were meant to sit on the palm trunk benches on the left side of the aisle, but they had come in such force that they spilled over to the male side on the right, where I sat squashed between a few young boys. Women who were not preoccupied with their own crying were coping with babies burping, puking, having tantrums, or breast-feeding. The last to come in were two dogs, the first like an out-of-form Border collie — its coat bald in patches, its tail like a kitchen broom — the second like a yellow, singed hearth-rug. Once these two were settled, it was time to start.

There was a song, which with everyone's minds elsewhere, was not a success. A story was told by Johnny: Christ's triumphant entry into Jerusalem, how palms were hacked down and waved at him in salutation and adoration. Only the babies and the dogs must have failed to see parallels with their own lives: the son doomed to suffer, the adoration of the people, the cutting of the palms, the pain ... For some it was too much.

Johnny, standing at the front in his best shorts, his eyes so strong and dark against that strangely fair skin, said we must remember — women, boys and girls — that whatever we suffered, the Lord gave His only begotten Son to die for us. Despite the inconveniently audible snuffles and the slashing of crocodile-nest branches outside, the women were calm, and passively accepted their yoke once more. Johnny concluded: though we were many, we were one body – the Christian Church. He had seen that even Master Benedix carried a red Gospel of St John. It was torn and frayed, but had travelled with him through the bush of 'West Irian', among the hostile peoples there. The boys turned and gaped. Benedix had seen the hostile people – the Indonesians they meant. And sure enough the tattered Gospel that Paul Kline gave me was in my hands. The reality was that I had tried hard with the book, but with no luck so far. I had prayed for guidance, tried to appreciate the warnings – John 3:36, 'he that believeth not the Son shall not see life; but the wrath of God abideth on him' – and look where I'd ended up now: entering a nest of paganism.

The women stoically sang a final hymn, while a basket travelled from hand to hand along the rows, little one-toea or two-toea coins clinking into it. The tray came to me more quickly than I had anticipated as I fumbled for my change. The children watched to see how much rolled in. I gave what I feared was rather more than I could afford; the rattle of the money settling was very obviously the loudest so far. Before the dogs got up to stretch and lead the congregation outside into the sticky morning air, the word had got around that I had given generously – there were tears again. 'They worry on you, Benedix,' said Johnny.

'Oh dear.'

' "Oh dear," you talk,' he said impatiently. 'You must be *pleased*.'

The carving buyer, Head, left the village pursued by a trail of children bearing masks, a marriage payment belt of thick, culking shell discs, figurines on stools, food hanging hooks worked into life-size men and women, perched on by eagles, turtles, pigeons, bats.

I joined in yanking fence material from the river bank, the women standing by patiently, forbidden to cross our route through to the gaigo. Swaggering youths who had been through the ceremony recently at Timbun, the satellite village, helped out. They were bulbous, their bellies spilt over their trousers, which were giving at the seams. Their fresh crocodile markings stood proud, in bands either side of the stomach, up over their chest, down their arms, backs and thighs. These men could lash the poles into the fifteen-foot-high fence. As mere *koonongoo*, uninitiated boys, we could not touch it. We had only the privilege of climbing fifty feet up the smooth grey trunks of the palms to hack down fronds.

In the cool gaigo Rom was in oblivion, apparently undisturbed by the braying Timbun youths. He had been left to himself all night, and had accumulated ingredients from various rituals: a chicken feather, one chunk of taro, one citrus leaf, herbs, and a paddle like the short, woman's type. Journeying in his spirit world he sat mouthing strange words. You could hear him only occasionally, but you could easily see the ground dampen with spittle: 'lak . . . lak . . . lak . . .' The initiation was to be conducted according to his own Yaark clan traditions, in preference to those of the Posagos, Yargoons and Niowras, who also owned this gaigo.

Fumbling with his lily-pad green-coloured wrap, Rom pottered outside with the paddle to a gap left in the fence. With a chant, he covered the paddle blade in herbs, blew into them his red spittle, then clapped the bundle shut, trapping the magic tight inside with bark string. The fence was quickly joined up over the spot. He planted another of the same at the opposite end so that no bad spirits could enter the nest to prevent us learning the secrets: If he had done his prayers right . . .

Coconut leaves continued to drop like massive feathers from the sky and were bound into the fence. Among the screams of the construction crew was one from a pig. The scream was cut abruptly short, there was a gurgle, and the victim was dragged by its trotters through a slit in the fence – dead, but still with a baffled look to its face. The pig was slung over a fire to singe off its bristle; the midday air, already too hot, was now nauseous with that acrid smell. Two sprays of sculptured leaves, grasses and tender yellow palm shoots, like an array of church flowers, were hoisted up to stand like sentinels over the Niamé and Niowi fence ends. There was so much coming and going that worms tunnelled up around the wood crocodiles in the gaigo.

Bala, a *yanon'yan*, as they call a spirit priest, was presented with betelnuts, and in exchange looked for spiritual holes in the fence, ordering the Timbuns to stop up one invisible gap here, another there. 'Only one missed and you boys might die!' he laughed in Pidgin. However, the truth was that all but the most traditional of elders had been letting their spiritual devotions slip. None of the initiated were quite sure how the spirits would behave now that their co-operation for the ceremony was sought. Common sense said there was really nothing to worry about – of course not, in this day and age. We, the uninitiated, also could see the spirits had been neglected but the matter was irrelevant – we would be given a hard time, if not by 'spirits', then by the men. So we were on edge, exhausted by the weary business of continually brushing off the fear spread among us by the taunting men and the heavy doses of pity from the women.

A large, well-clothed man looked on, rubbing his full, black beard, rocking on his long, bare feet: Godfrey, the Catholic, forbidden to take bread and wine for a reason I had yet to fathom, wondering what to do about all this spirit worship, not entirely unhappy things were coming to a head here, I guessed. Biding his time to act maybe . . .

Certain clans, for the special safety of their boys, rounded up sacrificial chickens and ducks, which waited patiently with their legs tied for their execution, while clan leaders mouthed their own chants to their clan gods. Rom could not light his cigarette using flames meant for cooking up sacrifices, so he resorted to a *gandja*, a smouldering bundle of palm leaves for transporting fire in the bush. Johnny had done some arithmetic and said I put sixty-five toea in the church collection. That was a relief – I thought it was more like sixty-five kina – but he said, 'Because you are so very rich, Benedix, you may buy a rooster for Sebastian.' Sebastian, with the bright, scintillating eyes, was his young brother, and now mine, because his family had adopted me. He had a scar, a thick cord, running diagonally across his back. The jibe of the newly initiated youths, arrogant at this first chance to prepare a nest, was that soon it would be hidden under all sorts of new etchings, those cut by beating canes. Though he was only slightly built, barely fifteen and one of the youngest boys, his heart remained light and free. Martin translated Sebastian's Pidgin: 'That is because I am the good Catholic, and happily throw my troubles in the Lord's face.'

The door slits in the fence were covered over properly. A slit gong roared.

Martin said, outside, 'That is it now. The next time we journey into the nest is on The Day.'

'Ah yes, The Day.'

Under the soft rising sun the next morning, we ran to the canoes, holding coins tightly in our hot hands like children rushing to spend pocket money on sweets at a corner shop. It was our last opportunity to see Pagwi. Peter, a Moresby Riot Squad policeman, had invested a little of his salary in an outboard motor, which tended to be thoroughly overused by the whole village while he was far away on duty. On leave at present, Peter steered the dugout in the morning haze through the weeds and pink lilies, whose damp flowers were open at that hour. It was good to run your fingers through the water, which was warm and soothing in the shallows, picking sweet lily stems to chew on.

We surged through the confined water of the channel, open just now, fresh cobwebs snapping on our faces, the damp air sickly with the taste of overripe fruit, our wash cleaning the river banks of leaves. We slowed so as not to tip the canoes of Nyaurengai women fishing their territorial waters. The morning light glanced off the water ripples, shone intensely on those with younger skin, the dull slack breasts of the older women bouncing from the impact of our waves. They worked with spatulate

124

fingers, cleaning out the traps, fixing them between bamboo stakes to align them to the current. The water was clear, meaning today the flow was towards the Sepik – which is, people joke, the colour of Milo, the milk chocolate sold in green tins in all trade stores. The river must be low. The worst of the wet season was over.

We hit the choppy water of this big river abruptly. The prow of the canoe was tugged downstream for a hundred feet before we managed to turn upcurrent. Sebastian jabbed a finger in my back. '*Kumbui!*' Sure enough, loose squadrons of large, sedate bats were on their way home to bed. Egrets passed us on barely floating logs, intent on their fishing, their beaks barely out of the water, poised like closed scissors. Where I was sitting I received the full force of the spray spewing from the prow. The wind on this open water chilled the wet skin. Never mind, a whole day to look forward to away from the close atmosphere of the village!

White insects with the lacy look of mayflies skimmed with us over the water. They fluttered with urgency alongside, before destroying themselves one by one with the merest brush against a wave.

We drew up tight alongside the other canoes. Men walked idly along the track to market, women beneath baskets of goods. The boys in my party, led by Joel, the Smaark of my age with a square beard, surrounded a yellow truck containing a man with a baseball cap propped fast asleep against the driving-seat window. After five minutes' harassment he was well awake and had reluctantly agreed to give them a lift to the bigger stores in Maprik, four kina each. I hadn't enough spare cash so I had to wait there, with the old man Tovai. I waved the Smaark candidates – Joel, Sebastian, Stens, Kennedy and Martin – off as the truck ground through the gritty orange clay.

There are two stores in Pagwi and one belongs to Ken, perhaps the longest-surviving white man on the mid-Sepik. His is a box-like job with splinter-free floors, every joint flush; nothing warped or rotted or leaking, despite the tropical swelter. Ken came from Australia somewhere, and had a CB radio, black hair parted as neatly as windblown grass, and black-rimmed spectacles which irritated the bridge of his nose. He has been part of the riverscape for decades and he now features, due to an unfortunate oversight, as a part-time canoe dealer in a backpacker's handbook which recommends that he be sought out.

By nine o'clock the sun was a discomfort. Under the darkness of heavily foliaged trees, women squatted before neat heaps of market produce – mostly strains of mottled bananas. I saw you could also buy dead slimy eels here, turtles stacked like crockery with pale belly plates and shackled feet, singed opossum, bush kangaroo legs and tails, or more eels, but cooked like burnt toast and ready to eat. The mosquitoes did not like the thick screens of grey smoke from the cigars or pipes of

125

the women, who sat cheerfully colouring the ground puce with spat betelnut juice. They nattered away among the fishy, fruity smells, and if the silvery eels started wriggling, they gave them a club, sometimes until the eels' button eyes were red.

I passed between the rows of women self-consciously, tempted to cling to crowds of other shoppers. There was not a person out of these hundreds, representing a dozen river villages, who did not know of 'Master Benedix'. Their eyes slid after me. When I tried to pay for a branch of betelnuts, old dears waved away my money. Buying breakfast, a hand of fat bananas, I put a ten-toea piece in the palm of a youngster and her mouth dropped open so far that I could see the length of her pinkish tongue.

The young woman who gave me the tobacco had a mannerism I originally mistook for haughtiness. She held her head tilted back and so high that my eyes easily singled hers out from all those staring. She had an untroubled mind, I sensed, and a fully lit smile which she was offering me unreservedly, as to a soulmate. She stopped me walking right by with a hand held up to my waist, clutching some tobacco leaves. '*Yargee*,' she said, using its local name. 'I belong Kandengai,' she added.

Thinking about the turmoil in store from the initiation I felt like saying, 'Oh dear, that's very bad luck.'

'I present you.' She waved the *yargee* at me. I took it up. Her hands were quite beautiful. The nails were scrubbed as a surgeon's, and as smoothly trimmed. Her fingers looked about as sensitive, yet they must have been worn and scratched each working hour.

'Thank you,' I said.

'Thank *you*,' she said. Her teeth were very bright in comparison to the usual sets stained dark red with betelnut. Her lips hung open: thick, curling out, framing that clear enamel, from which sharp light reflected. With her head borne back like this and so high, her unlined forehead captured the sun as a clean disc. Shadows were unable to hide under her firm, light brows, but she made no effort to shade her eyes. Deliberate or not, that let me see that they were clear, tender and – this might or might not be detrimental – only a child's.

'Thank you,' I said again, trying to maintain the flagging conversation. Already I was beginning to think I would miss her, being stuck in the crocodile nest.

'Thank you,' she said once more, amused. Then we both saw we were the nucleus of a growing crowd.

I sat with Tovai in the verandah of the store which is a rival to Ken's, periodically accepting gifts from the shoppers. The boys must have reached Maprik by now, if they were not in a pothole. Tovai's son, with the traditional name Saun, 'egret', was with them; a small boy despite his long adolescent limbs. These two were just about the last representatives of the Bowee clan, which is allied to the Smaarks. Saun was a hyperactive clown of spectacularly awesome cheek, and he knew that inside the crocodile nest he would be given a particularly ghastly time by his elders and betters.

We waited for hour after hour, our throats dry with dust. The penny dropped that the Smaark boys were not buying stores at all, but drowning their worries outside the drink stores. It added to our depression. What a last day out!

The market women left in twos and threes for their canoes. I waved at the *yárgee* girl. She smiled in reply – more to her girl friends than to me. They nudged each other, looked to me, giggled, looked back to each other, shared and spread laughter again.

The sun having soared up and almost plummeted fully down, the Toyota came rocking back, the boys leaning over the tailgate with pallid faces. By the time everyone had pulled themselves together enough to step into the canoe, I had lost all hope of overtaking the girl.

The channel had been closed by the floating salvinia and grass and we had to abandon the canoe and choked motor, heaving our supply boxes along a human chain to neighbouring Nyaurengai, walking from there. The twilight mosquitoes were so bad that soon my chest was freckled brown, and with no hand free I could only watch as they drew blood. Withered yellow palm fronds left from their Palm Sunday service surrounded Nyaurengai church, mirroring the palm fence around our spirit house. Deliberate? I wondered.

'Benedix.'

A soft girl's voice came from a Nyaurengai house. I flushed – the *yargee* girl? No, but when I saw it was Augusta who stepped down the ladder I was pleased. She was the only girl I knew at all well; about the *yargee* girl's age. Perhaps they were once classmates.

'I have been visiting a girl friend, and I am walking homewards direction now. I can aid you to carry somethings.'

We walked side by side. I asked her what she wanted to do with her future. She was not going to waste her brain, I hoped. Though she had failed in her first bid to become a nurse, she still had expectations of the outside world. This was the face of the future, the future of the individual.

'For now I stay in the village. Who knows? Now I only worry on you boys. You be with care in the men's house, Benedix.'

'And you, out fishing for our food, Augusta.'

'Yes, and I.'

When we entered the village, children ran up and slapped at the mosquitoes till I was wet with their corpses, then took our boxes and ran alongside.

127

Chapter Eleven

The village was waiting. Boys and girls, fathers, mothers – even the bigmen fidgeted. Only headman Rom would 'know' when the time was right; the day his blood spoke. We guessed it would be with the rise of the full moon. Now it was over half, and growing . . .

On Wednesday, 3 April, out of the blue, a Polish priest materialised to announce that he would conduct a slightly premature Easter service. The third white man here in about ten days! He could speak only a smattering of Pidgin, and had not conducted a Mass on the Sepik before. The first I heard of him was while I was trying to get some peace and quiet in my corner of the house.

'Hello, hello!' The voice got nearer and the rungs up to the front doorway creaked – someone heavy and far from agile. 'Hello, hello! Are you in? Hello, hello! Is there an Englishman please here? Ah good. I am looking all over for you having heard you are present.' The shake of his hand – hot, soft, damp – was so violent it pulled me off my *t'gurt* as I rose.

'Hello.'

'Ah, thank you, yes. It is so good to see a man of Europe. I haven't had one for two days. My name is Jan, and yours, please?'

I told him who I was, gathered he did not know what I was doing here, and decided to keep it that way. The children outside discussed in loud whispers whether it was proper for them to come in, decided it wasn't, but did. As the priest and I yakked together astride *t'gurts*, they danced about us, stirring the air with shadows, like the bugs around the lamp.

'Ah, the mosquitoes are very, very bad. Too much. You have to fool it with your white skin very much too, I think?'

I reassured him that he only had to last out two more months before they declined, as the waters went down and the crocodiles were more visible. I wondered if he was a Brother rather than a Father, and what the difference was.

'Ah, I am already looking to see the crocodile face to face. Do they know the Polishman tastes of the very best meat, I wonder? Ha, ha.' He said he was about to receive his first posting on the Sepik: Angoram, a long way downriver. He joked about the hell hole he was expecting it to be, while he squirted his neck liberally with Off from an aerosol. I was sure the crowd was waiting for his bulky frame to slip off the *t'gurt*. It was only a question of time. He could not stop talking and yet, because he was so radiantly happy, no one had the heart to interrupt him, not that he would have heard anyway. He was regaling me with stories of the Pope's recent tour of PNG.

'Of course I am being very proud. He is another Polishman like me, well not like me, no one is like me, I know I am the very outgoing person as you have certainly made a guess but he is from the same country of birth like me, and . . .'

By candlelight outside the church was a ritual washing of three boys' and three girls' feet, then the symbolic lighting of a little fire. It was very exciting for the children – the magic of the golden, softly licking flames glowing on their teeth and eyes. The exact meaning of it all was lost because, as Father Jan threw his hands enthusiastically forward explaining about rebirth something or other, a boy took his gesture as a signal to fling on more outboard motor fuel. The inferno cleared the mosquitoes and sent sparks so high that the crowns of the palms were singed.

The service was relaxed, but moving. It need not have been: Father Jan, after all, did not have a language in common with the bulk of the congregation, but his conducting arms and irrepressible grin were enough for the occasion. And it was an occasion: so many families, barring the older men who were absent as usual, assembled under one roof probably for the last time before the initiation – mothers about to be separated from sons, sisters from brothers, brothers from brothers. A last sing together; a last smile together. And a last chance for confession as well. The queue to whisper a word in Father Jan's Polish ear stretched right out of the church across the smouldering ashes of the fire outside. And Father Jan had no idea why.

Afterwards, he played hide and seek with small almost bare girls who tittered, flitting with the bats between the palms under a large moon – it was only about two nights from being full, I suddenly noted. Johnny's sister Rhonda said she would cook up some *makau* for Father Jan to eat when he had finished playing. We had been waiting an hour.

'Fish? But he will hate it,' I said.

'Fish! But I love it!' Father Jan said coming in with a candle borrowed from the church. It was his first *makau*, he said. 'I was thinking I am eating bread and butter only.' He had brought with him to the village a loaf of sliced bread.

Father Jan overslept and had to leave next morning in a tearing hurry.

'God bless you, Kandengai village. You are the most lovely people. Where are the *men*, I do wonder? And God bless you, Benedict.' My hand is large, but he managed to envelop it with that soft, strong grip, like a monkey wrench in kid gloves, before marching off into the trees with a brigade of naked infants, between them tugging along a holdall containing his robes.

I was left with a feeling of regret, of missed opportunity. Father Jan, the last European I would see for a while, was so innocent – I wished I had told him what was going on in Kandengai. Our last entertainment gone, it was like the window being closed on a fuggy room. We could think only of what the bigmen were cooking up for us.

Sebastian and Stens, another Smaark, who breathed intimately into your face when he talked, were constructing a little bachelor's home opposite Johnny's house and occupied themselves with that. I spent time with Edward, the Assembly of God leader. His Church forbade him to chew betelnut and his teeth, in strong gums, were as china-clay white as the *yargee* girl's. He would not be coming into the nest. It had nothing to do with his religious scruples – none of the Christian boys tried to get out of the initiation.

'The little baby Christ's body was initiated,' he said. 'Remember this.'

'Yes, but it's hardly the same, now is it? Spirits . . .'

'Exactly. The Holy Spirit.'

'You think the spirits in the church and gaigo are all one and the same?'

'I do not know. I am too young.'

Whatever the Church leaders thought, and Johnny and Edward were clearly not sure, there was one thing for certain: ultimately all sisters and mothers took pride in the boy proving his worth, and girls turned their noses up at those without the beautiful crocodile patterns.

The slit gong spoke out to neighbouring villages: it *would* start on Friday night, under the full moon.

Jimmi, the gentle man who wore woven arm and leg bands as a sign of mourning for the loss of one of his wives, heard that the bigmen had got *gwak* from the Korogos – it was an oil extracted from a forest tree, said to heal cuts.

Only today to get through, I thought: 4 April. Then tomorrow evening, Good Friday.

The village was cold in its quietness next morning, punctuated only by dusty races to capture chickens and by the knocking down of coconuts: one each as offerings to the spirits – seventeen coconuts, seventeen boys. It was tempting to stop, stand and stare at the slightest excuse – women coming in under the weight of firewood, feathers flying from the chickens, coconuts being eased from the trees and dropping to the grass with a thump.

Families kept themselves to themselves. These were the last moments of intimacy. Married boys like Alex and Willi disappeared into the forest – with their wives? Sebastian and I were together indoors, helping Glen, Johnny's one-year-old son, walk his first steps and catching him when he was about to crack his skull. Rhonda and Imelda, Sebastian's quiet, smiling sisters, were pleased we had chosen to spend our last day with them in the house.

At dusk, I swam in the peaceful river with Johnny.

'Any good advice for me?'

We were naked side by side on a log looking out across the water, gouging the weed from between our toes, his only a few tones darker-skinned than mine. Black ants climbed from crevices in the log and gathered up the mosquito corpses as they fell between our legs.

'I have one advice for you. You accept all that is done to you. That is it.'

'But I don't know what's to happen to me, and I've come here to *learn*.'

'Good, your head is too messed, like all boys. You know nothing. It is funny. The white boy knows nothing!'

Johnny took my jacket towel to hang up. He would be seeing me later, he said, and, still walking away nonchalantly, he added, 'Ah yes. One something: You boys can have your head hair taken from you before tomorrow.'

'*What?*'

He said he would hack mine off in a few minutes when I came in to supper. 'It is fish and sago.'

I sat wondering where the villagers were – the place was dead. Where were the other boys? Stens with the hot breath, shiny-smiled Edward, Joel, the Smaark my age, Vincent, a boy whose mouth always hung open. The *yargee* girl, with her head held high, her poised lips, the unflinching honest child's eyes and other features composing her disarming, generous and full face.

The river was very tranquil too. Earlier it was windy, and heavy rain came in with showery rainbows. Considering headman Rom was meant to be clearing the sky for tonight and tomorrow, it did not do much for my confidence in their spirits still being around, or in Rom having sway with them. The fishing birds were already off the water and fretting in the forest for preferred sleeping branches. The hazy patches of rain were so thick above the far bank it was some time before I realised the sun I was watching was not in the west, and it was rising. It was the full moon, so cold with its pure silver sheen. I traced out its mottled surface and, catching the silhouettes of near birds against it, I saw they had no flight feathers and were bats.

The men were gathered in the gaigo. We could only guess what they were up to in there behind the fence enclosure. Letting their Western clothes drop to the ground, stepping back into nature? Fashioning leaves into skirts? Smearing their faces with charcoal and the red *wareekupma* greasy seed pods? Oiling their skin so their muscles shone?

An explosion, a giant clap, tore through the fence, and village. 'What the hell is that?' I said out loud, but no one was around to answer. Cockatoos squawked, rising in alarm from the trees. Soon after, a sound of enormous drains clearing – blurp! Then the smack again. I could not identify the noises. What were they?

Johnny came up. 'Why are you stayed here? You hear the noises of a [sacred] crocodile, *avookwaark*?'

'Crocodile?'

'He is splashing in the muds. He is coming out of his sleep, in the gaigo, and he is beating his mighty tail on the muds.'

'Oh, that's what he's doing.'

Clearly, the crocodile was taking a walk now. The steps were aggressively loud – tick, tock, tick, tock – accompanied by flutes, hand drums. The impression was of a very heavy beast patrolling its stretch of river bank, stamping its feet to the simple beat of music. Then silence.

'Oh well. That was very realistic,' I said, sad at not yet being able to loosen myself free from my Western, rationalising bonds. But it was not over; two screams pierced the air. 'What . . .?' And the crocodile was at it again, strutting about. Tick, tock, tick, tock . . .

The village was waking out of its sleep. Children peering from entrances in the direction of the nest. News spread that one of the fence ends had been opened so that the uninitiated could see the dancing going on inside it. It was very colourful, apparently, but you could not see what was making the mud-blurping noise. Hiding it was a separate inner fence.

'*Yagua!* You come!' said Rhonda, dropping her Pidgin now, her bronze cheeks more burnished than ever I had seen. But quite frankly I wanted to restrain my curiosity, remain in ignorance. Sebastian told his sisters he couldn't care less about the ceremony, that he wasn't interested. The luminosity of his eyes was yet to be dulled, but his remarks did not ring true.

Tick, tock, tick, tock . . . It went on interminably, with occasional breaks when the crocodile splashed about and smacked its tail. Children like Elijah scampered back and tugged at our hands. 'Martin! Sebastian! Benedix!' They pointed through the dark to the spirit house. '*Waark, waark!* Crocodile, crocodile!' They did not appreciate the state of our minds, nor did the women, who satirised the men's dancing, to me trucking like youths on a Harlem sidewalk. We continued to mooch, waiting for the lopping off of our hair.

Outside under the moon, the river shimmers like near-boiling mercury. The tick-tock racket stops. I squat patiently with the Smaark boys, by the moored canoe as ordered by the increasingly bossy Johnny, waiting for our elder brothers to come with their blades and scissors. Young Saun's hair is removed first, his skull shaven. It is the first time I have seen this clown cry. Kennedy's round, angry opossum's face is soon shiny, without the facial fur. Martin breathes stiffly, seeing him wince as hair is snagged. He is next. Joel, my age, without his beard, now looks as young as the others. His face is revealed as gruff, heavy, intolerant. Johnny's attempts to shave my straight sort of hair end in failure, so he trims me to the skin as best he can with scissors, and decides to leave Sebastian in that prickly state too. There is nothing much to do, except to swap friendly insults. 'Boney head!' 'Monkey face!' and we go back for our own family meals, not even wishing each other good luck. All over the village, other clans will be doing the same.

The tick, tock, tick, tock again.

The boiled fish is soggy and tastes, somehow, of rancid cheese. Can my stomach take months of this food? I chew it as I sit beside Sebastian, under the gaze of Imelda, Rhonda, Johnny's wife, his little brother Elijah, whose skin flakes off like dry potato skin because of his infection. These family faces are only part of the audience, those given the front row. Behind are Smaarks of various small sizes who hold and stroke fistfuls of my blond hair recovered in the dark outside.

Outside, tick, tock, tick, tock . . . Inside, the people who fill the room with such silence occasionally let their eyes settle on Glen the baby, who drools and splutters on the banana he is being weened on to. Otherwise the eyes are on sparkly eyed Sebastian – his slash-scarred back held by the lamp beams – and on me.

I am very bad value in entertainment terms, though they appreciate my efforts to clean up the whole fish, the eyes. I wash my hands in a bowl, but instead of slipping away to bed, as I intended, I discover I am at the end of a long line of women and children wanting to shake our hands. It goes on and on – mostly hands with palms thickened from canoe paddling, and fingers strengthened through handling fish traps and sago. Though some hands are softer than others, none are weak. Onlookers block most of the useful light and I do not know who is who. Perhaps the *yargee* girl is among them. Augusta's hand is. It is so obviously smoothly mannered, long, matching her height, and confident. When I show recognition by saying her name, she squeezes my fingers a second and third time warmly. Where *was* the other girl though?

Sitting down again, the women filing out, one of the bigmen comes through the doorway. Sebastian leaves. Outside the moonlight is very clean. The man has an apron of green foliage around his loins. His sparse chest hair is stuck to him with sweat. Some smears of soot are all that remains of his face make-up. The leaves of his skirt are well bruised from dancing. I look to Rhonda, who can speak some English.

'This man is Pinga. He is now father of you, because he is bring the rooster and the coconut of you.' The chicken is white; trussed but lively. He puts it with a coconut at my feet, scaring a mob of mosquitoes. The other sixteen will go through the same ritual. Their chicken, their coconut, handed over by families, like sandwiches being packed into a satchel for a first day at school.

'*Apman gun, bandee*,' says Pinga. 'Good night, bandee.' He has a receding hairline, stubble like black moss on his chin, and a permanent bump like a black chicken's egg sitting on his forehead, not quite squarely.

'It's "Benedict", not "Bandee",' I tell him politely. ' "Ben-ee-dic-t." '

'No, you are bandee now,' Rhonda says. 'You have not name now. You only bandee.' And that is the name I am to answer to, like the other sixteen. It is better than a number, I decide.

Tick, tock, tick, tock . . .

The sacred crocodile, the *avookwaark*, seems to be up and about again, and getting friskier by the minute. My stomach is knotting up. Trying very hard to sleep beneath my mosquito net, I know I should be enjoying this, my last night of comfort. But I can hear Joel's heavy body tossing on his woven mat, and Sebastian's small cough. Are any of the sixteen boys asleep? This clamming sweat of insomnia must have covered generation upon generation of Kandengai males on their last night as free boys.

From the gaigo, tick, tock, tick, tock, muffled by the hot, heavy atmosphere prevailing in the village.

'Benedix, are you awake?'

'Of course I am. Is that you, Johnny?'

'Shut up.' That confirms it. 'You must sleep. I can call you later in the night, and you can get up and walk after Joel. He knows where you go. We give good food to make you strong. Then you go asleep once more. You understand?'

'Yes. What—'

'Shut up.'

'Yes.'

Some time later the tick-tocking dies, as if that crocodile has slipped into the pitpit to have a light nap. Good riddance.

Have I slept a little? Possibly. Someone is tapping my arm – Joel. I put on a pair of shorts. We feel our way down the rungs of the ladder, under the moon with its fleece of cloud. The village is quiet enough for us to hear the frogs splash into the water as we walk along the bank, all the Smaarks – Martin, Kennedy, Stens, Joel, Sebastian and Saun – and myself.

'Be quiet, *kukuks*, you make too much noise,' says Saun.

'Who's he talking to, Martin? No one's making a sound.'

'He's a silly little boy – he's speaking to frogs.'

We all squat along both sides of a house floor. Everything is red in the paraffin light. The women sit behind and try to whisper comfort to us, who pretend to ignore them. We have left a big space along the centre of the house. We are waiting for something; and that something will fill the space. The men are tick-tocking agitatedly in the nest. Indiscernibly, the noise gets louder. But nearer? We decide yes, it is coming towards us, and imagine, correctly, that a chain of men is stamping in our direction and the rhythm is accompanied by a high dove-cooing sound, and clapping hands.

They stand in a line in their finery: feathered headdresses, rust-brown cuscus fur hats, leaves flapping between their legs from a belt. The men's skin has a pink sheen of oil and sweat lit by flame light. We are still half asleep, and as if in a continuation of our tortured dreams, find ourselves on our stomachs, being forced between the legs of this rank of about twenty clapping men, one after another. I squirm after Joel's wide feet through the bruising tunnel of wet swaying legs, scoring my knees and elbows on the floor. At last, I am out – I can rise to all fours, but as I look up a sago pancake, *sownow*, is jabbed into my mouth, then a hand forces a dollop of coconut between my lips. I almost choke. There is something gritty on my tongue with the coconut. A third man wipes a stinging leaf across my forehead. Before we are outside I catch a sight of a few old women joining with some younger men to crawl with the agility of lizards through the line of men's legs.

'Ug! The bones taste badly of my teacher's chalk,' says Martin, walking back. It seems we have just eaten the bones of some famous forefather. 'Are you strong now?' Martin asks. 'With his spirit?'

'No, I don't feel it.'

'I do. *You* will soon.'

'Yeah,' I say vaguely. I wish I could shout 'Yes' with the conviction in his heart.

We are back to lying on our mats, back to hearing the men slapping their feet on the ground, and back to the game of conquering our fears alone. I wonder if, on this Good Friday, the more Christian boys hope to take Jesus as a companion into the nest. I go alone, as unsure as most of the rest.

It is a woman's touch which disturbs me next; the dance, I notice, has stopped. Rhonda, nudging me gently, says we must get some coconut and *sownow* into our stomachs. No sign of the other Smaark boys, no sign of the brazen redness that used to show in Rhonda's cheeks. As the light comes, so again does that dreadful tick-tocking. The women regard me with a strange curiosity, wondering what I am thinking. Johnny pops his head in and sternly says I am to hurry up. It is almost time.

Outside, the Smaarks are being herded together by Johnny. I join them – the grass blades slip damp and cold between my toes. We drop our shorts and hang fresh sheaths of leaves over our loins from bark-string belts. Saun giggles. Joel is sullen. We stride by grim, tight knots of women like dutiful troops to a front. The boy with a savage opossum's face, Kennedy, snaps his muzzle at me for holding the Smaarks up. I can see he resents my intrusion in Kandengai's affairs. I can only try and work harder to blend here, and not accept special treatment if I am offered any.

The seventeen of us gather below the palms. The fence is closed up. The dance – tick, tock, tick, tock – is uncomfortably loud here. The women are standing dumbly. No one seems to have any last messages. I look for faces I know in the crowd: Rhonda, who usually dresses in scarlet, but who's in a salvinia-weed, burgundy-tinged green today; Imelda, with her, hugging her and looking towards Sebastian, who is the only one here bright-faced; Augusta, a head above the rest. Our eyes lock together. She manages a smile. Her eyes fill. The *yargee* girl – where is she? No one has left the village today, that's for certain.

I have very few people to say goodbye to and I do not feel the wrench from the community like the other sixteen. There again, I am the least comforted. Just think, I could be back at Jeff's riverside retreat having a lie-in or a natter:

'Jeff, what's the national sport of PNG – football?'

'No, tax evasion.'

We stand apart from the villagers, as flighty sheep before a dip. Chat – in Pidgin, so I feel included – is trivial: 'Did you get any sleep last night?'

'*What*, with that noise going on?'

Or boyish: 'Watch out, your thing is showing through your leaves.'

'I don't care.'

'*You* don't have to look at it.'

Shivering in our nakedness, or excitement, we are given betelnuts to chew. Some of us get one, some a half, and some do not see them come round and so get none, which is a shame because they have been worked on with chants and are to deaden the coming pain. I find myself next to Martin. His shaved-smooth skull makes his thin moustache prominently comic, the one boy to have got away with keeping some facial hair.

It is not clear what we are waiting for; the end of the monotonous dance, we suppose. Our waus stand with us.

'You believe the betelnut works,' Martin says, 'or you can feel lots of pain, like Joel. He only believes Jesus is mighty.'

So, the issue is laid before us by the bigmen, fair and square. The sooner we believe in the spirits' power, the better for us. On this occasion, the ceremony will not just be an initiation of boys into the adult man's spirit world, it will be the elders' battle to win the minds of the New Young.

I am saving my betelnut in my cheek like a hamster. The juice is acid and colourless without lime and pepper leaves. The women are working themselves up into a frenzy. We mostly stand chewing the nuts like gum, trying to be casual.

The tick-tock crocodile dance stops – the silence bites into us like a cruelly cold wind. The crowd draws breath. Before they breathe out again we are marching forward, in a line to the nest. From behind the fence, comes a marching beat on hand drums: thung, thung, thung, thung. The Timbun youths are singing raucously to it, but no individual words can be heard above the cries of the women, who are hysterical. Our waus' eyes are wet. Johnny cries for his father, who is dead and should be here to see Sebastian go into the nest. Andrew, unrecognisable and looking less skinny, all blacked up and under a head of feathers, again apologises: he cannot be the friend he has been. I *will* understand, won't I? Thung, thung, thung. Our waus slip into the line, and put their hands on our shoulders. Johnny acts as Sebastian's, mine is Imanwell – a quiet friend composed of fold after fold of muscle, sheaths of it disguising his ribs.

Last looks at loved ones. Some women restrain themselves and stand by, holding their children; some run as if to yank their sons out of the line and have to be gently fended off by Jimmi, Johnny and Andrew. In the passion of the moment, I find I have almost chewed away my betelnut. Reserving it *matters*, I suddenly feel. It *can* work to numb me . . . Immediately in front is Johnny holding Sebastian; we are near the back. The first boys are already being squeezed through a gap in the fence by their waus. Last chance to look around. The crowd follows as we move forward and some women run their hands along our bare chests and shoulders. Augusta's face is upturned, looking at the grey sky; her eyes very wet and swollen. Is she looking up to keep the tears off her cheeks or to miss the sight of the last of us disappearing? We have little idea when we will next see her or she us. A month or two? Three? Johnny's little brother Elijah is running amok at Rhonda's feet; not crying, just confused. I salute boys we are leaving behind: shining-teethed Edward, of the Assembly of God, strong Nicholas — tubular-necked, thick-shouldered, who paddled the canoe with me from Pagwi market on my return.

Just as I think I have finally spotted the *yargee* girl — I have been too busy looking for her combination of child's eyes, sophisticated grace and white teeth (parted by deep but light lips), having forgotten that she was not going to be smiling right now — my wau shouts that I must face forward, from now on keep my head bowed, and my hands together between my knees. Sebastian is dipping through the wall of leaves. I am next: my head plunges in for my dose of 'animal nature'.

Chapter Twelve

One second we were in a world of maternal care and grief, the next in an inhospitable environment created by men. Because we had been led to expect brutality during our imprisonment, our natural instinct was to brace ourselves as we stepped into the nest, emerging into this walled-off arena. However, steered by our waus through an avenue of stamping men, though wincing at their song's violent screams, we had received no blows yet. A leaf of the *yangut* was wiped on our foreheads and we marched with our faces to the grey mud – a posture of submission. To our sides were feathers of the Timbun youths, hand drums, clacking coconut shells, bigmen orchestrating, singing words so old their meaning was obscured; the air moist with the men's breath and sweat. They could not have slept last night and their hands and feet beat heavily.

The song had stopped, yet the noise was continuing somehow – the women outside. We had done two or three anti-clockwise circuits of the gaigo; more maybe. The other boys looked weak, as if the blood due from them had already been taken, all except Joel and Alex – a married bandee wearing his habitual fed-up expression, lips squeezed tight. Now that we were allowed to look up, I saw that there was a fleet of inverted crocodile-prowed canoes around the broad strip of grass. We could very easily guess what these smooth grey bulks were for, and they were not a seating arrangement. Really, they were more like operating-theatre tables. We dropped our leaf aprons, *soopwees*, but only actually felt naked when our waus were told to step out from among us. We were next marched over a heap of fresh *largee*, and the herb rubbed on our backs. The juices released on us were 'an extra precaution to ward off bad spirits', we were told, and we had too many concerns just now to disbelieve.

The first half-dozen waus lay down on the hard canoes, made themselves comfortable on their backs, then received their boys. I watched Joel being laid in the cradle of his wau's body – flesh against flesh, both face up, the shining bald head settled on the man's breast, the boy's pelvis nestled between the wau's open legs. These Joel was advised to grip. This was the day Joel would have longed for and feared as a small child. He would have smoothed his little fingers over the ploughed fields of grown-ups' skin in awe. Today was the day of *waarkvaru vakaak*, the day when the crocodile bit you. Soon, he would also have the marks of the Niowra people. The bigmen, who were now apparently *avookwaarks*, embodiments of the giant crocodile spirit, bent over these first shivering boys, who were told to keep their mouths shut, close their eyes and – could I have heard it right? – sleep.

The rest of us slumped to our allotted canoes and waited, not knowing where to look. The Timbuns, like roaming minstrels, played to the reclining boys lest the women whimpering outside heard their noise. The sun came in short forays from the clouds, then nipped behind them again. My watch had been confiscated by Johnny for my time here, but the sun was strong on my back and it must have been about 8.30 a.m.

The dance party wove between the canoes, bare feet avoiding pools of vomit and blood – it was said that it was our female blood we were losing – from bites around the nipples in crescents, down the chest, in two narrowing bands, also over the shoulder and almost to the elbow. Each boy was very slowly stood up, laid on his flowing chest, and the bites continued either side of his spine extending outwards in two pairs of wings, then down his thighs. There were family variations. Gabriel, a thin goaty-faced boy, a few paces away, was coping so badly the *avookwaarks* hissed that a malevolent spirit was attacking him, trying to stop him from joining the men's company, from sharing their knowledge.

A strange thing: about a quarter of the bandees being cut were asleep with dreamy smiles. Joel, as Martin predicted, was one of those who flexed and unflexed their toes in the mud, their waus wincing under their charges' claw grip. The dance group swooped in and ridiculed the *avookwaarks* for being so cruel:

> *Gramba-maree, tambermang,*
> *tamber,*
> *tamberlan, liko, liko, temblo dee!*
> *Yeeeeeeeeeeee-a! Yeeeeeeeeeeee-a!*

'Gramba-maree, your arms and legs are short, and getting shorter [you're so decrepit and worn out], *liko liko, temblo dee!*' We loved the Timbuns for this, and our bond with these newly initiated gave us an unexpected strength.

When each job was done, the bandee was peeled off his wau and warned not to try to stand upright; the happy band was called over, the boy advised to clamp his teeth tight together and when the singers got to their loud chorus – *Yeeeeeeeeeeee-a! Yeeeeeeeeeeee-a!* – a pitcher of water was emptied over him. A long rolling roar of either Yo-anga-mook! or N'iangandoo! signalled that another crocodile offspring had properly entered the nest. *Gwak* oil was painted over the bites with a feather. One by one the other bandees were led into the shade of the spirit house.

Fed up with staring at my feet, and at my patch of grass – as yet unspoiled – I asked for my camera and did a photographic tour, for the record. Martin was stiff, splayed on his wau, two *avookwaark* heads down over him. The boy opened his eyes, which looked shrunken and tired. His expression said I was brave to be hanging around watching, but I was just frustrated with the waiting, and told him to smile for the camera. This he tried to do, but as the charms dictated, he was already drifting into another sleep. Back at my canoe my wau said, sympathetically, that because I was here to learn Old Ways, the *avookwaarks* had agreed to carve me with the traditional bamboo blade. That was the instrument rendered haphazard through its bluntness – more force had to be applied compared to the foreign metal blades, and I wondered if it accounted for the death toll of the old days.

'And where did you get *that* from? It's my razor! And that's the last of my soap!' I said.

'Your legs are too hairy,' my wau said in Pidgin. He splashed soapy water around and drew the razor up and down my thighs.

The sun shone bleakly through the palms now. I swigged water from coconut shells to prevent dehydration. Jimmi, the young man with the bands of mourning around his ankles and wrists, came up and said he would be near me. I asked for a betelnut.

'Here. But it is not prayed over. It does not know to give sleep.'

My wau leaned back, his hands under his head as a pillow, his black-haired chest drawn high and up. I slowly placed myself on him, leaning steadily backwards from sitting between his legs astride the canoe, conscious of my great weight as the small of my back settled on his genitals. I adjusted my muscles and bones to his; my head rested in the nook of his breast. My back and shoulder stuck tightly to him with the sweat of both of us; our forms were cleaved together. Our platonic snugness was beautiful.

Now I was conscious of two figures looming over me from either side – faces of folded old flesh which had been blackened up with charcoal and so were yet more formless against the bright sky. They angled their heads across me to confer, and light spiked through the holes in their noses. I closed my eyes – not firmly, but enough to shut out other stimulations. I wanted to confront this pain, not to hide from it by seeking out distractions. I wouldn't hum, I wouldn't sing.

The first stabs, around the left nipple, took me by surprise, and involuntarily I lifted my head in defence, my eyes focusing to the source of the shock, a strip of bamboo slithering in and out of me in wet fingers. My eyes closed. I pondered on that liquid being spilt – it tickled as it ran down my ribs – my lifeblood flowing from me through this deliberate act of submission; my shot in the arm (and chest and back and leg) from animal nature.

I would not fall asleep, I came to see: that was the cost of not being able to believe unreservedly. My soul was prepared to embrace these spiritual forces – instinctively I had felt their presence in nature and had been drawn to this land to find them – but my Western mind, hostile to otherworldly notions, was now fighting acceptance. My rationalising upbringing said I needed proof of these spirits if they were to be a reality. So, whatever my questing soul *knew*, for now I would feel the pain of the unbeliever.

I became weaker, and as my thoughts floated I wanted to inhale the spiritual conviction of these two old men craning overhead. I was drinking in the breath they hotly spread over me. I held it deep within my lungs. I lay there before them, offered naked and vulnerable, accepting of their will, waiting with desire for this transformation into a human crocodile. Perhaps, before I left the nest, I might have assimilated their allegiance to the natural forces, and my mind would join my spirit in acceptance.

My breathing began to couple with that of my wau. My slow chewing of the betelnut accompanied our movement, which was uninfluenced by the irregular rhythm of the piercing blades. Our greater, combined rhythm overcame the pain. If my skin suddenly seared or my pulse quickened in panic as I had to vomit the too bitter betelnut, my wau's chest was always there raising and lowering me in tranquillity. By virtue of my body being locked in his I could restore my harmony by thinking of *his*, by meditating on *him*, the already initiated, the already crocodile.

The Timbun dancers came around every now and then. The wood crocodile, roaring with triumph at the completion of each bandee's marks, had roared a great many times now, and I sensed I was the only boy left out here. I rose from my wau's belly, and as I parted from his open legs it was as if he had given birth to me, in this his female role. I came away with blood, born. The crocodile sounded for me. The Timbuns fell silent. I felt the tender lick of the feather and the cool oil under the sun.

I was united with the others, who were spread indoors on long canoes, three or four of them laid side by side, at both ends of the spirit house. Our chests were cushioned by thin sago skirts, our hands propped our chins. The dry threads of sago material issued a sweet cosy hayloft scent, but the fibre was working into our incisions. We could not sleep, but only waited.

'Rule One:' a gruff voice was saying, in Pidgin for my sake, 'bandees may not touch any part of their bodies with their hands. It is tambu [forbidden]; so is touching another bandee.' The youngest men – called *g-eenjumboos* – Johnny, Andrew, Jimmi and so on, hovered over us and bashed mosquito clouds away, when they had time off from constructing swats from yellow palm-leaf shoots. I felt I had been drugged, but clung to the words coming down on to us, knowing from the tone that they would not be repeated.

'Rule Two: this whisk must never be seen by women. Its name, ——, is to remain secret.

'Rule Three: your head must remain extra low as you walk past *avookwaarks*. When walking keep your hands below your knees.

'Rule Four: you will never look up at *avookwaarks*, or *jinbungees* – that's the less senior bigmen. It is tambu.

'Rule Five: you will not listen to what the bigmen say except when they're addressing you. Then you will not look up. It is tambu.'

Food came in baskets from somewhere – boiled fish and sago pancakes, surprise, surprise. None of us wanted anything and that was no surprise either.

'BANDEES, KAIKAI NAU! Eat now!' We tilted ourselves upright. I was next to Sebastian, on a canoe. *G-eenjumboos*, some of whom were waus, took a *makau* in one hand, a *sownow* in the other, and put them alternately into our mouths as if we were babies. Our hands remained limply at our sides. Water came in cups later, and was poured down our throats.

'BANDEES SLEP NAU!' We closed our eyes, as we laid on our full bellies. Those who did not were yelled at. We uttered no word of dissent – we would see how far we could push our rights later, I thought dreamily. Unfortunately we were down here near the cool floor, they were up on the benches in silhouette. We could do nothing, or precious little, without being observed.

Above us, in the smells of our oil, drifted soft flute music. Opening my eyes through my fingers I could see it was a duet, two *avookwaarks* standing face to face with seven-foot bamboos, the old men with skirt wraps swaying and dipping as those notes fluttered; parent crocodiles singing their little ones to sleep. The music stopped. The silence was unnatural. Why were the men whispering? The canoe under me was trembling slightly, I could feel it under my hands: either Kennedy or Sebastian, lying on the same canoe at my head and feet, was sobbing.

We were relieved when it started – whatever was coming. It was a brutal knocking on our canoes; fast, then a slower drumming, getting stronger, nearer, working in from both ends of each canoe – the crescendo instilling fear – until your hands joggled against the dugout, and a few treble voices cried out weak pleas. Now there were soft thuds in place of the canoe-wood bangings, and this was the sound of our skin, tightly stretched in its swollen state, as the men walked the canoes, dropping green-husked coconuts and clubs on us, as we lay prone. The knocks were so violent on the second round of this *yanoo* ceremony that my teeth clicked together in time; but by drawing in my shoulder blades and spine much bruising could be avoided. I felt for the smaller, skinnier boys.

The heat of the day passed. We sat, shoulders stooped, brains dulled. Saun was bent over in a little ball – no clowning now. Martin was crouched looking at his fingers. I could hear Stens' normal heavy breathing. Joel was humming, as if to a sleepy baby. No one opened their mouths even to whisper. Risking raising my head a little, I saw the black and orange face of the wood spirit Wunjumboo, his spiked black hair and wild eyes painted on the main posts; the tail ends of dusty, crumbling Yo-anga-mook and N'iangandoo in the centre blocking our view to the Niowi side, where the married bandees Alex and Willi were, and Vincent, his mouth always in a small perfect 'o'. The air was calm, fire and tobacco smoke stacking in a layer. Legs, thick and thin, hairy or bald, passed my eyes. I took in little else of the men, but wondered on this power I had given them over me. I fought to clear my mind of its cloudiness, but couldn't. The Timbuns were outside whirling the sacred bull roarers – blades of wood – which released to the air screeching, whooping voices of their crocodile spirits. The uncanny sound flew out of the nest and for miles around.

Of the seventeen bandees, five, including myself, required additional surgery to finish the patterns to headman Rom's standards – he fingered us like braille. It would be done tomorrow.

At night we walked, hunched almost on all fours, hugging our gory sago fibre skirt mats, out of the nest to sleep in our houses. We whistled like the *swé* bird to warn women to turn away and close their eyes. The oil on the skin of Joel's broad back ahead gleamed white under the moon as we split into clan groups, to our own portions of the village. There were glows from fires, but roofs and stilts were black against the silver river. There was no family chat in the air, only the crying of babies, our clumsy flat tread on the grass, and our haunting whistles, drifting with the fire smoke.

We filed up the ladder into Johnny's house, glimpsing the turned backs of Johnny's wife and sisters, Elijah ducked down stiff, terrified, and slipped into a cubicle Johnny had made from coconut fronds. The *swé* bird cries we killed in unison, and the women started up their chat again. Food was handed over the screen; we winced as we stretched for it. We could feed ourselves with washed hands in silence, but we could not use our mosquito swats, and suffered the mosquitoes sucking on us.

I cursed my white skin for being so sensitive. As I was the biggest, Johnny said I would have a mosquito net to myself. It sounded great news – privacy at last! While we were outside having a quick pispis, I whispered, 'Martin, how's it going with you?'

'Shut up,' Johnny said. 'And sleep well. That means on your belly. Or bigmen come and stick you.'

I eased under my net and stretched out. The sago fibres seemed alive, gnawing at my chest. The air temperature dropped with the clear sky. I wanted to curl up on my side, but it was forbidden. I could not rub my naked skin because of the slashes and bruises, nor put my arms around myself. They had removed almost all my hair – was it true that a third of your body heat is lost through your head? A lot, anyway. I heard other bandees snuggling up close to each other, sharing warmth. I opted for curling to a kneeled position, and was still like this just before dawn when there was the deep whoop of a large wood blade flung in the air, the crocodile calling. We must return. We took up our sago skirt mats.

It was good to get around the fires (which had been burning continuously for the bigmen) and to be reunited after that lonely night. The men were as yet sleepy, the gaigo unlit, and quiet chat tolerated. The first thing to do was to reassure ourselves that no one had slept on his back. No one had.

The completion of the crocodile marks was done casually; I sat astride a canoe and, as some thirty bright red beads ran down my chest, in the eyes of my audience I saw the same fascination for lost lifeblood as had gripped Bundam Sole, when he had cut his nose in the highlands. The sun poked above the fence, and my white skin alone lost its stiffness, and so I alone was to be completed the next day.

In the first hours we adjusted ourselves as best we could to what seemed to be the rhythm of life here: bouts of anxiety caused by men raging irrationally at us, and lulls of protracted boredom as we waited for the first of the inevitable beatings that we knew were a feature of the initiation programme. We sat folded up on our canoe seats, the jeers of the men spreading over our bald necks and scabby backs. The *avook-waarks* were vying for the most extravagant boasts regarding their prowess with beating rods – in the old days Kumbui could bring a boy down with only a flick of a light reed across fresh crocodile bites; and Rom, how he used to wield those glancing, downward strokes! Ola-man! Did the bandees used to start flowing! 'Tears or blood?' we who were seated on canoes below, feet patting nervously on the cold mud, wondered. We were able to confirm from the chat that when beatings came they were in the form of a dance outside. Saun, promised for years before now that come his initiation he would be beaten especially hard for being the village fool, wanted to relieve his bladder. Though free to go to the lavatory shack he was too scared of the attention it might arouse, and so he doubled up his short torso and squeezed his long gangly legs tight together. I was close enough to hear his faint whimpers.

At last the Timbun youths were ordered to pluck down the hand drums from the rafters and lead us outside. Joel, Martin and I exchanged dreary looks and half-heartedly breathed good lucks. For the very first dance though, our backs were shielded by those of our waus, and we marched in a squad, heads bent, all in time together. The Timbuns set the beat with the drums – thung, thung, thung – singing '*tambermang, tamber, tamberlan* . . .' – and our guardians, both waus and fathers, actually seemed to be enjoying themselves, showing off their fearlessness and resilience. They shrugged away the canes and green twigs with howls of laughter – never an admission even of discomfort.

If only we could skip our schooling and acquire their courage and strength in some gentle way! But that was not feasible. Their example told us of the long haul ahead – in our present state it was hard enough to stretch to put one foot in front of another – and as the canes rose and fell in blurred arches around us, cracking loud on our waus' backs, smaller bandees wept. As we paraded around the gaigo I smelled spilt urine.

The second dance was half an hour later, and '*Saun bunguernian! White man!*' – I was called to go indoors. I would be quite safe. They wanted me to learn by watching, on this occasion. A snap from Rom stopped my unspoken objection.

The parade stomped around the spirit house, the waus laughing at Lamin Wogoo, who was trying to bring his stick down on to Jimmi, but kept falling in the mud. Bala, a bigman with a round hot face and laughing eyes, was breaking off from beating the unflinching backs. I became uneasy; he was veering towards me, raising his switch, as I stood vulnerable, all the more so for my two-hour-old cuts. Then I knew with certainty he was coming for me, that I was going to be the only bandee beaten on this occasion. What had Martin said once? That I had to be made an example of, 'Otherwise you can tell the whole world Kandengai village no longer makes their boys into men as strong as the crocodile.' More likely, the Kandengais could not hold back from the unique prospect of beating a white man at his invitation. Before I had moved an inch towards the cover provided by the marching squad, Bala's rods were square on my back. The stinging lines were less than the sting of the trickery, the lie that I had been separated to learn by watching in safety.

'Do not even think of lifting your head to him,' said Johnny, embracing my shoulders. 'Just sing.'

'*Liko, liko, temblo dee.*' My head down, I saw that Steven, the smallest of bandees, plodding behind under his human shield, was grimacing. I followed the line of his eyes to the passing ground at my heels. I was leaving a crimson trail and Steven's little feet were paddling over it. The sight of the blood served to make a loud announcement: that I was not getting special soft treatment. That was how I wanted it.

Back indoors Fredalin, a bandee whose earlobes were pierced with splinters of wood like cocktail sticks, was ordered to stand up from his canoe perch and entertain the gaigo with a certain traditional song. Old calloused feet of bigmen swung over us in our positions beneath the benches, as the bigmen rocked with joy. There was no such song that any of us had heard of, and the quandary of the scared boy was good sport. I did not know Fredalin well. He stood in a crumpled stance near the giant wood crocodiles, his head dropped low, submitting to his mood, to physical discomfort and to the rules. Being down at his feet I could smell the *gwak* oil on him and see that his eyes were shy, mouse-like. In an effort to please, the boy smiled winningly and commenced the first line of a hymn, hoping it might do. He piped words along the lines of 'Onward Christian Soldiers'. The benches creaked and groaned as the men buckled up with laughter. Fredalin dipped his head lower to hide his own grin. His song had gone down beautifully, he thought. Ban, a man with a sour temper today, unexpectedly leapt from his bench and brought the boy down with a broom stick. Jimmi, the nearest available *g-eenjumboo*, hurled himself on the boy's back to block more blows.

The Timbuns sluggishly moved their fat legs to take us outside for another punishing dance. Beatings were rarely handed out individually, we discovered: it was all of us or nothing. We were offered no more rules of behaviour, we were to discover them for ourselves as we broke them. Guessing whether it was right or wrong to go to sleep, go to the lavatory shack, whisper, was hard because we were also punished at random. Some of those men senior enough in the hierarchy to beat us showed mercy, others chose not to. It was not worth asking for any — weakness was the most terrible thing in a bandee.

I noticed that Godfrey, the Christian, was up on the bench, which sagged beneath him. He was asked to do a special variety of drum roll, which he had learned in his pagan years between initiation and conversion. To my surprise, he obliged. If he did not want the initiation, why was he co-operating?

Using two clubs on the slit gong, Godfrey announced that visiting bigmen from Korogo, Timbun and Nyaurengai would be holding a sacrificial feast all night.

'This is not food for us,' Martin said. 'Or we get boils under our armpits and *siks* [genitals]. This is how the spirits speak to the bigmen we break rules.'

'What if we get them and we haven't broken any rules?'

'You do not.'

This was very worrying. The diet was so alien to me that I was a very likely candidate for pimples.

At night, Rhonda said, 'Good night, bandees,' through the darkness. Her voice was content, I imagined her cheeks wore that warm reddish glow again. We could not reply, but acknowledged by stamping our feet. It was another bitter night of no sleep. Saun or Martin cried continually. Once a paraffin lamp disturbed us, flickering as it rose up the house steps, the shadows shifting in its beam – the *avookwaarks* come to check our sleeping positions. The boy's crying stopped, with a series of last gulps. My mosquito net was gently lifted and I knew the light was on my back. Later the sobbing started up again.

From the third morning we had to squat on the floor at meal times; not just anyhow, it had to be with soles on the ground and almost two foot apart. It was a new position for me and tore at my knee ligaments; even the others found it hard. Crouched among the skulking mosquitoes, we opened our mouths to be fed, well after we wanted to stop, and were forbidden to touch our whisks. If we stood up to stretch, sticks pushed us back to the ground. Poor Alex, like Joel and myself, was too old to accept easily being pushed around. If there's to be resistance against the bigmen, it will germinate from either of those two, I thought as Alex came over, stooped like an old man, from the Niowi half of the gaigo. 'Come. There is a boy who is bloody,' Alex said, his lips pouting even more than usual. 'Rom says you can finger him. But do not stop his skin pains.'

It was Vincent, the boy with the round mouth. Rags had been wrapped and wrapped around his upper arms. Unwinding them was a slow and heartrending business; dried blood had hardened them to his wounds. I had smelled the smell before – the sick Obini baby, with grotesque creamy sores in West Papua. When Vincent's wounds were bare, though, I was startled. The cuts, though gushing, were clean.

'Rom's spirit prayers,' said Vincent dubiously. But Rom, it seemed, tolerated a modicum of unspiritual medical intervention, and I couldn't resist the comforting spasm this realisation sent through me. Andrew was allowed to fetch my little medical kitbag from Johnny's house and Rom told me to take the bandages and quickly bind Vincent up. It was his family's tradition that the crocodile was always asked to bite especially deep.

'Hey, Doctor Benedix, do not go. Tell me. *Is* this spirits?'

'Well, we'll know the answer before we leave the nest, I think.'

Soon afterwards it rained, washing the grass clean of all the red stains. Rom stepped into the downpour chewing a betelnut and mouthing words. His dustiness was washed from him. He thrashed the air with *kamuin* leaves, threatening the clouds: sure enough they swept away.

In the afternoon we were ordered to line up on the steaming mud and the bigmen of other Niowra villages moved along shaking hands. We had to remain silent, not look up. We were to lose the Timbuns, and it was a blow. Seeing them, recent survivors of an initiation, had given us hope. They chucked away their leaves, squeezed their fat-laden hips into shorts and walked out through the fence, free.

Also leaving were the towny Kandengais, those drawn away from the village towards Western life. Peter, the riot policeman, had shaven off his beard and was going back to duty in Moresby. John, a teacher at Ambunti, went back upriver to his school, not knowing that he was fated to return in a hurry one day. Older Kandengais had grown soft and fat in the towns, their links with the village loose. They could not remember what was secret, so their children learned much of what was sacred here. These men found it hardest of all to part from us. We must not look them in the eyes, were not permitted to shed tears in sympathy, and they seemed to have forgotten the point of all our suffering. They cried a lot, and loudly. Our handshake was firmer than theirs.

Chapter Thirteen

'Two white men at Nyaurengai and walking this way!' The news spread along the benches. Gabriel must have looked up above the level of the thick, veined feet dangling in our faces because he screamed with surprise and wanted to clutch his ear after the rap it got.

The foreigners could have been guided here to see the initiation only by Steven from Yenchenmangua, another village in the Niowra group. He had got himself a plum job with a tourist lodge under Glen Bolton, a large, generous, hearty Aussie, who periodically descended on Jeff with tins of stew and dumplings to give him a surprise feast. The last time I had seen Steven he was at Jeff's, wearing sunglasses on his forehead, steering the river truck for the pink, multi-chinned orchid lady.

The bigmen shouted at us that a *very* special beating dance was going to be laid on for the white men. 'Man! Man!' they laughed, enjoying our cowering. Later, they seriously debated whether the foreigners should be permitted in. As they were only passing through, and were non-Sepiks, it was decided that if the tourists were to glean any secrets, these would never be used to compromise Kandengai; to them, Kandengai's status on the river or position in relation to the spirits were irrelevant. For the sake of village prestige they could have a very superficial look around. The sacred flutes and other objects were hidden.

Jimmi escorted Steven through the fence. The tourists had been left outside, and had probably been shown what the ceremony was about from the strident marks over his broad chest. It was the second meal of the day. We were squatting, allowed to feed ourselves now as long as our hands were thoroughly washed. Steven's sunshades crowned his head. He had on the clean blue ironed work trousers he wore for tourist outings. I dropped my eyes to look at his feet as they froze on the threshold.

'Benedict!'

'Hello, Steven!'

A wasted leg, probably belonging to grumpy Tovai of the almost extinct Bowee clan, swung at me for talking. '*Kai wow-ung!* It doesn't matter!' Rom's tired, mumbling voice said, expecting me to understand some local language now. I judged I could look up a little, and before I did anything else I took this first good chance as a bandee to look along the men's perches: above the pairs of brown legs stirring the air to outmanoeuvre the mosquitoes, were reclining figures – I could only see their wraps, a navel or two dipping and lifting sleepily – and the younger, more vigilant men who hung over us wolf-like, pectoral muscles developed from a life of heaving, chopping and paddling. The youngest men walked alongside the benches with heads respectfully low, just as we had to.

'Hello, Steven. What are you doing here?'

'What am *I* doing here?' He took his sunglasses from his head and clicked them together in his hand. 'I am so happy,' he said. 'All this,' he waved his hand across the spirit house. Our betters smoked, chewed, spat, as they eyed us bandees, bunched as we were over stacks of fish and sago laid on *bai*, palm-sheath trays, blowing at each other's mosquitoes with mouths crammed full, a thick stick waving over those who were not eating fast enough; swallowing more and more, and miserable all the time at the pressure on our stomachs, our stretching insides. 'All this,' said Steven, 'just to learn our customs?'

'How else?'

'Jeff told me a cock-and-bull story – you had gone to meet a sangriman in the bush.'

'Tell Jeff that Cursacaik never turned up. It was a con.' I was ordered to drop my head again.

The tourists – in safari suits, judging by the trousers passing our noses – were led, swinging SLR Nikons from their hands, to the far end of the gaigo, near Alex and the gory Vincent. We heard them laugh nervously: it seemed they were surprised to discover we were all naked. No one had warned them. Martin nudged me. He mouthed, 'What peoples are they?'

'Australian,' I mouthed back.

Joel and Kennedy were trying not to smirk – the men seemed so overdressed beside us. It was an ordeal – for the tourists – and it was lucky they did not know the bigmen were laughing at them as well. We heard disguised snorts above us and imagined the straight but meek faces the men generally reserved for carving buyers.

'And these initiates go round starkers like this all day . . .?' a tourist said. With my eyes low I could only just see the floor up beyond the hulking great crocodiles. Alex was barely discernible, squatting like a bull frog, food bulging his cheeks. The poor Australians did not know he could speak English. One man did all the talking – a bass voice, manner methodic, even-keeled, unexcitable. 'So how much do they get fed?' Looking at the Australian's sneakers and at the fine hems of their loose, lightweight trousers, Alex churned over the fish ostentatiously like a cow chewing its cud.

'They can eat as much as they like,' said Johnny.

'So the idea is that you are making these boys manly, for the time they leave, is that it?'

'Yes. We believe they are like little crocodiles, being taught by big mother and father parents to be brave.'

'Can you ask this one how much pain he felt when you cut him up?'

Steven dutifully went along with Alex's game of not speaking English. The Australians said they wanted it 'word for word, right out of the mouth of the boy. Just the way it was.' The men squatted down, and gave Alex a kind smile. The tourist with a bass voice also had a flourishing moustache. The second had not shaved for a couple of days. Alex was chewing – unspeakably rude from a bandee to anyone worthy of respect; and the bigmen seemed to be appreciating the joke. After Alex had told the highlights, the tourists juggled with their lenses and clicked away at Michael, a close-up of his curious crooked front teeth; at the 'fiery spirited one with the squeezed-up lips', Alex; and at Vincent with his photogenic swaddling of red-blotched bandages.

'Look at the way these boys are getting their food down.'

'It's a wonder they don't chunder.'

'Reckon they really starve 'em. Pity we can't slip them some sandwiches.'

The men were led past N'iangandoo and Yo-anga-mook – they fondled and stroked their crocodile snouts – to the Niamé side. They did not register surprise at a white man being here. They had heard back in Wewak, then along the river. Could they shake my hand?

'Only by the wrist, I'm afraid. Hygiene rules are very strict while we are eating.' Headman Rom called out I might sit on a canoe. 'Phew, that's a relief.'

'I'm glad we can bring you a little comfort, mate.'

They asked all the same questions, to get my story about the life of an initiate. Like all tourists, they missed the point, which was that the spectacular patterning of the skin was the least discomfort. It was the sleep deprivation, back strain from crouching, the 'dances' and the absence of individual rights. In talking I found I was consciously fighting involvement with the Australians, being short with their trivial questions. This Western contact was distracting to my bid to be absorbed spiritually.

'Is there anything we can do for you? Send some food in? Cigarettes?'

'Not really, but thanks.'

'This must be harder for you than them?'

'Oh, I don't know. I'm the biggest after all. Though the food might eventually kill me, I must say.'

'We'll get our friend Steven here to send through some ketchup for emergencies. Is there any chance of us two seeing dances here?' Martin's young eyes were pleading for me to say no. The tourist said, 'I'll ask Steven. Steve—'

'No, no . . . Look, this is going to sound selfish, but we would rather not. You see we, us boys, would have to dance and we . . . well, we are tired. There are much better villages. Try Mindimbit, downriver. They love dancing.'

'Oh, I don't mean you initiates. You are far too ill even to move. I mean some of the older men.'

'They'd get us to do it.'

'Surely not. Na, not in your condition. Steven, what do you think?'

I looked daggers, lifting my head to the leather belt around the tourist's waist. 'Bad here, aren't they?' I said. 'Dances, I mean.'

'Well . . .'

'See? Go to Mindimbit.'

The men sloped off to look around the village, after taking a snap of the 'sweet kid with large eyes like a koala' – they meant Saun.

'Well, goodbye, Benedict.' I looked up – it was worth the risk. Steven had his spectacles down. 'Look after yourself. Does Jeff agree with you doing this?'

'He should understand my motives more than anyone, but somehow I feel I'm trespassing on his preserve.'

'Will your people in Britain understand, though?'

'My family will. The rest maybe not.'

The moustachioed Australian stuck his head through the fence with a thought. 'Jee-sus. Some of 'em speak English?'

'All right,' Steven said to us. 'Keep your chins up. *Apman andinya.*'

'*Apman andinya.*'

'BANDEES SLIP NAU!'

We obediently lay flat and wearily took the blows, collecting yet more bruises. The bigmen, in a good mood, turned a blind eye to Joel chewing a betelnut he had discovered, and Johnny had to jump up to rub the boy's stained lips with clay when a Korogo party came unexpectedly. We could not have them thinking our discipline was slack.

From that day we had to leave our sago skirts in the houses and sit not on the canoes, but on the *bai*, the palm sheaths which were scattered on the spit-splashed mud.

On the fourth day, we were summoned to lean against the Niamé and Niowi ends of the fence. Water was poured from a coconut shell down our backs. It was cold enough to be a shock, but that was fine, because it numbed us as our waus scraped off the crocodile-bite scabs with a

156

mussel shell. Kennedy, as unashamedly cool to me as ever, was forgotten for a second after being doused; the scabs had time to soften. I congratulated him. He spun his round, marsupial's face away from me. Everyone was smeared grey with wet clay, over our ears, skull, eyelids, lips, genitals, between toes and cheeks of our buttocks, until there was no skin to be seen. We tasted the clay that was making our lips sticky. We understood it would be a twice-daily ritual, the only time that touching our own or our fellows' skin was permissible. The darkness and sheen of the mud was lost as it dried, tightening on the skin. We became ghostly, dull-textured. Once, I could be distinguished through colour of skin; now this coat united us bandees. It was a coat of anonymity – the features of our faces were rubbed out – our stooping posture already lessened height differences, and we looked as bald as each other. Before I could go to check on Vincent – he had been leaving a bloody trail since the scrape-down – we were lined up in a rank, facing the fence, bent over, and forced to prove our full sexual submission.

Afterwards, much weaker, we got a lecture from Lamin Wogoo in Pidgin about a secret twice-daily ritual we would have to enact; this stressed how important the number five was for the ancestors, although no explanation was given. Outside I could usually stand far enough away to get complete views, even with my inclined head. Lamin Wogoo was the smoothest-skinned of the bigmen, with steel-wool hair. His feet, I already knew: the toenails were like mother-of-pearl scallop shells. A coarse rope was plaited around our necks and fixed with a permanent knot. We might not undo it.

Pinga, my 'father', sternly advised me I must cover my neck rope with clay to prevent it cutting. It would be removed the day I left – and who knew when that would be. In a month, when our cuts were healed? Or like at Kubriman – where the village ran out of food for the final feast and took ages to accumulate it – a year?

Indoors, our heads low, we at last heard some men's thoughts on the spirits. (Godfrey had not been around lately; I noted that he was not here now either. Perhaps he spent his time away praying for the termination of our proceedings.) The bandees, Rom pronounced, had come through the first round. The spirits had not harmed anyone. 'Who in all honesty thought they ever would!' voices chipped in. The voices were youngish but their tone asked for respect, so these men must be middle-aged. We, the bandees, were fascinated: apparently even men this old doubted the power of spirits nowadays. We had guessed as much already about the faith of the younger, Christian or modern-influenced *g-eenjumboos* – they openly expressed spiritual opinions even to women. However, now we saw the full situation we wondered: if out of all the men only the senior *avookwaarks*, those who were actually steering the ceremony, believed in modern-day spirit power, what was the point in trying to indoctrinate us bandees? Or indeed of holding the ceremony at all? Rom was going to brush over the issue, it seemed. Perhaps they would discuss it once we were in bed. He said that because the spirits had co-operated, the rituals must have been done in a manner pleasing to them. 'We can proceed with more confidence.'

Now we were entitled to wear short aprons of palm shoots. Their name was to be kept secret, like that of the rope. Pinga pushed me about roughly, measuring up my skirt, cutting the supple leaves off across my thighs. Joel was invited to grab the string of one of the little bull roarers while it was being spun in the air. We were issued with others. From now, it was our job to keep, our young waark spirit whooping sounds, coming from the nest most of each day. Though the task was somewhat tedious, it was a way of straightening out our backs; and maybe, when you wandered free, around the gaigo, you might catch the sound of a loved one beyond the fence. The leaves of the screen had wilted and settled since they were erected: we could see chinks of daylight through; after dark the flick of a burning torch as it shed light for those wary of snakes. And each morning, when women queued up some distance away and called that the bandee food was ready – '*Bandee now eeya-kray!*' – there was a chance you might even catch a glimpse of a dress.

Today there was a traditional game – wrestling for the first sago basket brought into the nest. Johnny had been selected – presumably because of his no-nonsense manner. He had to jog with the basket, keeping us off as long as possible. The women, knowing of this sport, shouted blindly, encouraging their bandees, as Johnny put his knuckles in the face of any who came near.

'Jo-*elle!*'

'*Vin*-cent!'

'My-*caaaaaal!*'

It was sad to hear Vincent's name; the women could not have known he was strapped up indoors on his belly, swimming in his blood.

Fredalin, the shy boy with cocktail sticks in his ears, got a headbutt, and Johnny steamed on, trotting around the gaigo. Even Joel was rendered harmless with a fist against his inflamed chest. Alex limped away. Martin, Saun, Steven and Sebastian – all less developed boys – were easily sidestepped, and Michael, the boy with the crooked teeth, had them almost knocked out as he was tossed into a gaigo post. The spectating men cheered and bellowed, those who were reclining on benches this side craning their necks out, under the eaves.

Johnny charged at me, the bag hooked over a shoulder, apparently aiming to dispose of me by raking his fingers along my front – the finishing touches to my patterns had been carved only hours before. He plunged both his hands at me, spreading his fingers to the two swollen sides of my raw breast, as if plucking fruit. I bent, embraced his waist and was flung around to the rear as Johnny's inertia carried him past. My encircling arms began to slip down his pelvis. Then Johnny experienced his first rugger tackle. We flew together for a while, skidded through the ashes of an old fire, Johnny's feet trying to inflict damage on my chest. His head, meeting a fence pole, suddenly stopped our combined progress. The men cheered. The bandees, covered by the men's noise, joined in. The women shouted: Who had done it? Who had captured the basket? The men taunted them: Martin? The fool Saun? They wouldn't tell. A grating old female's voice swore, repeatedly, and we heard the women dispersing with chatter and amusement. I strained to listen to their light tones fading from earshot.

'Bandee, I am pleased on you,' said Johnny, seeing the blood smeared down on his legs and wondering if it was his or mine. It was mine. 'Your chest is leaking much now, go and layer on more clay.'

Our swiping of the food bag, as with the *waark* blade, symbolised our taking of secrets, our snatching rank from the initiated. Rom ordered all the other bandees to shake my hand. Kennedy, in doing this, produced a wry smile, which might have said, 'Congratulations on pulling off a cheap trick and impressing everybody. Well, it doesn't impress *me*.' Indoors, Pinga was proudly re-enacting his son's tackle in the gaigo. Andrew said, 'When the young girls hear, their dreams tonight can want to be on you, bandee.'

'Well, that will make my night more bearable.'

'Yes, bandee.'

'By the way, Andrew, has any girl been asking about me? Wondering how I am? Especially, I mean?'

'Hmm. Ah yes. There's one girl.'

'Oh yes?'

'Johnny's sister Rhonda. She's a good girl. Clever head; works hard. And yes, I believe Augusta.'

'No one else?'

'No, bandee. Now stop time-wasting,' he said, trying to be firm. 'Put on ground [clay] to stop your bloods up, before Johnny sees you are so slow.'

We had eaten. We sat on our palm sheets in the dampness under the bark benches, with the men's feet dropping dust in our faces. The bigmen were restless, and that infected us. We were all so fidgety the mosquitoes were whining everywhere, unable to settle. Steven, whose presence below Rom was tolerated as long as the bandee kept a fire smouldering under him, like a housewife, was called. His cousin in the Yaark clan wanted a word.

'It is a trick,' whispered Martin in English. 'He must not go.'

'Yes, he is to be sticked all right,' Joel added.

'He will be if he doesn't go,' I said.

The Yaark clan bellowed their heads off, understanding the dilemma.

'We all can be sticked if he goes or not,' Joel said. 'We must not play their game. Don't go. We lose anyways.' I agreed: our first stand. It was so hard to surrender up our pride as individual boys.

Ban, with a strained elbow from beating too hard, came stomping over, brandishing a branch of betelnuts. He spat on Steven's bald head. He was a 'fugging bustod', a pathetic, miserable toad. Ban had only wanted to offer him a gift. 'Oi bandee,' he said in Pidgin, 'I'm talking to you, you little runt.' Little Steven looked up, marginally, to the level of the bigman's lumpy knees, and got the gift of betelnuts across his face. The betelnuts separated, rolled and tumbled over the smooth mud, scattering out of sight, as if also sensing impending violence. From Steven's lips hung a globule of blood. 'Keep your nose to the ground when I'm addressing you, girl.'

For this bandee's insolence we were going to be punished. Martin stiffened his arms to his side in the way he did when afraid.

'You can cover my back up with yours if you like.'

'And you can mine, if you like,' I said.

We walked out alone for the very first time, no *g-eenjumboos* to shelter us. Ban conducted our marching parade with a smile, waving his canes in time and prancing between us, delivering the punishment, sparing nothing. He swooped over us like a bat, flapping his hands like leathery wings, a stick in each creating clicking noises as they met our hides. Those like myself with hand drums put their anger into their drum beat; those without screamed the words of the song; many were just sobbing – Saun, Gabriel. Steven was singing, but no discernible sound was coming out. His eyes were clear, tearless, gazing in shock.

Ban stopped us after one circuit. 'I've been cruel?' he asked. 'Oh, I am *so* sorry.' We could have a court session, if we so wished. He, Ban, would listen to our judgement.

'*Ow-a, ow-a, ow-a.* Yeah, yeah, yeah. And you'll be absolutely fair,' Alex said.

We were assembled before Ban, who had got Saun to place a stool for him on the grass. We stood trembling – not from fear, but from the shock of the ringing pain. We leaned forward with our weight on our knees. Only Alex stood upright, a shade nonchalant. Vincent was swaying and oblivious of me as I knocked the mosquitoes off his legs.

Well, what complaints would we like to make to the old man? He had his double split rods in his hand. Ban sat alone, waiting for an answer. Steven was thrown a challenge. If he was angry, what punishment would he like to give Ban? Steven, shocking us all, swiftly lifted the bigman's stool from under him. From a gaigo bench, indoors, Lamin Wogoo led a men's cheer at this smallest bandee's spirit. Ban tumbled furiously on Steven, slapping the boy in his flustering bat manner. Kumbui, the bigman with the limp, wrestled the rods from Ban and gave him instead pliant twigs, which would sting rather than bruise. Steven was fenced off by Kennedy, and Kennedy was walled by hot-breath Stens until he too was rescued from the smashing twigs. We were ordered to take our drums and dance – we were not going to stop until we had learned obedience.

When Ban's sore elbow was aching too much, his place was taken by Lamin Wogoo. His face burned keenly, his teeth biting hard together. His skin was as sleek as his manner, and, tightly muscled, he moved between us lightly, silently apart from the whoosh and slap of his twigs. An example was made of Gabriel who moved one of his bony hands defensively from between his knees. Thung, thung, thung, the drums sounded on around the gaigo . . .

Our stand had been a disaster. We patched each other up with mud, dully. We had seen our companions' souls laid bare – how we reacted to pain, and to seeing pain in our fellows. That, and our mutual feelings of anger at our impotency, bonded us.

At dusk, Jimmi tiptoed between our wounded bodies and said we must get up to see this joke. A boy somewhere behind began crying, softly, but it was not a joke on us, for once, it was on a bird. Outside, with the spinning bats, Jimmi thumped his foot on a canoe three times, and called into the overhanging palms, 'Kee-o-kay, koo, koo, koo, koo, kooo!' He said something about the call scaring courting birds off their perch, but we were not listening.

'It is going to be like this for months, Benedix,' whispered Martin, lying at my feet. 'Beatings, feedings, no sleepings.' I saw that his feathery moustache was gummed down with clay.

Alex, Willi, Joel and I – the oldest bandees – were the sum total of those up and about. I went to Vincent, who needed help, Alex said.

'Hello, Doctor Benedix. Look what they been done to me.

'Perhaps they don't like your dancing style.' I began the painful business of undoing the stiff, clotted bandages. 'Now this is going to hurt.'

'Eee! I always – eee! – am a bad dancer. The bigmen are – eee! – saying we dance like marching Indonesian soldiers, you know.'

'Oh dear.' Binding up Vincent again I saw he was shaking. 'You're scared of me?'

161

'Of course. Rom's medicine does no hurtings, it's secret words only.'

'Try and inch towards the fireside. I think you're starting to get a fever.'

Head bent, returning ignominiously through the men's breath along the right bench side, I was stopped by Rom, who said I belonged to his clan, the Yaarks. The Yaarks looked after the seawater spirits, and white people came to the Sepik from over the sea. I wanted to say actually I came by air.

Sebastian was bunched up with a fever, and Kennedy, Saun and Steven were looking like corpses. On the Niowi side Thompson, Fredalin, Norbet and Vincent were out of action. The aspirins I dished out were running low. It had better not be a cold night, I thought. But it was. We fought it by getting up continually for a *dee* or *weetgnia*. (That had been pekpek and pispis, but I was being weaned off Pidgin.) Before crawling out like worms from our mosquito nets we had to bang on the floor to wake Johnny's grandmother, who was so old she was sexually neutral, and would keep our secrets. She led us out warding off any women or children, the dying moon giving her luminosity – her dry wrinkled flesh like our clay-caked skin. These boys had to be more used to this climate than I was. If *I* get a fever, I thought, what then?

At daybreak I stoked the fire of my adopted brother, Sebastian, and kept the smoke out of his eyes, and the mosquitoes away, by stroking him with the whisk. Bands of fibre were twisted around most bandees' heads to 'squeeze away head pains', as Martin put it. Rom said the pain was the work of spirits. 'He will talk to them why are they doing this, bandee,' Andrew told me.

'More to the point, does he know what's going to be the consequence of hitting us today and letting us face another night stretched out in the cold?'

Andrew said whether Rom knew or not, no one had the right to tell him.

To cheer us up, Alex's little toddler son was brought in through the fence by his wau. He would be too young to remember anything he saw but he screamed loudly at us mud men, and wanted nothing to do with his father. He was given his own palm skirt and painted grey. He left, kicking and screaming, in Jimmi's arms. We heard the child calming down as he sighted his mother, then we caught her shrieks of laughter when she saw the boy dressed up, and the child's even louder screams.

I hummed a Beatles song. It was difficult not to think of the world outside. Joel copied. 'She loves you, yeah, yeah, yeah, yeah, yeah, yeah, yeah.'

'There are less "yeahs", Joel.'

He said he would one day escape to a town and learn to play the guitars he had seen in a magazine. 'She loves you, yeah, yeah, yeah, yeah, yeah, yeah.'

'What would happen if you walked out now?' I asked Martin.

'Maybe they can kill me.'

'And if *I* walked out?'

'The same. The bigmen can say you were attacked by a crocodile.'

'They wouldn't risk the publicity. Besides it wouldn't be true.'

'But if the *avookwaarks* did it – crocodile men . . .'

'They could place charms on you. Be rid of you that way,' Sebastian said in Pidgin.

'You mean poison me, then pretend it was due to the spirits? Some of the junior bigmen don't seem very convinced any more.'

'They have too many wrong foreign thoughts – like you,' Martin said, revealing that he was a traditionalist. 'You *will* see our spirits even now have powers. You will see. We *all* will. Maybe we will be hurt by our spirits for being careless with them.'

'And you know that can't be bad,' said Joel.

'What?' said Martin.

'I don't think he's listening.'

'She loves you, yeah, yeah, yeah, yeah . . .'

Right now our lack of interest in life was causing the ancient *avookwaarks* to peer down their noses at Sebastian, who was coughing more like a drenched bush kangaroo than a little crocodile. They were still resolute in their belief: how easy it would be to lose one of their clutch, if the spirits wanted it. Few of the middle-aged, and even fewer *geenjumboo* youths or bandees – the two classes that composed the New Generation – seemed to take the thought seriously. But Martin, at least, did.

Chapter Fourteen

A *minchin tumee*, a centipede which was the dark brown of dried blood, dropped from the roof. Joel, Kennedy and I tumbled over those bandees stretched out on their slats to be clear of it. Johnny squashed away the animal's life. To most of us it was a centipede with a nasty bite. To the *avookwaarks* it was a spirit; maybe a malicious one.

The next day headman Rom muttered that an enemy was putting a spell on the fence to bring it down and let evil spirits in to attack us. Most of us had recovered from the previous day's fevers, and Johnny, leader of the Catholics, put this down to his praying, the *avookwaarks* to their rituals. Godfrey appeared, but, well-built Christian though he was, made no comment; that seemed odd. To strengthen the fence, two more sacrificial chickens were knocked on the head with a drum stick, *largee* and *kamuin* leaves were bashed along the fence. We were ordered outside, so that the men could discuss the spirits in confidence – everyone was suddenly very aware of them, even if they *were* outdated and underpowered nowadays.

Bleary Lamin, the gambler, brother of Rom, and as little and dusty, summoned me over as a fellow Yaark. I stood before him, feeling Johnny's attention on me, his muscles tensing as he sat on the bench edge, poised to get me out of trouble. Lamin handed me a betelnut, an offer of friendship. I took it, permitted only to be mute. 'Nau yu tok "Me bilong Niowra. Me bilong Kandengai."'

He was expecting me to say 'I, Benedix, am from Niowra, I'm a Kandengai,' back in Pidgin, but I did not think it would be honest. I had come to learn, *not* to change heritage. I was here to build, not to swap. I was still a white man, still needed Hardy, Lawrence, Larkin, and all that; required annual stocks of Aunty Joan's and Uncle Geoffrey's tomato and apple chutney. Jimmi, upon the bench beside Lamin, was scratching his stomach nervously. I was getting ideas above my station. Eventually, I said the words Lamin wanted. I saw that in his mind this *was* building rather than swapping. He said, 'Nau naim bilong yu "Wumbunavan".'

So from now on I had a village name, in this case shared with the gaigo. I went back to join the bandees and mosquitoes.

Because the bandees' opinions were considered invalid, there was consternation when it was discovered that I had been consulting them about custom for my notebook, so the headman ruled that I could talk to any bigman I chose. Also I would be allowed to drink tea, which my wau would make. They worried how my clay layer flowed off me with my white man's sweat, and how my flesh was shrinking alarmingly with dehydration. Far from being a privilege, the tea was an important health requirement: without the extra fluid, my physiology put me at a serious disadvantage relative to the other bandees.

Now that I was a Yaark, I could not be told the secrets of other clans. It was a price I was paying for such close involvement. On the other hand Martin said a white man had been in Kandengai studying its daily – non-initiation – life, and many clans had not given up even their own various secrets.

Martin explained, apologetically, that times were hard for Kennedy; I should bear with his coolness. He had got back to the village only three weeks before, having been away serving his prison sentence. Separately both Martin and he had been caught larking about after they had got bored in the town. But whereas Kennedy's witness showed up, Martin's forgot to, so only Kennedy was locked up.

'Why do you not come in the low-water season, Benedix?' Martin asked.

'It's all right for you, you're used to the kubia bites. These are your mosquitoes. Look at Saun – the kubia are covering him like cuscus fur, and yet he's asleep.'

The bigmen were unhappy. There had been a quarrel between clans – initially about a chicken which had disappeared under suspicious circumstances. The argument brewed. We ducked down low to avoid the abuse. Men, as if on the boil, produced droplets of spit and perspiration, which rained unevenly on our heads and backs, spotting our clay black. Saun, his innate energy charged up again, began tapping his mosquito swat at the ground distractedly. The man called Warbee, 'flute', who had been accused of abducting the chicken, found it convenient to kick Saun and claim that the boy had touched his leg.

Right! Insolence again! Sebastian and Vincent were too ill to rise; the rest of us were summoned out to dance. The men's blood was already hot, and they spent their tempers on our backs. We sang, and only the biggest among us were not brought to our knees as if called to pray. We heaved the fallen to their feet, and cried our song:

Singro
ongora luga
bandee janguee maree
ongora luga.

'Stars, stars, stay up there, and stop raining down on us bandees like this.'

Yeeeeeeeeeeee-a! Yeeeeeeeeeeee-a!

Soon both Fredalin's cocktail sticks were lost from the boy's ears. Old Kumbui, whom I had mostly seen only at the far right-hand end of the gaigo, his legs, one longer than the other, hanging from the bench over Alex, hobbled among us, clumsily hitting out. Blood was whipped into the air off Joel's wide back, he buckled in front of me, lost the dance beat, then took up his stride again. And all because someone thought their chicken had been stolen. Two days later it was seen pecking at a lizard on the other side of the fence.

Afterwards, giving me time to sit down and catch my breath, Kumbui requested that I treat his leg pains, presenting little scraps of paper which he had faithfully collected from doctors' orderlies over the years. Some had been torn from notepads, others looked like wastepaper, bundles of chits issuing him aspirin. He said the actual cause was that a shaman called Wangee tried to clear salvinia weed from the river, telling some land spirits to jump into the water and tug it out. Afterwards Kumbui's daughter got into her canoe for a quiet day's fishing. The mooring line got snagged before she could cast off. It was caught on something big and obstinate underwater. Kumbui ran up to help. The line snapped. As it jerked back, a spirit zoomed up the nylon and into Kumbui's leg. He had been stuck with one an inch shorter than the other ever since, he said. I wrote a letter addressed to Dr Brown, the Englishman I had met at Brurui, asking that this respected man might have an X-ray, and was it osteoarthritis?

I had come to the aid of a man who was supposed to be schooling *me*! He had needed my help, the help of a white man, help from my world: just as all the old men had needed a white man's help, the confidence of his presence, to commence the initiation.

Kumbui's initiation had been about the same as ours, he said. The holes through the top of his ears were made with palm spines on another occasion, but he had worn nothing through them for years, the same for his nose — he stuck my ballpoint pen through to demonstrate — and earlobes. Yet he was saddened by the modern world of lapsed tradition. Even the Blackwater villages with big gaigos, like Govmas and Kraimbit, did not school their boys properly, and elsewhere the boys' fathers seemed to take many of the blows. At Chambri they used a mediocre fence. To cheer himself up he showed me the parade drill the Japanese had taught him as a boy during the war, but that set his lame leg throbbing again.

As I stood by the fence trying to straighten my spine, Andrew called,

'Bandee!' After a fifty-foot flight, a coconut plummeted past my nose and buried itself in the mud at my feet. Milk flowed out from cracks. 'That nearly crunched your head shell.' My wau came out to deliver a message in Pidgin from the bigmen. 'The palms look over the fence, so their spirits are hazardous. You stay away from there. Got it?' The coconut fell not on a windy day but on a still one, *and* it was an unripe coconut! The evangelist Godfrey wore a balmy smile which seemed an anachronism just now. He was looking at those men displaying worried frowns about spirits.

Martin and I, ostensibly having only a stroll in the sun, flying our *waark* bull roarers, softly conversed. The Kandengai dead men used all to be buried beneath the gaigo, Martin said. Hence, despite the new Christian graveyards, the ancestral spirits were all around us. So were a few captured Palembeis, the bad people downriver, who were deposited under the main posts as gaigos were erected; the spirits preferred the victims to be planted in the foundation holes alive, he thought. Also, Alex had overheard that I was not to be told any stories of times when the spirits were angry, or they might be reminded. The bigmen had agreed on this only moments ago.

'Before you came into the nest, were you told any secret stories by men?'

'Many, but they were lies, I think. Also, there is one thing funny: old women talk that *they*, not men, were kings of the Niowra. In long ago. They had all the secrets and the men were sticked by them. That is how, today, the men are too afraid of the women taking back the secrets.'

Before dawn each day, we could now wash in the river in front of the village. We threw ourselves between the fishing canoes and splashed in the salvinia weed, around us that smell of washed-up algae. It was not a penance, though the water could be cold if the current had stirred it. Starlight tinkered on the lapping water, and in the east, over the river, its silence broken here and there with abrupt occasional splashes, the first sunlight rose in a screen of darkest red. Running back through the black village naked, skin taut, goose-pimpled and streaming with water, gave each day a delicious injection of freedom. The route took Alex past the stilts of his young wife's house. I pictured her sleeping up there, her chest quickly expanding and contracting in lonely troubled sleep. On one occasion he hesitated, not noticing he was blocking the path of Willi and myself. He gazed upward a moment, twice breathed a word I could not understand – a name? – and moved on.

The *avookwaarks* had been arguing about my physical condition. Pinga summoned me but was so heated up with chewing betelnut that he could not express himself clearly. He shouted at me for not understanding and formed a fist with a view to wheeling it into my face. Alex shuffled along to me. (How did he manage always to compress his lips like that? It must be so tiring.) It was not necessarily sensible to get involved, and he did not want to hang around here, so he spoke quickly. 'Pinga says the bigmen are going to stick us all, all right? Sebastian and Vincent are too sick to move, they talk, so they have luck. Also, Pinga says your cuts are too bad. He is your father trying to help you: you have breasts as heavy as a woman's, he says. It is not a insult. He is trying to save you. All right?'

'Can I object to not being treated like you?'

'Don't even open your lips up.'

'Well, I hope you enjoy the exercise.'

'Do not have jokes with me ever. *Ever*. I am your brother not cousin. Keep up your silly words for *him*. Or you understand *nothings* of us Sepiks. *Nothings*.'

We were pushed back to the floor by Jimmi who wanted us out of the firing line. However, the argument was knocked on the head by Rom. He was worried by the meaning of the coconut incident yesterday, and sided with Pinga.

Beyond the fence called out a slit gong of Maree-ruman spirit house. The village produced a chaotic series of yelps and screams. Martin whispered, 'Oh, how horrible – this is the dances of the *mie*.' Women would be dropping their babies, dashing to intercept two men handling pliant rods, and running the grass space from that spirit house to this. Girls apparently ripped off their dresses – we could almost hear the tearing – and bared their backs to the men, offering themselves in our place. Augusta and the *yargee* girl might be doing this for us, arching their spines to the fresh morning sun and whipping sticks. Unfortunately, the tradition was that the *mie* were never satisfied with venting their anger on the women, even if they screamed. But we heard no screams of pain, just the urgent yells to volunteer and the smacking. We imagined a line of soft shoulders with rising welts – mothers, wives, favourite girls. It was enough to make us want to jump to our feet and gladly receive our punishment, which was what we did. I was going to disobey orders and I did not care. The two *mie* were old, titchy Lamin, coughing with all this running, and Lamin Wogoo, the cool cat, faces blackened with *gook bangur kupma*, clay from Torembi, and with a white clay, *g-owindee*, cheek stripes. From their shoulders flew capes of banana leaves, they wore *swoopwee* skirts, and pretty hibiscus blossoms lay entwined in their hair.

There was too much flustering for anyone to notice me as we squabbled to get one of the seven *kwangoo*, hand drums.

'This *vee-oo* is broken,' Joel said, tapping the grey lizard drumskin.

You would have thought there were better things to worry about than whether a drumskin required another blob of beeswax to adjust its pitch.

There seemed to be a slight delay in our dance squad starting off. I knew that Kumbui was passing the bandees behind me only when he swept a knotted palm-fruit stem, usually kept for cleaning the floor, down my spine. It was very neat – he avoided all the crocodile bites. The other bandees lurched forward for their first steps, leaving me winded behind. Thung, thung, thung . . .

Singro
ongora luga. . . .

The deeper, stronger tones of Alex, Joel and Willi guided the lighter, intermittent voices onward. The air smelt of clay and the twigs breaking on the backs.

I sat indoors, alternately with Sebastian and Vincent. The dance shuffled to a halt, the slit gong sounded, women again threw themselves in front of the *mie* with valour, and again the *mie*, unsatiated, dashed in.

Afterwards wet clay did not plug the open cuts, so the bandees were covered in dust scraped off dry blocks with river mussel shells. *Kupma*, ordinary clay dust, did not help, so then a white clay, *andesaun*, was tried. Next a light sprinkling of the red *beesit* and so on.

Willi, the married bandee who never spoke, who always sat apart and who had strange, well-embedded wolf's eyes, now looked so brooding that the younger boys like Fredalin, who had established floor space near him at the far end, were scared to sit down close by. Though everyone had by now learned to pretend that any tears of theirs were only from firesmoke, Saun, for one, was desperate. He wanted to know the rules. What could he do to avoid beatings? Whether we behaved well or badly they beat us. What did they *want* of us?

Rom then announced above our heads that the spirit of the *gapmakamin*, nailfish, had used its spine to puncture Sebastian and Vincent, and *that* was why their skin was not healing.

Godfrey appeared to make his very first move. 'I will pray hard tonight,' he comforted us openly, moving between where we lay, in huge, long-trousered strides. 'The strength of Jesus is greater.'

As dark came and we left, we each had to tread on some herbs at Rom's feet. Having done this, we were cleansed. During the night I thought over Martin's answer to my question 'Why isn't Godfrey allowed to take Catholic bread and wine?' 'Arr. That is simple,' he had said. 'He keeps more than one wife.' I had given a slight snort. But Godfrey's predicament was hardly humorous, any more than it was simple: he had been polygamous before his conversion, and I wondered if his exclusion from the Christian rituals accounted for his religious fervour. Guilt?

Around the gaigo, from my left we had Tovai, the ailing moaner victimised by the spirits; young, lithe Jimmi, in mourning for the loss of a wife; Godfrey, Catholic, who seemed more relaxed today. Up to now he had sounded fed up, as if waiting for some long-overdue event; Lamin, the gambler on a bad streak; his brother Rom, his mouth audibly bubbling like a lobster's as he mumbled prayers over us. Beyond him and Yo-anga-mook and N'iangandoo at the Niowi end, was Now, 'sago', the man distinguishable by the peace that emanated from his bench space, with the smoke and sucking noises of his pipe; Anderloo, who had been known to gather fruit from the forest, and lay it before us like our collective wau – while others grew hot in angry debate, this man at most grew tepid; Kwaark, named after the hard wood which some slit gongs were made of, his voice slow and very sure; Martias, the forceful old man of severity and the long, swift stride – it was he who had helped found Timbun village, as a youth, and had leaned on Rom until he agreed to the initiation. He was positioned above Alex, Vincent and Willi. Kumbui swung his different-lengthed legs on the right-hand bench at the far end with Lamin Wogoo – whose legs had the suave, polished look of snake skin; Ban, the bat man whose knees were unattractive lumps and who had torn the ligament of his beating arm, and Bala who had helped carve the proud male figures on the posts of the Banking Corporation of PNG's Wewak branch. He had a red, burning face, I recalled. On the right, this Niamé end, was Warbee, who had gums as empty as the rest; adopted father Pinga, who shared his pliers to crack betelnuts; Johnny, who, though only a youth, leaned back confidently in debates to out-shout any of his rank, and Andrew, who leaned forward tentatively – over the Smaark bandees and myself – to help project his opinion. On each of these people – a cross-section of bullies, the bullied, the dozy, the generous, the spirit-worshipping, the God-fearing, the spiritually ambivalent – hung our comfort: even our lives, some thought.

A slit gong softly sounded one morning, warbling gently like a finch to us from through the village, near the Smaark clan. The Catholic church. It must be a Sunday. Had only eight or so days passed here?

Lamin had had a brief flirtation with Christianity. But, he said, as a punishment a crocodile ate up his son, so he converted himself back. A good gambler, he kept his religious options open now by agreeing to give the young men and boys permission to sing a couple of hymns. He left after a minute, trailing behind the other *avookwaarks*, leaving me to wonder why on earth he didn't think hymn-singing would upset the spirits, or at least undermine our belief in them. Compromise with the less spirit-fearing, soft-line bigmen for the sake of unity was surely a heavy price to pay for the potential wrath of the spirits.

We did not push our luck. The first song was subdued and rather repetitive:

> God i-gutpela
> God i-gutpela
> God i-gutpela, gutpela long mi.

'God is good, God is good, God is good, good to me.' But there were more of the same, from the *Niu Laip Singsing Buk*, and the Assembly of God at the Niowi end also did their repertoire – lots of hymns with 'Hallelujahs'. The Catholic and AOG tunes once or twice were in harmony, refrains occasionally echoed, but more often collided over the central giant crocodiles and seemed to fight for dominance. Johnny led the Catholics; the AOGs got on with singing their own favourites by themselves. The remaining men yakked to themselves regardless, or looked at their feet, awkwardly humming the tunes.

Long after the words we had sung had died away, their message of love and charity hung above us, like a protective mantle. Though Godfrey was away – at church? – he must be delighted: the Christian God had made it into the spirits' house at an initiation. Instinct told every bandee to foster this newly arrived Christian love-spirit, whether we had formed any religious convictions about it or not. The *avookwaarks*, on returning, induced by the atmosphere of good humour, made us drunk with betelnuts for sport.

'What are we doing, Martin?' I asked, as we hallooed and stamped up and down the gaigo in a rolling conga line.

'We are being a man crocodile who is lonely for a girl crocodile who is pretty.'

The dance got wilder. Swaying, I turned my palm apron round, then waggled it from my rear as if I were a dabbling duck. The bigmen clapped, hooted, bawled: 'Haaaaaaaa! Man, man, man!' When they had tired of us, we were sent outside to sober up by running five circuits around the spirit house. Alex and I raced to the finish, and for that we would all be punished – no reason given. Stens, delivering one of his hot, loud breaths, said 'We are sex brothers. Bandees can love not fight bandees.'

In the last light, after the more septic scabs had been peeled off in the usual way, with a mussel valve, the egrets sailed through the sky from the river to their night roosts behind the nest. We were positioned around the grass in a semi-circle. Lamin was sat on a *t'gurt* in front, we at his stubby little feet, waiting for him to speak. Watching through our eyebrows, we saw the egrets time their awkward landings on the slender branches. It was good to think they had been out with the women, fishing all day. At dawn we saw them flopping off their perches to accompany the girls on the river. To us the gentle white birds had come to embody female loved ones. If only, I thought, one clean plume would sail down here to me, then I would spring to catch it before it touched the dust. I would smuggle it out of the nest and keep it in my mosquito net for nights. One day, I thought, I would give it to the *yargee* girl, return it to that free bird.

'We are Kavaaks, Niowras,' Lamin said in Pidgin. 'We, as you all know, are of the senior Niowra village – the originals, the greatest. Our fathers were founders of Nyaurengai, Japanaut, Japandai, Yenchen-mangua, Yamanumbu and,' Lamin spat, 'Korogo.' Was it a bad betelnut or the name of the rival gambling village that left a bad taste in his mouth? 'Head lower, bandee,' he said, kicking Saun. 'We are Amwaarks, crocodile people – other Sepiks are scared of us. Of course they are, because when *you* are hatched into crocodiles, we make life nasty. The Chambris, Palembeis, Blackwater villages – you name it, their ceremonies are pathetic. The boys aren't beaten sufficiently, if at all. What's more, your crocodile marks are more extensive than any in Niu Gini. When you leave, you'll lift your head high and say "I've been schooled as well as any man in the world – that means like those yellow [Chinese] storemen in Wewak, the whites and the blacks." Yeah, you may well smile, bandee,' he tweaked Norbet, Now's adopted son, with his short, fat toe. The boy lowered his head to between his folded knees. 'You wear these marks, yet you don't even show respect to fellow bandees. You compete. You tease – if one boy tends to a sick bandee, another sniggers that the first is the bandee's wife. You certainly don't revere *avookwaarks*. You want me to spell it out? All right, here: I'm telling you that you will honour your marks before you leave the *waarkdumba*. You will honour them with all your heart before you are with your families again. It will take . . . about a year at this rate. You won't like a stay that long, I expect . . . That is all I have to say. Bandee, pick up the stool.' Saun picked up the *t'gurt*. Lamin shuffled off.

'Shit!' said Joel. 'Kumbui was six months in the Aurimbit nest, Benedix. Bigmen, they planted a banana [palm] when he went in, gave him a more long and more long neck rope. It was like a snake strangulating him, and they didn't unwind him free until the banana was flowered.'

We sat, hating the mosquitoes, waiting for dark, and Johnny chucked betelnut shells from his bench and laughed when Saun, 'the koala kid', winced.

'Pick it up, bandee.'

Chapter Fifteen

The poor women; on Thursdays they paddled north to Torembi, and swapped fish for sago. On Fridays it was to Pagwi market for more. If they were not capturing the fish the women were boiling or smoking them on the clay bowls traded from Aibom, the Chambri Lakes village.

It was as if we were dead there in the nest, daubed in the same grey as the mud ground. Now we were dead; eventually we would emerge spiritually 'born again'. Joel discovered that by building up clay on our heads, we could harden it into a helmet to keep the heat in at night. That was not the problem at present. We had not been beaten for two days, and a pride of bigmen was pacing up and down.

Lamin Wogoo was fretting and strutting, with his cigarette hand behind his back at the upper limits of our permitted view. He had that silver hair, with well-toned rolls of muscle which I had already seen on occasions when he came out to scourge us; but what sort of face? Martin had once whispered that his eyes had 'the glints of the crocodiles'. I could imagine those eyes skimming up and down our backs to see how we were healing. From the sacred heart of Yo-anga-mook, he drew out three green rods, which he must have cut the previous night.

Saun could not contain his fidgeting fingers, and for our sakes went outside before it was too late. It was a sign of responsibility from him — his first? He walked with slack shoulders, loosely swinging his spindly arms and his long, juvenile legs. As he hurled a *waark* his short apron rose; Lamin saw his chance to pounce: the bandee's sparse strands of pubic hair showed no sign of grey clay. They were starkly black, unpainted. Punishable! The gaigo rumbled, banged, and clattered as men spilled from the bandhus and swept us outside to work us over.

Later, Rom had a hacking cough, and bruised his ribs straining with it. He, the man meant to be watching over the gaigo, pottered off home. He had never before left us like this. If God, offended at the paganism, or spirits — bad or angry — had wanted to punish, now was the time, I mused, not very seriously. *He that believeth not . . . the wrath of God abideth on him.*

I had fresh watery blood from some fissures on my chest. Pinga said I had scratched them. I could not contradict, so said I did not understand, and in his language, not Pidgin, to stress my link with Kandengai: '*wun ana yaravok kowoon*'. Jimmi gave me a warning raised eyebrow. Would anyone have believed me anyway – that my digestion was not coping with excess sago, raw waterlily pods, shrimps whose feelers irritated the mouth, and the never-ending fish? I strained so much over the lavatory pit that my wounds opened up. Joel whispered 'Shit!' with apprehension as I was run out into the daylight for an inspection – the clay over us faithfully recorded any scratch marks we made while soothing our itching marks. My clean coat validated my unspoken claim, and I was let off the hook. Who would have thought that these were relatively carefree moments. They were to become steadily rarer.

In the yellow light of the evening the *avookwaarks* 'suggested' we should play. We played, teased the *mondeavan* bird by goose stepping.

Wavee mondeavan
tamba mondeavan
man cloandoo
tamba cloandoo
beegor maroome ree
kambu dumweavan.

'*Mondeavan*, close your legs, close your arms, the spear is missing you.' We kicked our feet out three times, first left: 'Ka, ka, ka!' Then right: 'Ka, ka, ka!'

The *kwaik*, a nasty bird said to hang around graveyards and to have a taste for human flesh, was satirised by Martin, who shared its clan. He crow-hopped, while Sebastian yelled, 'Ko, ko, ko, ko, ko!' – the cry that gives children nightmares.

It was an earth tremor, one strong enough even to raise the sick to their feet. And it was the very first 'odd happening'. We were staring up at the black shiny timbers afterwards. Jimmi told us that it was the twelfth day we had been in the nest.

Earthquakes were not uncommon in this locality, every two years on average; however this one, the *avookwaarks* were murmuring, was centred on the gaigo. Rom was summoned from his house. We waited. Martias, the Timbun bigman, pondered aloud: why are the spirits angry? Saun was smoothing his fingers through his mosquito whisk, Steven was working his toes into the floor mud. They were a little apprehensive. Joel, Sebastian and Alex thought it amusing. If the spirits actually existed these days, then their Christian faith would protect them anyway. To me, an earthquake was a geological adjustment, nothing more. I wanted attainment of these crocodile people's knowledge of the soul of nature, not the superstition that they had spliced into that knowledge.

Rom broke the news. As a result of the quake a girl had plucked up courage and revealed what for ages had been an open secret among the market women: Koma, who had finally promised to sacrifice a pig for the Niowis before the initiation, was seen on a wild spending spree in Pagwi soon afterwards. The pig itself had disappeared, but one with the same pretty black polka dots on its ears had been bought by the Bruruis, and was settling in nicely. The bigmen had been made a laughing stock. And the spirits had not received half the main sacrifice. I glanced up to Godfrey — it was worth any consequence — and I thought that, deep within his beard, he was smiling again.

Koma was summoned; a canoe was sent to Pagwi for him. We waited. Our *waark* paddles sighed and whizzed in the afternoon air. People said the adult-sized ones could be heard in Suapmeri, twelve miles down the river, near the Palembeis.

Koma arrived; he had been on the meths. He ignored the curses flung at him from the benches and said he did not know what the fuss was about. No one had died; no one had been seriously ill even. Come on everyone, let's admit it. The spirits had lost their power to Jesus and to the up-and-coming generation of his converts. Rom had a coughing spasm and was led away to have a quiet lie-down.

At the evening meal, the frogs were loud in their elastic-popping din. On the other side of our screen Rhonda, presumably around the wall fireplace with other girls, spoke up so we could hear: Imelda was sick. Before they slept, the girls lined up outside our screen, and as was the custom from time to time, shook our hands through it. We had to be silent, but they sighed, said their names, requested us in turn and our touch reassured them that we were all right. Rhonda's grip was strong. I closed her hand in mine and squeezed tenderly to express my gratitude for the (ghastly) food she was supplying me with. Imelda's hand was absent.

Sleep seemed further away than ever. The frogs chirruped, cicadas grated. My chest was raging hot. I waited on all fours until called to the nest before cockcrow. Could the earthquake have been stage-managed by bigmen to reinforce the fear of spirits in the bandees? To state that *these* forces, not the Christian God, were in control? It was odd that it had occurred then, linking in so conveniently with the unhappy news about the pig sacrifice, but it was inconceivable that it was centred on the gaigo. Nevertheless I felt uncomfortable about the whole incident. It was so claustrophobic in the nest: the walled-off world was no doubt designed to stop us initiates thinking objectively. I wondered why Godfrey the Christian had chosen not to act against the initiation yet.

Or was he mixed up in this somehow, and just *had* acted, and aimed to give us an overdose of evil spirits so that we would run to Jesus? It really was getting very difficult to think sensibly, being removed from all the usual Western reference points of rationality – Oh for an encyclopaedia or a compendium of *facts*!

In the morning the *avookwaarks* reflected that our bites were healing up, no one was noticeably ill and it was a fair gamble that the spirits did not mind not getting the pig. The last initiation had been in 1977 at the Aurimbit gaigo, yet now it seemed that all the rituals *had* been remembered correctly from that time. That little flush of panic yesterday was over. Indeed, why not bring more boys in from the village as planned?

Anderloo brought us *paniangra*, the star fruit. The juice was sweet and stopped us vomiting as we ate fish after fish. A splendid man, almost an *avookwaark*, hairy and grey and proud, it was the third time he had put a tray of food down for us, ignoring the derision spouting from the benches – we were his *keeandas*, wives who bickered incessantly with one another. His bare feet trod carefully between us as if we were pieces of broken glass.

Stens said, his hot lips in my ear, that if we picked the yellow, shiny *paniangra* fruit which hung like stretched stars over the fence, 'we drink our bloods'.

'You mean our blood has been licked up by the tree?'

He shied away. 'I must not talk. I must not make you plenty stories to your notebook. I too small. I have mother's blood. I am belly.' He scuttled off.

Willi, the tall, sunken-eyed, silent bandee, who roamed alone and pierced you with one of his notorious stares if you disturbed him from his lonely longing for his wife, had to abandon his carving of a mask because he had *yapalli*. It was a wrenching stomach pain caused by angry spirits, Rom said, so we all had to walk religiously on herbs to cleanse ourselves. Everything had to be correct before more boys joined us in the nest, to come of age.

With only a delicate, sharp slice of moon in the sky we trudged homeward, uttering our *swé* whistles. I slipped into my mosquito net early, suffering from diarrhoea, and suddenly had the chance to watch those who queued up to shake hands with the bandees through the screen. Several girls, including Rhonda and Imelda, who was apparently no longer ill, were waiting passively in the diffuse, smoky light behind Sebastian's little brother Elijah, whose face looked at our cubicle with awe and reverence. The girls' uncovered breasts were smooth globes which looked soft and warm in the firelight. Three girls were obviously the favourites of these Smaark boys. They tied string gently round the bandees' wrists as tokens of their thoughts. When the girls withdrew their hands they too had a bracelet of string, which they held up to display to their girl friends. There would be trouble if either boy or girl let the tokens drop off before they next entwined fingers. Joel next morning said he no longer wanted to escape to a rock group. The bride his family had been forcing on him he now longed for day and night. He was in love, he confided.

The morning breeze from the village was silent. We chucked no *waarks*, and were silent also, as the new candidates without chat dragged new fronds up to restore the withering fence. We caught glimpses of their unpatterned skin through the old brown, curled leaves. Did they occasionally glimpse us in our prison?

Rom offered a branch of betelnuts to the Niowi and Niamé halves; a peace offering to settle any unknown disputes. We must be united, and there must be no neglected rituals *this* time. There was mounting excitement, but also the daily inconveniences, the scraping down of those milky sores that remained.

The air hung empty without our crocodile 'breathing' sounds; the village hush was expectant. Smoking fish smells never came our way. The crocodiles desired more boys and the families were troubled. Soon the fence would be opened and we would dance, as the Timbun youths had for us. We put on an extra smart grey layer, and *swoopwees*, to replace our sacred aprons, which were hidden. Our neck ropes were taken off – it felt as though shackles were being removed – and we laid one scarlet leaf each in the clay bed of our hair stubble. This was our entitlement – one *nambumangua*, to say we had already witnessed one intake of boys: ourselves.

The women were hopping and chattering like sparrows outside, waiting to see whether a crocodile would come out of the nest, or not appear at all, like the last time. Only Rom knew.

We, the bandees, were ushered together, and crowded round the screened-off pool adjoining the fence. The screen was parted and we watched one of the most secret of all sights – that of the sacred crocodiles, threshing in the ooze, and rising and gurgling in the water. The palm enclosure bowed over the pool, shielding it from the sun, but there was enough light to see the *avookwaarks   not human these – side* by side, lurking in the muddy water, in the grip of two naked men, who were adorning the forms with *largee* leaves, and a sago and coconut mix, *manchan*, parcelled up with red and yellow ribbons of foliage, worn like a scarf around their necks. I may not describe them to you more. 'They are getting excited,' Jimmi said, holding his *avookwaark* more tightly between his thighs.

The glare of the New Guinea sun was fast softening; time for the crocodile to begin stirring. Johnny took the adult *waark* paddle and raised it high on its bark string. It hung, twisting, untwisting, as Johnny paused, taut. He looked to Rom, and Rom nodded. The *waark* flew high as Johnny spun his arm; it released a heavy, throaty whoop of a vast crocodile. A *gowa*, a flat palm spathe, was smashed to the ground – the crocodile beating its tail. Five, *tambanak*, times the sounds were made. Rom pummelled Yo-anga-mook, and with the roar released by the spirit, the fence was parted, revealing – though we were forbidden to look – freedom, compassionate femininity. We sensed the wall of pretty cotton materials and waving soft bodies, and so wanted to caress and smell them.

Now, a first burble from the pool, and another, probably the second *avook*. They seemed to surge alternately, *tambanak* times – the revered number – responding approvingly to each other's pulsations. A final smack from a tail and we were orchestrated to let out two cries: 'Yeeeeeeeeeeee-a! Yeeeeeeeeeeee-a!'

The *provook* dance began; no words, but pounding of drums, feet, hooting of *kook*, the conch shells. We hardened out the muds, and jerked to a halt; into our silence flowed the hum of women and their offspring. We screamed and the two hidden *avookwaarks* were thrusting their bodies through the waters in time, now as one.

After the fifth *provook* dance, the men, the crocodile spirit incarnate, began to weave a line outside, Rom at the head, *nambuwaark*, Lamin rear man, *giniwaark*, dragging a leaf flag, the tail itself, *avooknagini*, behind. We were slipped amid the men, soft yellow palm-shoot sprays in our hands. We stepped out, heads down, to a painful, transient freedom. Hundreds of eyes darted along us, checking us off. *Yes, seventeen all safe*. But in what condition? I listened above our song for the characteristic tones of various girls, strained to twist my line of sight up to the bright splashes of favourite dresses. It was little use, and we ourselves could not be easily distinguishable to our beloveds in our dirt uniforms, bloated and bent double. But each apparent recognition of a bandee was signalled by a pitiful wail.

Are you out there watching me, Augusta? Is that your poppy-red dress I can see from the corner of my eye? And yargee girl, with your open face (tilted proudly back), which I only remember wearing an unrestrained offering smile – are your child's eyes on me?

Ours was a song of the Yaark and Posago clans and we named their crocodile ancestors:

Maingowee,
Mainbangur,
Rurumbit bangur,

Kwarimbit bangur,
Savoowarn. . . .

We sang a verse:

Veendoo-a kwandoo-a
Karavee-a karaniaga
Vindoo-a kwandoo-a
Sévee-a Sétambanja.

'You fighting men, muscle men, strong chicken [called] Karavee-a, gather your spears, gather your *tambanjas* [fighting trophies].'

The crocodile was noble, self-assured in the knowledge of its strong pedigree. We, its clutch, were proud to march with it on our five outings, and when the old women began teasing, jabbing at our feet with pronged fishing spears, as they might fend off any crocodile, we did not flinch.

In the last light we reappeared, sloping out to a plaintive tune. 'Ooooo-a! Ooooo-a! Mothers, you have given up your boys before. Please, the time has come. Please gather up some more.' We circled as if in a search for more bandees, rounding them up.

Bunjim, bunjima bunjime
Bunjim, bunjima bunjime
Nianandige bandee andege
Eniana a waar
Eebandee o waara

Ooooo-a! Ooooo-a!

How many boys were out there waiting, shaven-headed, I wondered? Had the bigmen chosen to risk putting all their eggs in one basket? And why not – who seriously could believe in the power of the spirits any more, anyway?

Chapter Sixteen

Our dreams were swayed by dance noise from the gaigo and in the morning we were witnesses to the last throes of a feast – our Niowra neighbours had come for a party. We blinked through the smoke haze at benches crammed with flaking paint on flesh, crumpled feather plumes and leaves on the wilt. We had to push discarded betelnut shells to make sitting space, and drunk uncivil Korogo men spat on us with saliva red from the betelnut.

The shaven boys, we knew, must be lining up, strapping on their *swoopwee* leaves, treasuring their betelnuts, and trying to be brave in front of their weeping sisters and mothers.

The crocodile slapped its heavy tail and shifted in the mud, bubbling and lolloping. The front of the fence was opened up. The women peeked from a distance as the dawn air cleared, and we manoeuvred in five flag-waving dances. The *avookwaarks* left us, fastening the fence up, to perform the dance of the crocodile, *kuta*, one time. Six men beat both Yo-anga-mook and N'iangandoo, who produced a thunder that blotted out every other noise. The *avookwaarks* set out again, the second time, *vrerook*. We upturned the dugouts which had been brought in under cover of the dark. Jeff had once said that if you turned a live crocodile upside down it would lie still and helpless. These smooth canoe bellies were like those pale undersides, the carved snouts and cowrie eyes pressed against the mud.

The outsiders were wailing by the time it was dance number three, *koowook*. The *avookwaarks* walked out while the crocodiles rumbled again. The bigmen showed the mothers their hands – empty: the crocodiles are ready to take their boys away. A fourth dance, *vruk*, and the fifth, *tambanak*; the final, awful crocodiles' deafening roar, and the quiet that followed.

Kumbui was outside with the *koonongoo* boys. They had no right to walk in here – this was *our* nest – the nest of us seventeen bandees. They must break in. Kumbui beat a hole through with a *waarleeyaark*, a special staff. But we had anticipated that and created a blaze from firewood and crackling dry leaves. It greeted him as he fell through the fence. He stamped it dead with his crusted old feet, and beckoned the boys in. At last we could see their shiny smooth heads, like oil-dipped coconuts in old husk surrounds. That was *all* we could see, as their fathers or waus were splayed over their shoulders, about to walk the gauntlet of *avookwaarks* who would club them, while we sang on either side. Thwack! Thwack! went the blows. The men had their eyes shut, and the bandees beneath steered them forward. Lest they went too fast, Kumbui at the front blocked their way, slowed by his arthritic leg joints.

Thirteen new bandees! The village must have been emptied of older boys, and there was Edward with his holy grin and ox-shouldered Nicholas who paddled me to Kandengai. The thirteen waus' shoulders were lumpy and striped; pieces of flayed stick and green bark hung off them. The new bandees looked around, bewildered. We went from boy to boy, shaking hands with them, pretending it was not as bad as it was. They did not say a word; their eyes were fixed on the bellies of the canoes awaiting them. The day was overcast. Outside the women's moans sounded exhausted; they would stop soon. We felt it our duty to sing with all our might, to beat the drum lizard skin, regardless of whether our palms were sore.

Not before time the new bandees lay indoors glistening with *gwak* oil, the rags used to mop up were tossed to the river, the crocodiles' habitat. The *avookwaarks* walked out to the women, bearing leaves in their mouths to show that the biting was finished. Rom, in rare exuberance, directed an additional performance: each new bandee was heaped naked on to the back of his wau, dried cruelly with orange balls of flame from old fishing traps ignited and pitched up to him, and paraded outside the fence, looking as lifeless as old suits taken out for an airing.

The new boys were sent to sleep with the *gowi* flute tune – you could hear the eagle soar, hover and drop to its prey – and woken with a rain of clubs. That night one of the new bandees slept on his side, and so, instead of hymns, this Sunday the new bandees were pushed up to the fence to call for protection from waus who, a little too optimistically, were having a lie-in. 'Sangeeran, come quickly! The dark clouds [bigmen] are about to bring rain [sticks down on us].'

When it came the dance was a game of heroics; we, the older bandees, were learning the art of self-sacrifice as we shielded the delicate new intakes.

Nee-aitoo neeambundoo
boonee, boonee, ana cowoontee
yaark, yaark, cowoontee

Yeeeeeeeeeeee-a!
Yeeeeeeeeeeee-a!

'Father and older brother, I didn't sleep on my back, back, I slept on my belly, belly.'

The bigmen, not in a mood to tolerate the Sabbath nonsense today, drew more blood from us than ever before. Maybe too much. Many bandees were feverish by the afternoon, and I was not feeling one hundred per cent myself. I was also low on aspirins and restricted my general distribution service. That was something few boys could accept – white men could produce anything. Martin alone understood: 'Go away, you silly boy. His medicines are small, and he is saving them for dying bandees.'

Joel's fever was bad. He was lifted on to a bench and covered in a sheet. Allowed up on to a *jambur*! But he was not authorised to curl up or lie on his back, of course.

The new bandees lay like polished brass ornaments with freshly applied oil. They had smooth, tight folds of muscle, whereas our skin was inflated, lacklustre. Our smothering of dry clay made us corpse-like and sprayed from us if we swished mosquitoes. 'The *bynaypee* is flying overhead,' Martin said, lying downwind of a fire, hoping smoke would sting the eyes of the mosquitoes more than his. A *bynaypee* is a bird that comes this far inland prior to a storm. Martin was referring to an air of foreboding over the bigmen. They were definitely unsettled by the sight of so many bandees spread flat before them. Rom said it was the work of spirits – they probably *were* angry at the lack of Koma's pig. *Now* he tells us!

Outside, black-freckled chickens squeezed through the fence and fought for possession of a grasshopper. Japanese and Sepik, Lamin's dogs, sat at his feet. (The third, Boss, had disappeared, 'taken by spirits'.) All had the pink blotto eyes of their owner. If we accidentally touched them or they us, while flapping away the flies on their raw ears, they had to be eaten.

My father, Pinga, called me to cheer the gaigo up and we hopped together like two fighting cocks, getting two encores; even Kennedy smiled at me. 'You are a good boy,' he said afterwards. 'You have made the bigmen better.' This, from Kennedy, was like an affectionate kiss.

Day by day the bigmen's hot sticks had been doing their work, welding us together.

A parcel was handed to me: my heart rose . . . then sank. It was an extra large fish and a colossal slab of sago. But the label read: 'To Benedik from Augusta', in loose twisted capitals, each of which gave me a warm *buzz in my stomach. How I long for your company, Augusta, your tender presence.* I wrote back, 'Augusta. *Thank you* for the beautiful food. I enjoyed it very much. See you again later. Benedik.' If only she knew her present was a torture. I could only hope next time she would just send a note – *but please do send a note, Augusta. You, or your friend.*

No *waark* called us from our houses the next morning. Something was wrong, and we could smell worry in the last cold dark as we were led back to the nest. Inside, we heard that a man had died at Nyaurengai.
   'He was old, Martin?'
   'A young man.'
   'He'd been sick for ages?'
   'A night and a little.'
   Was this it? The punishment from the spirits? Rom tackled the problem quietly on his bench. Until the man was planted in the ground we could not eat or swing the *waarks*; it was as if the crocodiles were absent, in hiding.
   Soon, life went back to 'normal'. The man's death was nothing to do with us, it was Nyaurengai's problem, Rom had divined. Once their slit gongs called that the man was installed underground, our crocodile spirit came to life with a slap of the tail, a rupturing cry and a rolling bellow.

Now aprons had been issued to the new boys, they had been coated in grey, and had neck ropes chewing at their throats just like us. When the time came for the food chase, Nicholas casually enveloped Johnny in his huge arms – like inner tyre tubes – and plucked the basket off him without giving him the chance even for a struggle.
   New and old bandees were starting to look similar, and the bigmen sought to join us emotionally more tightly. In the sunlight, we were stood in a ring, facing inwards, stepping to the beat of our drums, while circled by the bat, Ban, who swirled and flickered over us using a dry, knobbly palm stem across our skulls. It was the sound of a heavy man wiping his feet on a coarse mat, and we were not singing, so any vocal noises we made – gasps, yells, coughs – were exposed for all to hear. When the time came for the striking of Sebastian and Steven, who were doing a drum duet in the middle, the thump of their palms and soles neither slowed nor dulled.
   Alex's jaw ballooned up; Kenny, brought here from the town and six feet tall, had an eye that puffed out like pastry. Joel's nose pumped out blood. It was all the biggest bandees – the potential leaders were being quashed. I was let off lightly, presumably because I was not about to

start a rebellion against a ceremony I had prompted myself. Lawrence, who anyway only had one useful eye – the second was milky, like that of a boiled fish – could hardly see to get back indoors. The other older bandees were seething with resentment, and thus so was I. Our individuality had been worked on so hard that now our loyalty was mostly to each other. We hated the cruellest bigmen, and would not submit by respecting them.

To keep us from brooding, the bigmen kept us on the move while putting on our evening clay, forbade us to cluster, sent Johnny to space our legs and bend us over, so bigmen could check that absolutely every square inch of us was coated. Our stomachs were prodded to see how well we were putting on weight. When we dried off, circling around in the last sunlight as it came through slits in the trees, men indoors yelled that I must have been evading the force feeding, because I would *dee*, shit, more otherwise. The younger bandees – Florian, Steven, Sebastian, Saun – had already been broken and were quiet. They spent most of their time staring – not tearful, because that was an offence.

Martin whispered that night, 'The *avookwaarks* do not know all things, you know.'

'Shut up, Martin,' said Sebastian in Pidgin. 'Why don't you surrender, like us?'

Martin's theory was that once the *uk-kung* owl called in the night, it was sufficiently late for the bigmen to be asleep; we could turn on to our backs. He would try it that night.

After the owl called out 'uk-kung', I opened my eyes sharply. Something was moving about near me in the night. It was heavy and threatening. Could it truly be that our senses had become so attuned to danger, because of all the persecution? Thunk! The sound could have been from fingers slapped across a loosely stretched drum skin, but it was not, because it was chased by a terrible cry, clear and loud. It echoed in two sentences. 'Ha-eee-haa! Ha-eee-haa!' A Sepik boy does not cry out 'Ow!' in pain; instead he makes a yelp with his throat stretched out. The dark was almost absolute, and because my body was programmed to expect punishment, I defensively doubled up on my knees, swelled my back muscles, for a blow. No pain came, there was only the sound of fast, choked breathing from the neighbouring mosquito nets, and, fading away across the village grasses, the padding feet of two men – each presumably carrying a *mie si jai*, slit-gong club. I heard a deep snigger – Joel's. Martin's little experiment had failed. The *avookwaarks did* know everything.

Towards morning the fishing women were setting out; a laugh, impatient murmurings – they were waiting for a latecomer. They spoke through their teeth – from the chill? The paddles knocked on the canoe sides; women coughed and hissed as they worked hard, steering through the weed.

Willi, with his lonely eyes and his ear mauled like one of Jeff's dogs', pining for his wife, had decided to risk a visit that same night. Martin said next morning, 'He slid across the *gepma* [house], to her as she lay asleeping. He put his hand on her little mouth, and whispered she can not scream out. "Sssss. It is only your big Willi." She was too frightened, because the bandee was daring to talk. "Will you make a *yargee* cigarette, my darling lovely?" he said.'

I said, 'What then?'

'That is all. He was sliding away like a grey snake. He lay lonely with his cigarette. Morning came up and you know that the women talk when on the waters, hunting for *makaus*. She talked to Alex's wife, and Alex's wife talked the story to the whole world.' So now the broken custom had been discovered, the initiation suspended while the spirits were appeased. A man called Patrick had also struck his wife: not uncommon, but occurring during an initiation, the violence was also an affront to custom and so to the ancestral spirits.

It was possible the whole village might be punished, the men blacken their faces and sweep through Kandengai killing any livestock or dogs in their path; but the women – now restricted to their mosquito nets, awaiting a decision – were too weak from fishing to keep thirty bandees stuffed full. Rom said the spirits might only want a duck or two from the offender. We would risk it.

The crocodiles roared that the initiation was in progress again. Soon a present came from Imelda and Rhonda – a *yimbununga*, giant mosquito swat they had made for Sebastian and me to share, a painful souvenir of the world out there. Now the Yenchenmangua bigmen wanted to come along and beat us. The last time, in 1976 maybe, the Yenchenmanguas almost did away with some Kandengai bandees, Martin said. Later the Kandengais asked very nicely if they might return the favour to the Yenchenmangua bandees. The Yenchenmanguas said no.

Lamin stood to make a speech beside N'iangandoo. He said if those 'fugging' Yenchenmanguas laid one hand on his boys, he would quite simply order the bandees to 'kill 'em'.

'Man, man, man!' The men hooted.

'Yes, fugging kill 'em.'

'Man, man. Haaaaaaa!'

'With their bare hands!'

'Man, man. Haaaaaaa!'

Lamin was in his best brawling form, his gambling mode; how everyone liked to see him, his eyes without that blotchy look. Martin said: 'Benedix, they love us really.' As if to prove it, that day they beat us only lightly. Anderloo, whose feet usually negotiated around us so considerately, today was remarkably clumsy and heavy. He tripped over Steven and spilt the sugar cane he had brought us as a treat. He said he was overtired. That was about the last we saw of him.

'Can't you stop his weeps?' Alex said, tutting the way only he did as he slackened his lips to speak. I was sitting over the young bandee Florian, who had a rabbit's-like nose. Rom had been making chants over him; my only medicine now was outboard-motor fuel to close the cuts. We all had back strain, but Florian's was worse than anyone's, because he could not stretch himself – it set him 'leaking' again. I got permission to knead his lumbar vertebrae with my knuckles, trying to press his spine back into shape.

'*Koa?* You are all right?' I asked, in the local language.

'*Kai,*' he sniffed. 'No.'

Alex wiped Florian's eyes so the bigmen would not see he had been crying – such a waste of much-needed supplies of cotton wool.

Apart from Florian, we were all in reasonably good health. It seemed a funny time for Rom to be sitting on his bench, curled up worrying about the spirits being angry with us. His blood was hot, he said. More than it had ever been.

Chapter Seventeen

I asked Godfrey what was so wrong with spirit worship. He brushed down his smooth town trousers to his fleshy bare feet. He spoke with ease in his practised English.

'The gods of the clans are never pleased. They are greedy. They always want sacrifices.'

'Doesn't the Christian God demand prayers and praise and ask you to give up your goods as well?'

'No. Well . . . yes.'

'But, anyway, the spirits do exist, you think?'

'Of course. A Gama woman disappeared. She had only walked into the bush to cut bamboos. Her clan didn't know why the spirits had taken her, but they made peace with them two moons on – killed a pig. Before nightfall, she was returned. It was like she has fallen asleep all that time.'

Was Rom perhaps losing his nerve? Did he think he ought to let us leave the nest while the going was good? The spirits were definitely troubling him.

At evening meal time Sebastian, Joel, Martin, Kennedy and Stens looked less pensive than usual in the firelight. Saun never looked pensive anyway – as we sat cross-legged, he ground imaginary mosquitoes to death on the ball of my left foot, with the handle of his swat. The pots smelt of fish and *tulef*, the tasty greens, as usual – all except mine, in which bobbed chicken. This was *my* night, my turn to hear the sacred words, to be given a secret name, and my wau had killed his best rooster for me.

We all crouched in the shadow slashed firelight, eyeing the chicken growing cold. The women were silent. A chant wafted through the fence over me, the voice of Lamin Wogoo. It spoke in his mechanical way, but fast, as men do when sweating with the heat of betelnut. The chant was a list of what seemed to be ancestral crocodile nests:

Tornagundumba,
Maivernavundumba,

Waymareedumba,
Waynagwandumba. . . .

I was hypnotised by the rhythm, now of the names of ancestral bandees:

Jeerangoomaree,
Vandungoomaree,
Kee-kee yoweemaree. . . .

The end – the only movement the smoke and the mosquitoes filtering up through the floor from between the stilts, driven by the special anti-*kubia* fire lit down there for us.

I rose, stepped up to the fence. I put my left ear to where it rustled, warm hands extended and clapped around my head. This would be my secret, spiritual name; handed down with clan-lore over the generations; it would be unique to me; die with me. Having it would give me the strength of the ancestor to whom it once belonged. A hot breath was against my ear; a jaw, chewing at the betelnut, panting. The smell of betelnut breath – like the crushed laurel leaves white men's children put in jam jars to gas moths for specimen boxes. 'Ahhh,' he breathed. He was remembering. 'Ahhh . . .' And the name tumbled from his mouth. It was very long, about eight syllables, and I worried that I would not remember it.

'*Hay*,' he said, not using Pidgin. 'Go.'

I nodded, though he could not see me. Our heads parted, I was one step further to being 'a crocodile'. And somewhat more strongly tied to nature, to the life system. But would the crocodile transformation be real if the Niowra spirits did not convince us of their direct involvement in these ceremonies? I could only say no.

The new bandees had been in the nest a week, we for three. Their neck ropes were as hard, their skirts as brown and dry. With a brood of thirty, this crocodile nest – which I had started – to my knowledge dwarfed any the mighty lowland Sepik had lately seen. And still no evidence had appeared to point firmly to the spirits' active contribution, I thought in the quietness after the second morning meal.

Crotchety old Tovai laid a slither of *yargee* on a fire log, to steam some water off before curling it up for a cigarette. A cream-coloured grub worked its way out of a hole in the log, which was getting hotter as the wood was shunted little by little into the fire, burning up. The grub decided to work itself back into the hole again, then out, then in, and a compromise: half in, half out. Kumbui and Lamin blew the sacred flutes, releasing the call of the spirit lodged inside. Each of the tunes' moods were triggered off by the lead flautist touching the foot of the other. The grub in the log turned brown, stiff and crisp.

That evening Steven, swinging his *waark*, struck down a shrew-bodied bat. He stretched the wings between his lips and made them whistle, as the bat gnashed its needle teeth. Later, Sebastian, who said it was a *buym-bway*, lifted it into the air. We watched as the bat climbed, spiralling up to the freedom denied to us.

Another Sunday passed by, only the odd prayer or two allowed. The rain came down in irregular splutters that night and the puddles along the path were warm to our toes at dawn. I made a worrying discovery: boils under my armpits. The bigmen would say I had been breaking customs.

'What's wrong, Benedix?' Martin said. 'Your *kisegraak* [armpit] is ill?'

'Nothing, nothing.'

I later confided in him.

'What? This is badness. I can tell the men quick. This is you breaking rules.'

'You don't really believe all that. It's superstition. Poppycock.'

For now Martin agreed to keep quiet.

Though we worried we would be beaten in the rain – we could easily imagine how the sticks would feel on wet skin – again there was no beating. Why not?

'I tell you, Benedix, the bigmen are afraid. Somethings terrible are to happen.'

It was easy to laugh away Martin's remarks, but soon it appeared that everything was not well in the village. That very night there was not enough food for us and we discovered that our stomachs now actually *required* to be stuffed four times daily. In the night women were crying, feeling they had failed us.

Other unusual things happened. That morning, Rom called me before him to extract a promise that I would not tell certain things to anyone once I had left Kandengai: especially thirteen secret words labelling public and private parts of the male and female anatomy, the nature of either spirit in the mud pool, names of neck ropes and mosquito swats, and a few customs more that I have not mentioned here, such as a type of string we used. Rom said bandees might not talk about their crocodile marks, or venture down the badly screened path to the loo unless wearing a long, long wig of palm shoots, a *nambu mais*, to disguise themselves. Nor might bandees touch the benches from now on. All rules were being tightened up, we gathered. However, Wumbunavan, the *saun waark*, white crocodile, might use a stool to help him when writing. The inference was they wanted me to get my recording done *now* – while there was still the opportunity.

Kumbui took us outside, whirling a stick like a shepherd's crook. He said this was what he would remove our heads with if we ever breathed

193

any secrets to the women or children. Wide-framed Nicholas, in his hovel under the bench, overheard that we were not being beaten because the bigmen wanted us stronger. Why? Why? Why?

Rom was growing weak eating so little. Though he had no teeth, he could not slice up food with a knife – it would, he mumbled, be like cutting a hole in our protective fence.

Two coconuts dropped together from a tree, almost cracking open the heads of two bandees. Another accident? For Martin it was the final straw, and he stalked off and told Now, the gentlest of the bigmen, with a pipe like a Sepik woman, that I had got boils. Kumbui paraded us. Five bandees were found to have been hiding boils. What I would like to have said was 'Between you and me, Kumbui, it's the odd diet I'm on.' We were not punished. Why not?

The *avookwaarks* rowed over what we were doing wrong to cause the boils and Rom's instinctive unease. Accusations flew: Godfrey was accused, outrageously, of using his position as acting village Kansol secretly to undermine the initiation. To everyone's utter horror he admitted it. The truth was squeezed from him. Men of the old Gama clan had walked through Kandengai on the eve of the initiation, checking for signs that the spirits were unhappy – even a doorway cobweb might have boded ill. Godfrey, it now emerged, had coaxed them into cutting certain of these rituals. He had managed to keep it quiet all this time.

Johnny brought in reassurance: Bibles for anxious bandees to consult. Those who I had once thought uninterested in Christianity, like Kennedy, thumbed through the pages for inspiration. Edward assembled an AOG Bible-study group. Bigmen did nothing to stop these things, but meanwhile grew hoarse shouting at each other.

Precisely at this moment – yes, I can truthfully say precisely – a four-foot snake, the blotched colour of an overripe banana, chose to slink along the inside of the fence. Vincent, now liberated of bandages – it had taken three weeks – clubbed it to bits. Edward said maybe it was Satan, and reached for his Bible. Godfrey suggested it was a bad spirit – he had avoided the word 'devil'. I saw why. He liked the spirits to seem threatening. In fear, rather than thinking on the spirits, the young unquestioningly chose the alien religion to cling to. *Had* the initiation come too late for the spirits to hold their and my minds and hearts?

'Edward, has anyone actually seen a proper spirit?'

'Like the bush spirit, Wunjumboo? Ishmael and Steven seen him. They were washing their bodies in a stream. A black little man with big fingers and too big black claws, and hair growing on his face, watched them horribly from a *meeamba* [tree]. No clothes were over his *sik* [genitals]. He hung from the tree like the cuscus and climbed down the tree belly to attack them. Steven heard Wunjumboo land on the clay. He screamed out. Ishmael saw him, and cried also. They were too afraid and left their trousers and ran home way. On the path a woman walked with *noo* – what is *noo*?'

'Firewood.'

'Yes, and she dropped the fire sticks and ran with a branch to hurt Wunjumboo . . . But already he had gone away.'

'Brave woman.'

'The womens of Kandengai is strong and good.'

Joel crouched beside me, searching for truths in the Gospels. He seemed to agree that the snake was just a snake but was no longer so certain that Jesus had overriding powers. As I sat writing, he looked up from time to time at the coconut palms we could see swaying out towards the Smaark territory and his lovely girl awaiting him. Getting out there was becoming less and less a desire, more and more a need for both of us.

Chapter Eighteen

We were united with the men against a common fear, a fear real or imagined, planned by Rom or out of his hands, that effectively diffused any bitterness we, the older bandees, felt about the cruelty of our captors.

Beating dances were recommenced next day and the only people to sob were Rom and Lamin, fathers of the gaigo, hearing us clobbered. We, the more strongly made boys, had learned to grin and bear pain, our youngers to see inspiration in our strength. The men went cutting up the grass islands blocking the channel. They would flow away, now the Sepik was too low to back up. This told us we were approaching the dry season and the first of the pitpit along the shrinking river must be carrying pale banners of flower.

Lamin, meanwhile, let me step up on a bench to see two secret Yaark masks hidden in a sack on a shelf across the rafters. The masks were very, very dirty, crumbly and raised choking dust clouds; they had aggressive eyes projecting in an awful stare from their serrated, restless and unhappy faces. A glimpse would turn a child into an insomniac.

'Why have I been shown these Yaark clan secrets, and not Yaarks like Michael, Thompson and Job?' I asked Martin.

'The bigmen think you're the most manful bandee. The bigmen have finished you already. Or . . .'

'Or what?'

'Nothings.'

Was it that Rom did not like the responsibility of having a white man here if the puzzling spirits really did punish? That night the handle of my pot of *jungwoo* came away and the steaming coconut and taro soup flowed over Joel. He jumped in the air, and maintaining silence, apart from hissing '*Goo! Goo!* Water! Water!', was splashed down by Kennedy. He was badly scalded, the paraffin light revealed. The skin rose from his shoulder in soft balloons of yellowish water.

'You cook him,' Stens said. I felt bad about it. However, a month ago even Joel would not have had the will to preserve silence like that. Surely we were mature enough to leave the nest now, weren't we? Couldn't the *avookwaarks* see that? Now, though, there was so much bickering between the bigmen it was as if we did not exist. With the absence of their habitual pressure, we did not feel relieved, we felt neglected.

Martin crept about between bandees and gathered all our intelligence. 'Long time ago, the bigman Martias secretly learned himself the secret name of the spirit in the *mie* [slit gong] Yo-anga-moook. Now at the time of the *waarkdumba* he has powers on all bandees. Also, the fathers.'

Good grief, I thought: the reason why this initiation came about was because Martias campaigned on my behalf. Now it looks as if it had in fact been only a personal power bid, the nest giving him a hold on the entire village.

'Does Martias admit this?'

'No, no. But Lamin and Rom say, and all the bigmen agree to them because Rom and Lamin have care for their sons.'

Martias was finding the tirade against him intolerable and he stormed out. He beat Lamin's name out on a slit gong at Maree-ruman gaigo, calling him to fight. However, Lamin was miniscule beside Martias and knew all about bad odds from his gambling. He said he was prepared only to rub Martias' face in the dirt inside the fence (with the protection of Yaark spirits).

Martias returned. It was about time, he said, that the little crocodiles were taken into the bush to be dipped in the water. 'The eggs are hatched.' Rom intervened now. He had just come back from a call of nature in the woods. Allegedly, he had encountered a spirit dressed in the form of a bandee. The spirit had said to Rom, 'You may go. We know it is Martias' fault. I will not harm you.' Martias walked off, still noisily fuming. Rom made an announcement that everything was under control. '*Apmanda!*' Good thing too, everyone agreed.

The reassurance lasted fifteen or maybe twenty minutes. Its end came when Steven – standing in the pinkish dusk light, his short height stretched in a shadow which climbed right up the fence – dropped his *waark*, said 'Eeee!' and ran into the gaigo. 'The *waarkdumba* is *moving!*' His face looked distorted, as if, the clay being not just a coating but his entire substance, a sculptor, now desiring a form more grotesque, had thumped in the cheeks, so jerking the eyeballs forward into unnatural prominence and displacing the jaw downward, the lips outward. Rom ordered us indoors.

The bigmen inspected the fence in and out. Rom munched his gums calmly. Even I was finding myself wanting to be able to look up to his tired face for reassurance. Yet this was so irrational.

The men came in: nothing. Maybe it was a pig having a good scratch of its back. Their relief at this only served to remind any doubters of their true belief in the power of those spirits. A complicated game was being played here – though I did not know who it was being played between. Us and the men? The Christian God and the spirits? Superstition versus rationality? I did not like this feeling of being manipulated by an unknown.

It was not a temporary feeling. The very next dawn Ishmael, Pinga's son, found himself staring face to face with a dead ancestor. He had a yellow skull, and the bandee had uncovered it while digging a drainage hole under a Niowi bench. It was barely dawn but anyway the bigmen were so distracted these days that none of them would have noticed. Quickly I dug further. The spade chinked in the soil, and I recovered two incisors and some molars. They shone brightly from the clay – I had half expected them to be stained red with betelnut. Someone was coming. I winced and offered my back for the blow. 'Close that hole!' It was only Jimmi. He agitatedly tugged at his mourning wrist bands while I shovelled the soil over the disturbed remains. Before any other men knew of it, the evidence was gone.

The finding of the skull was not extraordinary – once, all the men had been buried in these soils. But death had forced itself into our minds. We really had looked it in the face.

The gentle bigman called Now, took out his pipe and told us to gather around for a story in Pidgin. He was trying to keep our minds occupied.

'I was out in the bush, hunting one day . . .' Joel groaned – he had heard it before.

Now had once gone off with his shotgun and wife, pig hunting. It was dawn, the grey haze licking the water as he left his wife spear-fishing. He looked high and low for fresh tracks, chanced on a fresh series and lost that after spending all morning on his hands and knees tracing it along like a *wara*, or dog. The sun was by now dropping slats of light vertically through the tree canopy. He slumped against a *kwaark* tree trunk and had a suck on his old pipe before starting back for his wife. In front was a *miaark*, its branches casting a heavy shade. A *kwaik* – that detestable bird which longs for graveyard flesh – flapped clumsily in the upper limbs. Then it took off from the crown and circled around the trunk, descending lower and lower, looking bigger and blacker, as it came down to Now, who sat slumped there watching. It alighted, spread its wings and, behold, it was a grubby dwarf. His fingernails were extended; his skin was as dirty as a pig's. His hair was greasy, long and tangled and he carried a shoulder bag which, Now guessed, held potions. He had already decided he was seeing Wunjumboo. It was obvious – for Heaven's sake, the creature's beard hung to his *arangee*, his navel, which was plugged with muck. The spirit was a hideous spectacle, and it flashed his eyes, trying to intimidate Now. But Now had been well schooled as a bandee, and fear did not enter his head. Instead, a thought did. 'Olapukpuk! I've got no cartridges loaded!' Slowly, he slipped one into the breach of the barrel, which lay across his right thigh. The spirit looked disconcerted. The man was not behaving like most men. Your typical Chambri, Palembei or white man ran a mile, but not a bit of it. This one was sitting there, puffing at his stupid pipe. And now he was loading a shotgun! The closing snap of the firearm startled the spirit into action. He brought his hands up, and with a flap was a bird again, lifting into the air and out of sight.

Now found his wife having a lucky day fishing, back at the canoe. 'Never mind that,' Now said. 'Grab your paddle. We're off.'

The story was such an obvious moral tale – we had to be brave bandees – it was appalling. However, Now would not lie to us; so every word of the tale was true to his recollection. Thus they, Wunjumboos, *did* exist even now. But would this confirmation in our minds increase the spirits' hold on the Kandengais? Force Christianity back?

The night was peaceful; too much so. By daybreak we had very good reason to believe news was being kept from us. Andrew kept coming up for more 'potions', and wagged his head forlornly when each time I said I had only got aspirin. I had given most of my own chloroquine to sick bandees, thus ensuring I would come down with malaria myself, sooner or later (once back in England, as it turned out, and two different species of the parasite). It did not seem a sacrifice – I now felt that my fellow bandees were an extension of myself – but I did wish it could be understood that white people could not summon all needs with a click of the fingers.

So we had guessed someone was ill. Who? The bigmen were mostly out of the nest, presumably stooping over the sick patient, breathing chants in his face – perhaps that of the old man called Saun – after all, he was 'one hundred and twenty' years old.

We were called to dance, but we were casual about the beatings, and did not register much pain. Were the bigmen bringing the sticks down more softly nowadays? As a body of thirty bandees, we outnumbered the bigmen and sang so loud – '*liko, liko, temblo dee*' – that our voices easily carried through the village houses to beyond the waterside canoes and on to the women out fishing. As we danced, Alex said that lovesick girls lingered near the fence, he had seen them through the leaves: maybe Joel's girl. Nicholas had a nudging technique – lodging his massive body close to the bigman's beating hand so he could not get a proper swing. The younger boys were finding bravery within themselves – their worry now was that they would not get the chance to show it: we sensed an end.

It was hard to resist straining to hear the village sounds – children bickering as they swung long knives to cut the grasses; their clacking of coconut shells *en masse* to scare the mosquitoes away – a joke passed on from ancestors. When the breeze floated from the river, sometimes we heard the moored-up canoes nudging together, and we breathed in the sweet smell of grass clippings. Firesmoke perhaps meant a woman was outdoors burning a woven palm leaf sheath full of shells, for betelnut lime. We were all so filled with food that even Steven, Sebastian, Saun and Florian, once in gangly adolescence, strode along with a heavy mature gait.

Two days on we knew it was Anderloo who was ill. It explained his recent absence. Why Anderloo, the one bigman who had been prepared to ride the waves of abuse just to display a little generosity by presenting us gently with trays of fruit from time to time, as if we were princes? The *avookwaarks* were so preoccupied with Anderloo, they were no longer bothering us. It must be very serious.

The sun was bright, but the day grim. Anderloo was worse, we guessed. Men in the gaigo moped, so we did. Rom and Lamin looked as if they had been dazzled, smoking tobacco and chewing over their prayer chants. We were huddled up together, Johnny and Godfrey on stools, praying monotonously for the Holy Spirit to drive the evil spirits away. By 'evil' did they include the spirits of the gaigo, which were protective if not abused or neglected? Johnny didn't, Godfrey certainly did.

'*Bandee, yagua!* Come!' The voice yanked me from the floor, and I walked, head down, to Rom. Jimmi stood by my side to help translate – today the headman could not manage Pidgin. Jimmi said, 'Listen, Benedix' – he had not called me by my name for over a month, and I knew this was my departure. The words came just as I feared they might: 'Benedix, you have to leave the *waarkdumba*.'

'*Ha?* What?' I said, avoiding Pidgin, stating my bond. I did not want to understand; my place was here, with the boys, until the end. During recent nights I had lain wondering when these words would be spoken, preparing myself for the shock of early separation by saying 'Yes, maybe tomorrow,' but the news when it came was still choking.

'*Ow-a.* Yes,' I said slowly.

'*Koa?* All right?' Rom asked. A bigman had never before asked me for an opinion. Already I was hardly a bandee.

I knew Saun, Lawrence and Kenny would be bunching up under the bench at my feet to be within earshot of Rom. Now they would be silently spreading this news. In a few seconds it would have reached Alex, Edward and finally Willi, who sat right at the far end. I was shattered – the prospect of freedom and the wrench of leaving. 'Why?' I asked simply, in Pidgin. I did not know the local word – it was not one a bandee could ever use.

Jimmi said, 'You listen, bandee' – back to my more correct label – 'the bigmen think two things. One thing is, you come to Kandengai to learn. You ended learning as a bandee now. It is over. There is much Yaark stories you must be learned, but first you must leave the nest and be growed up. Another thing, you can help the man who is sick. The bigmen thank you – it will be nice.'

'I have no medicine left. What about a doctor?'

'The *avookwaarks* do not wish the white doctor,' Jimmi said. 'Now your wau kills a pig for the spirits. That is correct for a bandee which is let go. Pinga can splosh you in the forest waters, like the mother crocodile, and you are free.'

We talked about this beyond the time for the dressing in mud and I alone among the bandees did not join in. I watched them smoothing on the clay. They kept looking indoors towards me, where I stood beside Rom and Jimmi. Tonight I would leave the nest as usual, tomorrow I would not come back as a bandee. I could already sense the freshness of air untrapped by the nest.

Alex said, 'You shake my hand?'

'The *avookwaarks* will see, and anyway if I shake hands it means I am leaving for good, but I'll see you later.'

I wanted time to reflect, but was given little. 'Bandee!' Kumbui called me over to the Niowi end. He was pleased that I had been in the nest, he said. This man, who only the other day was raging 'Kill 'em! Kill 'em!' as we danced and he applied his sticks, was now sobbing. I stood head bowed, wondering whether I was permitted now to cry too. From the far end of the gaigo came the tuneless weeping of Pinga.

A contingent of bandees came up, headed by Martin, saying they wanted me to do one more dance. I was not in the mood, and most bandees, sitting in clumps outside, were not either. We were one body and my going was like an amputation. The Smaarks alone stirred themselves to dance. The handful of us hopped like cassowaries in mad circles, revolving around Sebastian slapping his hand drum. We laughed and smiled but we were fooling ourselves, the entertainment was forced, this celebration painful. A dance that had always made bigmen reel on their benches in passionate giggles, today was of passing amusement only. My clean bare skin, without its renewed mud layer, declared that I was not of bandee company any more. Today the bigmen produced polite, awkward coughs for laughs, and the thumping rhythm of Sebastian's drum was less to us than our own combined body pulse, which only wanted emotion expressed in tears.

I cooled down quietly under a bench with Alex, who said, 'I haven't learned you many somethings for your notebook, and I possess a story you must know.'

'There's still time.'

There were two brothers, he said, the elder one married, but unhappily because his wife was desirable and everyone was envious of him. One night, the other, unmarried brother overheard men murmuring downstairs in the tall gaigo. They were going to chop the head off his brother; he also heard them say, 'Curses! Supposing that smelly creep of a brother upstairs is listening?' They tiptoed up and found him snoring deeply. To check he really was sound asleep they slid a hot fireplace towards his leg. Still the young man feigned sleep, and only apparently awoke as the hot clay was pressed to his belly. His scream was awesome. The men were satisfied.

When he could, the scalded brother raced from the village to a lakeside tree where he perched, ready to intercept his brother, who would be returning soon with his lovely wife. Unfortunately, by a trick of the moonlight, the man looked like a *saun*, the egret with feathers whiter than betelnut lime. The older brother, approaching in the canoe, spotted this *saun* and swapped his paddle for his spear. '*Kai, yaguandoo!* No, brother!' the younger man cried. He jumped down from the branch. '*Darameré*. Sit down. I've got something to tell you.' Once he had explained the plot to kill him, the woman ran to their garden and made *manchan*, the sago and coconut mixture that crocodile spirits simply adore. Then the three paddled to the lake middle, lit by the moon segment. There they mouthed special words and threw the *manchan* to the *waark*. The crocodile did not like being rudely woken up like this, and jumped into the canoe to upset it. Another ritual calmed the *waark* spirit. He was now agreeable to their suggestions. Back in the village they lowered him secretly into a hole. Under cover of the night, they tore through the bush, gathering up one pair of every animal and plant — *banya*, betelnut, *mai*, taro, *mewk*, owl, *maree*, rat . . .

The lake water began to rise. The three quickly put finishing touches to a large canoe, hardening it with fire, sealing the cracks with clay and tree gum. Elsewhere all was quiet; every man, woman and child slept. Asleep, as the waters rose up the stilts of the houses. It was when a girl looked out into the night, wanting to go to the loo, that the alarm was raised. '*Lapmeré! Lapmeré!* To your feet!' Her calls aroused everyone, but it was too late. Up the house walls the water came, as the villagers scrambled on to the roof. Up the roof the water came and there was nowhere else to go. '*Tama! Tama!*' they cried. 'Stop! Stop!' But the water did not stop rising and everyone in the world was drowned.

Everyone, that was, except for the three in the dugout, who were beginning to get a little ruffled themselves. There they were floating on a world of water, and the crocodile was blowing contemptuous bubbles at the rituals designed to correct the situation. Living conditions must have been getting cramped and the shapely wife was becoming larger than ever – she was going to have a baby, she said. There was so little room on board they could only hope it was not twins.

At last the crocodile said he would lower the water.

'Then we are saved!'

'But on one condition.'

'Yes? Yes?'

He wanted the baby when it was born. The woman was appalled; her husband and brother-in-law curious. Why did he want to eat a poor helpless baby?

'You misunderstand. I'm lonely, and the child will be a girl.'

'I see,' said the men.

'Yes, to be quite honest,' the crocodile said, 'I want to marry her.'

The three voted to go along with the demand – they had little choice – and when the baby arrived, she was tossed to the *waark*, who, content, lowered the water and took his bride.

Edward had been listening in. I was interested in his religious slant, especially as he said he knew other Sepik versions of the story.[19] 'What does it mean, your ancestors and the Bible both having a devastating flood?'

He thought about it and chose his words: 'That the good/bad spirits and God/Satan are the same?'

Of course they were, I had already decided. Edward had suspected this for some time – he had called the snake a devil, rather than a bad spirit – but he was not even now taking on board the implications. The good and bad spirits were God and Satan, so the battle was only in our concept of what form these forces took. As man moved away from nature, humanised powers, like the Judaeo-Christian ones, became more relevant and attractive. If you wanted a force that loved, you preached love among your brethren. If you feared those forces, and in a civilisation close to nature you feared much in the world, your faith gave the forces power over you to realise your fears.

Darkness came too soon. Those bandees who could draw presented me with pictures of the life forms sharing their clans – bats, bananas, snakes – having secretly ripped up my entire spare notebook for paper. I stood beside the headman above the bandees, as they crouched ready to go off to their houses. Lamin gently loosened my neck rope. Then my palm apron fell away, also to be buried in the gaigo grounds. Judging by their limp postures, the bandees in the firelight were miserable. Envy was absent. Because of their bowed heads I could not see their faces, or tears. I was given a stool, so however near I sat I could not be at the level of the bandees.

'The silence is presented for you, Benedix, not Anderloo,' Andrew said. 'The sick man is not too sick now.'

I had been a bandee for almost five weeks. A moon had gone and come again, and now was waning, its outline furry with cloud. I waved to the bandees as they peeled off to their clan territories. Joel was gently humming, 'She loves you, yeah, yeah, yeah, yeah . . .', and no doubt thinking of his sweet girl.

Godfrey came to the house while we ate behind the screen. That was strange. Then he asked me to show my marks to the women, Imelda and Rhonda, even though we both knew it would be an affront to the Old Ways: I would not be fully *waarkvarinango* until I went to the water tomorrow. No, I said, I had not come to undermine culture here but to build from it.

Even with the women nattering excitedly at the prospect of my appearance tomorrow, the luxury of being able to lie rolled in a heap of snug clothes, and curled on my side, demanded that I sleep.

The *waark* recalled the bandees before daybreak, and I patted each boy on the shoulder as he passed down the house steps. Their feet stamped out the warning of their approach through the wet, silent, dark village.

Pinga and Johnny were with me by the water's edge, almost invisible in the sparse pre-dawn light. We stepped out along a log. As the water glowed in the refracted first light, Johnny and Pinga plunged me deep into it – it was warm, delicious – then nursed the mud from me, and I was free, an adult *waark*. It was a baptism, an immersion which symbolised my final graduation. I was complete – with nature, part of nature; one with its spiritual force; I was part of that force.

Chapter Nineteen

Back in Johnny's house the women whose turn it was to have a day off from fishing were yawning awake. Children who should be running along through the forest to school were splashing at the riverside, refusing to leave until they had seen me.

I walked out in bursting trousers to be mobbed by the children – little more than silhouettes in the grey light. Given that disguise they felt uninhibited about grabbing my hand, stroking my back, running their fingers down my chest. A Timbun youth materialised, poked my fattened stomach and said, 'You are frog.'

'Ah, Benedix,' the women said. 'Ah, Benedix.' Their hands were so feathery soft – in the nest no one had felt my skin, except while smearing it with mud, and there the strokes it had typically received were with sticks. Though it could have been woodsmoke from the early morning fires, the women's eyes held tears. The children's touches were born of curiosity as they hopped about, clutching scribbling books; the women's were of happiness, pride, relief. For me the freedom and company was oppressive – the village was as yet dark enough to be the night-time place of cold shadows I had only ever glimpsed as a bandee.

My eyes were caught by Augusta's, and I knew hers must be a glassy red. I had forgotten how tall she was, how controlled and smooth her gestures. She was uncertain of how she should react to me; and I to her. We shook hands rather formally, aware of our shared thoughts, but unable to express them. She stepped back into the obscurity of the crowd. I felt her glowing at me, among all the faces and flapping hands. It was a sister's, not a lover's, pride, and that put me at greater ease – soon perhaps we could have time alone to share our thoughts about our respective fears and hopes.

There was news about Anderloo's health, and he was stable. I should nip away for a few days, the bigmen said, to answer some urgent telegrams that Jimmi had heard, through the all-pervasive network of Kandengai *wantoks*, were waiting at Wewak post office. Even before the sun was up, I was walking out of the village with Jimmi. Women dripping tears blocked our path, saying I would never come back.

New surrounds, the closed cover of trees and open waterscapes; new colours, the cool pink waterlily flowers already open; new tastes, as a Nyaurengai man shared a hunk of crocodile tail with me; new sounds, of water kissing the mud banks; the touch of leaves and shoots; the smell of overripe *laulau* fruit, the fug of the forest – all this was overwhelming. I would have been content with the freedom to stand up straight and fold my arms.

In Pagwi, the stimulation was that much more overpowering. I detested the fuss, of being showered with presents – peanut butter, biscuits, bottles of Sprite. My stomach could not take these, yet I was starving – accustomed to being crammed with four meals a day, and already having missed the first.

I had been away days now – Jimmi and I had not been able to find a truck back from Wewak. Finally, we were returning, approaching Kandengai in the canoe, with Moses, Anderloo's son, who had been called home. The river banks were crowded to greet us, and the women had a strange look of agitation. Their faces expressed an agony, as did their feet – pacing tiredly. And then we knew.

We consoled Moses, patting and rubbing his shoulders. He cried loudly, clear across the spread of water, wiping his eyes on the frayed white cuffs of his town shirt. Whoever said that Anderloo's condition was stable should have looked more closely.

His death was not the only thing I had missed; and I don't mean the funeral. Anderloo died on the Saturday evening, and as soon as the women's mourning wail went up, the *waark* spirits were silent, the initiation was suspended. Later, after the last meal, Edward went outside and, hidden in the dark, stood urinating. Looking up, he saw a man leaning against a coconut tree, watching him only a few yards away. He screamed – the figure was a ghost. It had to be, because it was Anderloo, who was meant to be growing cold, cradled by the moaning women in his house. Edward ran and bumped into the bandee Leo – another church leader. They both collided with Johnny, who had run up, responding to Edward's scream – it had been loud enough to drown the crying mourners. Imanwell, my wau, bounded up; then Godfrey and the bigman Warbee. While they were standing there discussing it, Leo also saw the dead man. Everyone else stared hard, but only Leo perceived the ghost, glowing in the pure starlight. Leo leaped on Johnny, gripping him tight around his brawny chest. The dead man's spirit was trying to yank the bandee away and Leo's paranoiac grip was squeezing the air from Johnny's lungs as well. Godfrey and Imanwell grappled with Leo, and at last the spirit gave up.

Edward and Leo lay all night with Godfrey and Johnny praying interminably over them. There was not a bandee who questioned the power of their spirits now, nor that they were angry – either they were offering no protection against bad spirits or they were themselves punishing the Kandengais. But why? Because of Koma's neglected pig sacrifice? Because Martias had angered the *avookwaarks*? No, the bigmen said, it was the Christian intrusion. It made sense; that was why the two most God-fearing bandees were attacked – Leo, from the Catholics, Edward from the AOG.

Though the bandees' *waark* calls emanated from the nest again, Rom was frantically trying to sort out how to appease the powers; no one disturbed him. The day crept on by, the bandees watching me with long, drooping faces as I passed in and out of the nest, fetching food from the cigar-smoking women waiting outside.

Once the bandees were in bed, I was instructed in playing the sacred flutes and listened to Yaark secrets.

Two days on, and Rom had not yet diagnosed what was wrong, or if it was safe for the bandees to leave the protective nest for the bush, to be dipped in the water. After dark, the fence rattled of its own accord again. The bandees were herded indoors as before. I ran round the perimeter to see this for myself – to witness the phenomena, not to disprove any more – and of the pigs that might have been happily scratching on the lattice there was not even a trotter print.

Paying no heed to Rom, who was incommunicado, sagging on his *t'gurt*, gripping his green skirt and looking cobwebby, Godfrey and Edward gave a bolstering sermon to the bandees, before they left for bed. On their way out Gabriel stepped over a snake. Before it was twisting in the fire, it was classified as yet another bad spirit. I found my mind surrendering to beliefs. All these phenomena had to be caused by something, and direct intervention from the spirits or God (I was sure they were the same) seemed the logical explanation.

Next day in the gaigo I was presented with an excessive meal of chicken and rice. I was put on a stool, the bandees were pushed outside; Lamin paid me the compliment of swatting my mosquitoes.

'Why am I being given this, Jimmi?'

'It is a feast. Special. The bandees see this is for you only. They know now you are leaving Kandengai soon.'

'Am I?'

'They will get their feast later. We are letting you enjoy your good food because you have loved us, and too we love you, but on the night-time before they leave the nest each bandee is given delicious morsels of egg, sweet potato and *jungwee*. He can not enjoy this. It stops too late – much is sicked up. It is completed only when the bandee's uncle brings much presents to the men filling up the bandee.'

At that moment, smelling my chicken, the boys were chewing clay pellets – a trick to help lessen your distended bandee appetite.

The bandees were lying on their stomachs back in their houses. Inside the gaigo was only blackness; the fires were smouldering low. As usual the men talked and cursed across the benches – 'Bighead!' 'Monkeymouth!' Rom was under pressure to end the *waarkdumba*. No one had risked beating boys for ages anyway, so why not? 'Rom? An answer please.' Rom announced slowly, tiredly, that, all right, the bandees might venture into the forest tomorrow, to be dunked in the river, but only quickly, mind. Then they would come back to the nest, still with the rank of bandee, and a few days later would be set free.

The bigmen had a brief ceremony to show they were all friends again, both Niamé and Niowi sides. Lamin and Martias broke a betelnut branch together with the call 'Woooooooooow', then words sounding like *nian bandee*, child bandee, and parted with exaggerated breaths, then grunting steps, of crocodiles.

In the night the Gama clan men walked through Kandengai looking for signs that the spirits were not happy. Rom saw to it that they did it properly this time. They sensed nothing wrong; we might go ahead.

It was dawn and in the soft light outside the gaigo stood two circles of boys, toes inward. In the centre of one was Godfrey, in the centre of the second was Edward. The bandees were told to hold hands. The preachers preached; from the gaigo came irritable mumbles that they should hurry up; but no one made a move to stop the Christians. For perhaps the punishment had been from the Christian God for this paganism, not from the clan gods or spirits. Rom looked defeated, overcome by events, and offered no lead. Godfrey's message to the Catholic bandees was that they had nothing to fear, the Lord would protect them. Edward, to the AOGs, was more vague. They must 'have faith' in the power above and in everything turning out for 'the best'. Godfrey finished with a loud amen: Edward finished, pronouncing it the other way, as two words, 'a men'.

'Well, here we go,' Martin said to me.

'Yes, here we go.'

The twenty-nine young stalked with us crocodile men in single file out through the back of the fence, using their whirling paddles to warn women that the brood was passing. We wound into the bush, towards the track called Kambynian. The men cut stakes into nine-foot spears for the juvenile crocodiles to fend off attackers. The bandees knew that they were to be ambushed by bigmen disguised as spirits: a final test.

The bandees tried as hard as they could to listen to the clacking twigs of birds fleeing, the fizz of a thousand creatures. No one had said they could raise their heads but their faces were tilted to the tree canopy, open-mouthed, bathing in the forest. Blue silken butterflies skipped in the sunlight as it came through, broken by the foliage, to end lying scattered with the leaves on the floor. The ruddy dragonflies skating and settling in the air indicated the closeness of water. I turned to see Alex behind, pausing, eyes shut, breathing in the air fully, forcing it into his lungs and bloodstream, taking the freedom with passion.

For a few minutes, we stopped and all but the *avookwaarks* were made to scratch the leaf litter for a hidden shred of plaited palm. It was only a game; crocodiles playing on their only family outing together. Good; quickly onwards to the water. We would soon have the children safely back in the nest. The bandees were paraded along a log which leaned down the bank to the river's edge. Rom said I could join in with my friends for their *mareewaark*, the immersion, so here we were together again, loosed of garments, all *kutandoomee-quieree-tam-buiree* – that is, thirty. They had lost their clay due to the wiping leaves of the forest, so among the new crocodiles I was now distinctly the only white.

Rom, Lamin, Now and Kwaark sat upon the bank, shaded by a profusion of vaulting bamboo stems, chewing smoked fish, enjoying this picnic outing, while we were tugged into the river in turn, cradled in the water by four men, two at the head to stop us taking in the muddy spray as we screamed in response to four irritant leaf species being scrubbed forcefully over our delicate crocodile marks.

The spears were sharpened and coloured in black spirals by removing bark strips in scorching flames. Light spiked down to us as we sat cross-legged, lining the path. Now we had been crowned with *namboo-garbia*-green, finely twisted headbands, which looked bright and young and delicate on our thickened, aged, skulls. We wore them, heads dipped in gratitude. In a further display of their pride the bigmen, drunk with betelnut, pulled off their shorts, and pranced around to entertain us.

It was way past time to get back. Godfrey repeated that the bandees had nothing to fear. He had been praying. Ask in His name, and it shall be given. 'Don't overdo it, Godfrey,' I said. 'It's only twenty minutes' walk back.' I too had fears, but what proportion was superstition and what religion? I wanted the bandees to work it out for themselves, I wanted an end to this manipulation.

'You do not go with the bandees, *saun waark*,' Lamin Wogoo said. I did not have to prove myself in the ambush. '*Koa?* All right?'

I stayed behind as the bandees moved off, headed by Nicholas; then

211

Edward, Vincent and Kenny towering above Florian. Rom walked with them.

'Let them be safe, Heavenly Father,' Godfrey said.

'As I said, I think you tend to the over-dramatic,' I told him.

'Wumbunavan!' Lamin Wogoo called, and we followed the quick route to select a good ambush site. The path travelled through a corridor of bamboo which was so thick it formed screens and permitted no easy exit. Three pairs of bigmen cut notches in the thicket, and prepared to spring out with sticks on to the track. Lamin Wogoo and Ban, who had cultivated a reputation as the most prominent beaters, would remain just visible at the exit to the corridor so the bandees would not be expecting danger until they got there. But the plan was more cunning still – I was to be placed in the sunlight beyond the corridor as a distraction.

We waited in our positions, and the bandees came, tiptoeing, but hampered by their spears. In the forest their hunched figures were grey shadows – they had been freshly daubed again. I tried to move out of their line of sight, not enjoying being a cog in the men's disciplinary machine. Short Lamin blocked my way with an angry few words in the local tongue. '*Ara!* Stay! You're not a bandee anymore, you're a *g-eenjumboo*. Call the bandees. Come on, call "*Yagua!*" '

Nicholas was now in the mouth of the corridor. He had spotted Ban and Lamin Wogoo ahead, and was looking suspiciously beyond them to me. I did not have to call, because he decided to come on, slowly, innocently drawing his soulmates into the trap, which was quickly sprung. Lamin Wogoo and Ban blocked off the front, the others brought down their sticks from the sides. Nicholas did not look in the least perturbed, but swelled his chest, dropped his head, closed his eyes and, like an angry cassowary, charged out. Lamin Wogoo had to sidestep him fast and ducking close behind were all the remaining bandees, all except one, who looked trampled as well as beaten.

'Praise the Lord,' said Godfrey, coming from the village, behind. 'For He has won.'

'Is that a quote?' I said, with sceptical interest.

He continued, 'The Lord has protected you. Yes, the bigmen have not touched the bandees.' Then his brow rose into a series of parallel ripples. 'Oh . . .'

Edward, the second bandee into the corridor, was the last out. He was badly battered. The most prominent Christian was the only bandee out of twenty-nine to have been whacked. I listened hard to catch what Godfrey would say.

'Edward, you are lucky. The Lord chose you to have the punishment for all the Christians. He is in control.'

*

The bandees came safely back to the nest, walking past the Maree-ruman gaigo, disguised under heavy garbs of leaves. Women stood counting them in – twenty-nine trotting shrubs, one lagging behind and, if they looked very carefully, leaving red dots on the grass. After that the Maree-ruman slit gong, Maree-me, rang out, and the women watched as two more bushes, trying to look much the same, ran after the bandees. They swayed and rattled, were tall, had lolling tongues of red leaves and panted at the children, making Elijah scream and Johnny's baby son Glen silent in Imelda's arms. Though the bushes had no eyes, they seemed to be leering: Wunjumboo. They dashed with their spear bundles into the nest.

The bandees inside had been forewarned, so they dropped their leaf coverings and marshalled themselves into two facing ranks, alongside the gaigo. The Wunjumboos hurled spear after spear and they flew fast and true, along the avenue of bandees, but each was parried and brought down by the boys' spears. Younger boys were grazed but the Wunjumboo javelins were inferior and wounds only superficial. The two spirits looked embarrassed, their spears were used up, and the two jumped about on the spot together. As the bandees advanced, the spirits dived for two exits, but too late. Kenny, Ishmael, Sebastian, Alex, Willi, Samuel, Aaron and Job had sealed off one, wide Nicholas the other. There was a violent struggle at each, but both the spirits were soon tossing in the air, borne at head height.

'What shall we do to them?'

'Into the crocodile pool!'

'*Ow-a! Ow-a!* Yes! Yes!'

'Into the pool!'

'Throw them in!'

But the bandees decided to have mercy and did not chuck them; the bigmen had been kind in not giving their protégés a proper going-over in the forest.

The bigmen were content: the bandees had shown compassion, shown that they did not resent their harsh tuition now. They retired to the gaigo's shade.

We, the newest generation, were now full with the knowledge that we had come through. We were strong and complete, knowing ourselves and each other. Though the coming world might pride itself in the independence it gave individuals, we had proven our selfless loyalty, and that for now was greater.

We circled the gaigo in a chain, a spontaneous celebratory dance to the beat of our feet and spirit, because we knew we had triumphed. And slowly, men began to join our circle, drawn to us. First Johnny, then Jimmi, Patrick and Andrew, and then they came more quickly, trotting out from the spirit house, bringing wuth them a hand drum, a conch shell, a clan brother. The benches emptied, the gaigo was soon gutted of all but the bigmen, who would remain the hub of our wheel, as we revolved, bound by our same marching rhythm, by our treading in the same steps in a continuous ring that enclosed the sacred building. Our ring had no beginning, no end: it was unbroken, and the spirits of the crocodiles were at the centre of our tight ring.

And, we had been assuming, the whole of Kandengai was also rejoicing for us. But it was not. We had been too preoccupied with ourselves, this important day. Only now we learned that lying in the centre of the village was a girl, and she was lapsing into unconsciousness.

No women can come into the nest to fetch men, so they have to let out shrill calls instead, like forest birds of a colony threatened by a tree snake. By the time I am bustled to the Posago house, all the senior men are there, starting off their ritual chants. The palm floor, which is polished by feet and would normally reflect the sprinkled sunlight, is covered in cross-legged women and girls. Rom and Lamin, sitting on *t'gurts*, hardly notice me enter – they are in a spiritual trance. The women do notice me, every one. They are looking to me for hope, maybe Christian hope – I last saw these faces together in the church; this new faith, in which women too may join in worship. By the girl's side is Augusta. She offers me a smile, her eyes as bloodshot as they have always been lately – occasions of joy, of sadness. I am beginning to wonder if they will ever not look sore. The sick girl must be a girl friend. They probably went to school together.

John Warbee, the Ambunti school teacher, is somehow suddenly back in the village. He greets me solemnly, and tells me the girl on the floor is his sister. I do not need to look at the girl to know the seriousness of her condition. 'We must take her to a doctor. Now! Is there a canoe we can use?'

'No.'

'There must be.'

'No. We cannot take her. The men want to drive the spirit out. They want to use their spirit medicine.'

'But she is your sister. You have a right to take her. *Take her!*'

'No. We must wait a little. Just a little.'

I turn to look at the patient the right way up, and see the bright teeth and honest face of the *yargee* girl. But it cannot be. It *must* not be. Yet it is, and I cannot begin to understand how it is possible. I bend over the girl, draw back her cover. She is naked, but for a skirt drawn low over her hips. In the spaces where the blanket has not been against her skin, she is dappled lightly in a dew of perspiration – under her chin, around her navel, between her breasts. She is murmuring, relaxed some moments, in seizures the next. Her child's eyes open and close. When they open, the expression is vacant.

Why her? I only know maybe six village women; six out of hundreds. Why has this been done to you? I hardly know you, I find myself thinking, but the sight of you in this state is worse than anything we went through in that crocodile nest. Then I feel let down – angry with her almost. The bandees have been fighting to be brave, partly just to see girls like you – what have you done to yourself? How could you do this *now*, just before they are set free?

When I push up the eyelids, the pupils dilate, very slowly. I look around at the women of Kandengai. Twenty-five or thirty of them encircle me; more are arriving. They watch my hands, and expect them to work miracles. They wait for the miracle of life – demand it, as they demanded it of Dr Brown at Brurui. I have had next to no medical training; and the girl is slipping away.

I lay her on her side – the 'recovery position', I remember vaguely. She breathes more easily for a minute, then screams horribly; even the bandees, through the village, behind the fence, must have heard. She tenses up. It is as if mains electricity has been bolted through her every muscle. Her eyes spring open, her knees are at her chin, her head cracks back on the palm floor-slats. Martias spoons a liquid from a cup, and blows it ritually over the girl. She tries to vomit, and cannot. Another scream. I grip her wrists and we wrestle. Augusta keeps manoeuvring a mat so that the girl does not smash her skull.

Her intelligently noble face is not unlike Augusta's – are they related? It is breaking Augusta's heart to see the girl writhing. It is as if the girl is trying to destroy herself. 'Yakarta! Yakarta!' Augusta sighs. That must be the girl's name. Yakarta. To me, 'the *yargee* girl'.

Yakarta relaxes slightly. I do not know whether it is a good or a bad thing – is she moving away from danger or further towards it? She must not give up this fight. That is obvious, but is this a fight against spirits who are furious at the customs neglected, as the Kandengais believe, or against . . . against what? I go through every disease I can think of. 'Augusta, I want to know how it started, exactly what she's been eating.'

Yesterday, I gather, she was out fishing for the bandees. She was with friends. Augusta was with her all day. She ate very little; a few bananas, that's all. Augusta ate the same. In the afternoon, Yakarta said she felt sick and, before she had paddled home, she was. Through the night her condition did not change – a mild fever. This morning it was worse. By lunchtime, when the men and the bandees were in the forest, she was like this.

I check over the girl's body. I am self-conscious with the audience here, I find, but it has to be done. I am looking for fang marks. Perhaps it was a death adder; but no sign. Cerebral malaria? It might explain the convulsions. I am just grabbing at straws, plucking at possibilities often remembered from my medical grandfather's ancient black *Wheeler and Jack's Handbook*. It has not escaped my mind that she may have been poisoned – by an enemy of her family? By Christians to blacken the name of the spirits forever?

I leave the girl in Augusta's arms. To Rom and Martias I say she must go straight to hospital. The women look from me to them. '*Apman n'iaman*,' I say. 'Please.' And I feel the female eyes offering support. No response. 'She should be fed plenty of water, sweetened with sugar to give energy,' I say to Augusta. Godfrey comes in 'to say a prayer or two'.

I walk the empty village, trying to think of something I can do. If there are other children or women in Kandengai just now, they must be waiting quietly, miserably, indoors. From the crocodile nest the bandees' *waark* calls sound lonely. I go to them and find most bigmen absent. The bandees look as if they have already begun their mourning.

'How is it?' asks Alex.

'Bad.'

He goes away to sit down, alone.

The bandees leave the *waarkdumba* at night and wind past the Posago house where Yakarta lies – Yakarta, the *yargee* girl at the market, apparently dying because the spirits were abused. The boys are given a heavy escort of *g-eenjumboos* to their houses. Who doubts that the spirits are not all around us now?

I eat with the Smaark bandees, behind the screen. Martin breathes, 'When you leave us?'

'When Rom and Lamin want. Soon, I think.'

'You stay to see when the bigmen stick Yo-anga-mook and N'iangandoo and we run bare-skinned from the nest, and our hands shelter our *siks* from the loving girls' eyes?'

'Maybe, if that's tomorrow, but I don't think so. The bigmen want me separated from you for a while. And maybe I've absorbed all I can for the moment.'

'We can all be worrying for you, when you go away,' says Martin.

'You must worry for us also,' adds Joel. Stens makes heavy agreeing noises. Sebastian and Kennedy sincerely shake my hand. We joke about Lamin's two dreary dogs, Japanese and Sepik, how we have managed to avoid touching them, and it looks as if they too have survived the initiation. Then the words suddenly fail to amuse.

I go to the girl's house. She is in Augusta's arms and they are alone together just now. Neither girl seems to have moved much since I saw them hours ago, though Augusta's head is propped by a *t'gurt*. It must be a good sign. Without disturbing them – Augusta is asleep – I listen and hear that the breathing of the *yargee* girl is less forced. Gently I ease the sheets over the curves of her damp chest, and tuck them around Augusta, within whose arms she lies.

I go to my mosquito net in Johnny's house, saying loudly, 'Good night, bandees!' They bang the loose floor panels to reply. Outside, the night is strangely peaceful. The village sleeps. No doubt Godfrey is awake praying somewhere, for something. A few men might later go back to be with the girl, their heads inclined over the herbs. Tomorrow, at dawn, I decide, I will insist she goes straight to hospital, at first light. I slip into sleep.

In the middle of the night, a yell rockets into the sky, cracking it wide open. There are screams, women's screams, and terrible wails, and they are incessant, wracking the night sky and on into the dawn.

No *waark* calls the bandees to the nest. Ceremonies are suspended. John Warbee, the girl's brother, comes from her house with a taper of grass, carefully marked off at what looks to me about five and a half feet. He brings it through the fence. A canoe is turned over. Nicholas is given an axe, and he easily applies his bulk to chop off a canoe length, which is just greater than that measured on the taper. Someone finds a few bent nails, and the canoe section is closed off with two small panels of wood. I walk behind the canoe chunk, now a long box, as it goes back into Yakarta's house. Inside, there is nowhere left to stand now. Girls, with faces streaming, sit looking at the girl, who lies with her eyes wide open, peacefully on her back in a white sheet. Godfrey stands over her with his Bible, and says words. Augusta looks awful, her eyes like cracked rubies. A screaming woman has heaped herself over the dead girl's chest and her saliva has made the white sheet stick to the black skin of the girl's breasts.

In the gaigo Rom says I am to leave the village with the body, in a canoe, which will go to the girl's family at Timbun. There is no time to think. A canoe is already being dragged through the bush to a back creek by gangs of children using rope creepers. 'Eeeeh! Eeeeh!' They heave the canoe along. I run to Johnny's house, and pack my bags, and Pinga comes to carry them for me. In a daze I find I have already shaken hands with the women who have fed me, Rhonda and Imelda; shaken the boy Elijah's shoulder, and told him to look after his brother Sebastian for me.

I pass disconsolate women, who reach out as if trying to stop me going the way of the girl. The gaigo is full. All the men are waiting to say goodbye, each in their correct place on the benches. Now I'm not a bandee I can look into the *avookwaarks*' eyes and they are distant, flowing. Not far beyond the other side of the fence the women are shrieking for Yakarta, who is disappearing from view into the coffin. I say goodbye: Rom and Lamin, the senior men who agreed to let me come and start this ceremony; Lamin Wogoo, who gave me my secret name; Kumbui, 'I'm crying too much, *saun waark*, you go now'; Pinga, my adopted father, who cannot bear to see me leave.

The bandees have already been ordered out to wait for me in the fresh morning sun, arranged in height order. I cannot begin to say what I want to say to each of them, though I have rehearsed a piece for each, starting with the town-fed, tallest bandee, Kenny. He came especially from Wewak to join in this crocodile ritual. I do not feel it appropriate to say Edward's stock greeting, 'God bless'. The shrieking of the women grows as the body is lifted from the house, and begins its procession past the fence, out of the village. It is time to go so I just say the bandees' names, and cup their hands in turn. Twenty-nine faces – Alex near the beginning with Willi, Nicholas, Joel, Vincent, Kennedy, Martin in the middle, my brother Sebastian, Florian, and at the end Steven and Saun, who earned us a dozen beatings. I cannot bear to look back at them, and pass out of the fence quickly. Johnny, Jimmi, Andrew and my wau, Imanwell, walk in the funeral cortège. Johnny hands me back the watch he had confiscated for the period of the initiation. The mechanism has somehow ceased to be workable.

The track has been ploughed by the big canoe, and we have to pick our way through the slough. In the river channel that leads through to the Chambri Lakes, and Timbun, a woman is splayed in the dugout across the box, groaning. Augusta stands amid the noise on the bank, so tired she looks serene. She says she will come with me to Timbun.

We go in two canoes. The canoe with the body is too heavy and gets caught on the roots. We walk alongside the shallow channel and tug and pull both canoes through the forest. Finally, we can scramble aboard and get out the paddles. Andrew flings us leaves to use as mosquito swats. He walks along the channel edge, Jimmi and Johnny and Imanwell behind, waving to me from where the path dies, sometimes crying, sometimes calling me to send them presents from England: boxing gloves for Andrew, football shoes for Jimmi and watches for Johnny and Imanwell. Soon, they are lost from sight in the dark leaves, and later so are their voices.

Timbun, the village called 'waterlily', is on the far side of the lakes, snug on a gentle hill. We speed across the water, forced on by our motors – they are loud enough to drown the moans of the women in the canoe alongside – bearing news about their girl Yakarta, the one that was fit and well the day before yesterday. We move so fast that no one can break the news gently to the Timbuns – we overtake anyone out fishing, and bring the story ourselves. The coffin is not easily visible from Timbun's shaded waterside, but the woman in the canoe who is rolled over it, and whose dress flies like a wind-whipped flag, is plain to see. The Timbun ladies who catch sight of her first, break down and collapse in the exposed mud bank. Gull-like shrieks ring through the village. Martias, in my canoe, bellows.

Yes, Martias, who Lamin and Rom said had angered the spirits by using the crocodile nest to his advantage; it is *his* family who has lost the girl. The power of the spirits? Or the power of poison? Even now I try to rationalise away the interventions of the spirits. All I can be sure of is that nature has its own life rhythms, and that I feel more closely in tune with them.

By the riverside is the gaigo used for the recent Timbun initiation, their crocodile fence in windblown tatters. The village is reduced to a heap of sobbing women, and pallid, whispering men. I linger quietly in the gaigo until, as the sun reddens, the coffin is dropped into the yellowish clay soil of Timbun, and two old women try to throw themselves in to be buried with her. The Timbun youths, who once beat the drums for us Kandengai bandees, now apply spades to heap in the earth, pausing every so often to pull women out of the grave.

'Well, Benedix . . .', Augusta says, leading me away from the crowd, wiping her eyes with the back of her hand. 'Well, I paddle back home now, and so do you to England. Will you write a letter back please, if I write?'

'Yes, please do write. Let me know about your career, and I'll tell you about England.'

'Too cold for crocodiles, I think England is.'

'Even white ones?'

'Yes, even. So come back.'

'Yes.'

With the Timbun youths, I paddle away across the waterlily lake. The sky is black, the water black. There is no moon. Dawn has yet to arrive. The breeze is damp, and carries a sweet scent of night flowers from somewhere across the Chambri Lakes. I can hardly see the other two men standing with their paddles ahead, taking me back to Jeff. Maybe Jeff and I will go spearing the fish which float sleepily on the surface at night. One day, before too long, I will return to Kandengai village and go out fishing with Alex and Martin. Joel could join us as well, if he has not been lured with his wife to a town by then. They can help train me up for a return visit to West Papua, a journey of less personal significance now. Perhaps we could slip over the border together from the upper Sepik and reach the Obinis, a surprise call from the east.

219

There is a lot to look forward to. It is the dry season now, the season when crocodiles are seen about, and if it were daylight I would probably see the pitpit in flower, promising days of plentiful food ahead. Martin said the river trees look beautiful when stacked with fishing birds – blue heron, *saun*, bright kingfishers – and there are no mosquitoes prickling your legs and back as you stand working your paddle.

And if I do not return to Kandengai for a few years, will all the bandees be away on the streets? Without doubt their sons as well will be known by Christian names, and will not be called after their clan animals and plants. And certainly the Kandengais will think twice about angering the spirits through being slack over rituals. The Niowra people as a whole may not risk another initiation, may lose this traditional spiritual connection with our natural origins; their youth may flock to the towns, adopting an urban culture. But the world is better off for the thirty men who have learned how to be as brave as crocodiles, and as selfless under the worst of life's calamities as the steadfast, loyal Kandengai women have been during each normal, toiling day. And what of the spirits? They have spoken out; they still exist in the minds of the Niowras. They have won a little victory over the encroaching future. They may lose here in the end, but it is a victory.

Notes

1. See the very brief history of the island which appears in the Preface.
2. For most recent substantiated incidents see, for example, *Survival International News*, No. 12 (1986). Also, *West Papua: The Obliteration of a People* (London: TAPOL, revised 2nd edn, 1984). TAPOL is the Indonesian Hman Rights Campaign, an organization based in London.
3. Sjovald Cunyngham-Brown has written the story of his life: *Crowded Hour* (London: John Murray, 1975).
4. There are many accounts of traditional life for the Dani-speaking peoples, particularly as a result of the Harvard–Peabody Expedition of 1961. An example is Peter Matthiessen, *Under the Mountain Wall* (New York: Viking Press, 1962).
5. Helmets were introduced for the MAF partly through the dedicated work of pilot Nate Saint who, with four others, later contacted the Auca Indians of Ecuador, who quickly killed them. See Elizabeth Elliot, *Through Gates of Splendour* (London: Hodder & Stoughton, 1957), and elsewhere.
6. A missionary version of the first Yali-area contacts is Don Richardson, *Lords of the Earth* (Ventura: G/L Publications, 1977). Another missionary story, set some distance west of Wamena, is Alice Gibbons, *The People Time Forgot* (Chicago: Moody Press, 1981).
7. A classic text including a catalogue of traditional artifacts is C. C. F. M. Le Roux, *De Bergpapoea's Van Nieuw-Guinea En Hun Woongebied*, 3 vols (Leiden: E. J. Brill, 1948, 1950).
8. Jan Louwerse, 'Notes on Una (Language of Goliath, Mek Stock, Level Family)' (unpublished typescript, Langda, 1978).
9. Asmat coastal people are renowned for their carving work, and are well documented, for instance Michael Rockefeller, *The Asmat* (New York: Museum of Primitive Art, 1967). A missionary tale illustrating the methodology and reasoning of the RBMU is Don Richardson, *Peace Child* (Glendale: G/L Publications, 1974), centred on the Sawi people, south-east of Agats — 'headhunting

cannibals . . . who would venerate Judas'.

10. See Robert Mitton, *The Lost World of Irian Jaya* (Melbourne: Oxford University Press, 1985). This pictorial study is based on his notes taken during years of travelling in the interior. Both his anecdotes and his geographical account differ occasionally from the RBMU missionary versions. The present author follows the place-name spellings and geographical interpretation of RBMU sketchmaps, so reflecting a more local understanding, and, in the highlands at least, a truer one.

11. The foundation is Yayasan Pengembangan Masyarakat Desa, Irian Jaya. YPMD then regularly produced a journal on current cultural and environmental activities, *Kabar dari Kampung*. The victim was Arnold Ap.

12. Later I heard a less elaborate version of this story from Martha Reimer, a Summer Institute of Linguistics (SIL) missionary based at Sumo, working on the Momwina language for Bible translation.

13. Margaret Mead, *Growing Up in New Guinea* (Harmondsworth: Penguin, 1942). See also Mead, *New Lives for Old* (London: Victor Gollancz, 1956), which documents 'Cultural Transformation—Manus, 1928–1953'. These publications show changes in a Melanesian village's life this century, and illustrate an anthropological approach. Relevant to the present author's experiences on the Sepik at Kandengai are Mead's observations that, among the Iatmul adults, 'temper tantrums are applauded as the way in which action can be initiated. . . . Rage means the ability to display the strength which will make others yield to one's demands. Among the Iatmul, rage is good.'

14. The classic traveller's tale, Frank Hurley, *Pearls and Savages* (New York: Putnam, 1924), tells of 'Adventures in the Air, on Land, and Sea', during a journey up the Fly river and along the south of this island half. Its style also frequently portrays the unfortunate perception of some early Europeans in New Guinea: 'These creatures are so filthy and hideous [in mourning apparel] that it is difficult to believe them human.'

15. Their former, colonial life is portrayed in Keith McCarthy, *Patrol into Yesterday* (Sydney: Angus & Robertson, 1964). See also the anecdotal Colin Simpson, *Adam with Arrows* (Sydney: Angus & Robertson, 1954) and *Adam in Plumes* (Sydney: Angus & Robertson, 1955).

16. The spelling and usage of Pidgin English, *Tok Pisin*, throughout the text is generally consistent with that of Father F. Mihalic, *Introduction to New Guinea Pidgin* (Milton: Jacaranda Press, 1969). Place names are in line with the present (undated) map,

Wewak: Gateway to the Sepik (Wewak: Wirui Press).

17. For detailed explanation of Iatmul society, and descriptions of traditional village ritual including initiation in the middle Sepik, see Gregory Bateson, *Naven* (Cambridge: Cambridge University Press, 1936). With the exception of place-names and Pidgin English (see notes 10 and 6) local words are usually written just as they occur in my four notebooks, in which the phonetic spelling accords to my own system, as I learned to communicate 'in the field'.

18. Kandengais think of themselves as the founders of the Niowra tribe, both a collection of villages composing about the most westerly of the 'Iatmul' people and a linguistic group. Iatmul is a term not used for Kandengais here, because it has no ready usage among them that I could detect. The Iatmuls – once so-called headhunters – occupy the marsh margins of the Sepik 250 miles to 150 miles from the mouth. The river width varies from 400 yards in the dry season, May to September, to maybe 900 yards in the wet season, November to March, when the marsh or 'fenland' – cane reeds, sago swamps, *kunai* grassland, low woodland and drier forests – is liable to extensive flooding in lower areas. Sago is a staple, the main protein source is the river itself, and there are gardens for yams, etc. See also Gregory Bateson, 1932, 'Social Structure of the Iatmul People of the Sepik River', *Oceania*, Vol. 2 (1932) 245–91, 401–53.

19. Similar 'legends' or tales are common to many mid-Sepik villages, and a variant was told to the author at Yentchan, downstream. Other tales are widely published, for example *Niugini Stories*, edited by M. Greicus and E. Brash (Centre for Creative Arts, PNG, 1973).

Travel/Adventure in Paladin Books

Journey Through Britain   £2.95 ☐
John Hillaby
It was a magical idea to walk through the over-industrialised land of Britain from Land's End to John O'Groats, avoiding all centres of population. Britain's master walker made his reputation with his book. Illustrated.

Journey Through Europe   £2.95 ☐
John Hillaby
John Hillaby gives a splendid pot pourri of factual account, lively anecdote, mythology and private comment in this account of his walk from the Hook of Holland via the Alps to Nice. Illustrated.

Journey to the Jade Sea   £2.50 ☐
John Hillaby
Tired of city-living and ashamed of his toleration of boredom, John Hillaby made a three-month safari from the Northern Frontier District of Kenya to the legendary Jade Sea. Illustrated.

Tracks   £2.50 ☐
Robyn Davidson
Robyn Davidson went to the dead heart of Australia in pursuit of a dream – to cross the desert alone. Her voyage opened tracks to the discovery of self as well as to the profound beauty and nobility of a threatened land and its indigenous people. Illustrated.

Hamish's Mountain Walk   £3.95 ☐
Hamish Brown
No one had ever climbed all 279 Scottish Munro peaks in a single journey, until Hamish Brown embarked upon his magnificent mountain walk. This is not only an unforgettable account of one particular journey, but the result of a lifetime spent on the mountains, in contemplation of the scenery and in deep conversation with the people of the Highlands.

Hamish's Groats End Walk   £2.50 ☐
Hamish Brown
For five months, the author and his collie Storm walked the length and breadth of the British Isles, taking in the highest peaks in Scotland, England, Wales and Ireland.

Beyond the Mexique Bay   £2.50 ☐
Aldous Huxley
A fluid and lucid account of Huxley's travels in Central America.

To order direct from the publisher just tick the titles you want and fill in the order form.   **PAL16182**

All these books are available at your local bookshop or newsagent, or can be ordered direct from the publisher.

To order direct from the publishers just tick the titles you want and fill in the form below.

Name _____

Address _____

Send to:
Paladin Cash Sales
PO Box 11, Falmouth, Cornwall TR10 9EN.

Please enclose remittance to the value of the cover price plus:

UK 60p for the first book, 25p for the second book plus 15p per copy for each additional book ordered to a maximum charge of £1.90.

BFPO 60p for the first book, 25p for the second book plus 15p per copy for the next 7 books, thereafter 9p per book.

Overseas including Eire £1.25 for the first book, 75p for second book and 28p for each additional book.